RON GALELLA

PAPARAZZO EXTRAORDINAIRE!

HATJE CANTZ

C|O Berlin

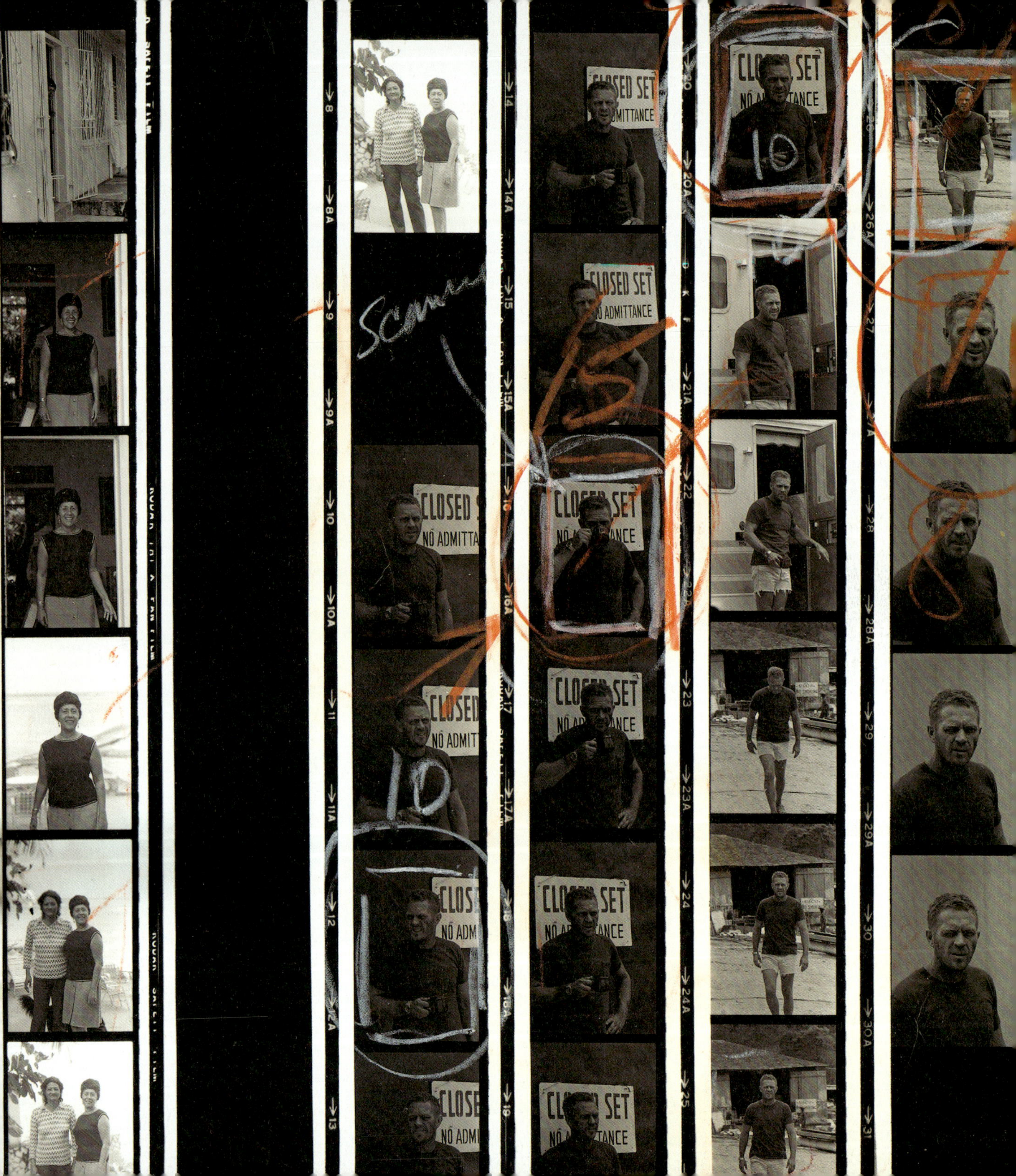

STEVE

15. April 1973: Steve McQueen am Rand des Sets von *Papillon*
in Jamaica. Ich wollte ein Foto von Steve und Ali McGraw – eine
heiße Romanze, die mit dem Film *The Getaway* begann. Steve
lehnte ab. Ich fragte ihn, ob ich Bilder von ihm alleine bekommen
könnte. Er sagte, ich hätte zehn Minuten, vorausgesetzt, ich unter-
schriebe eine Vereinbarung, das nächste Flugzeug zu nehmen,
das Jamaica verließe. Ich unterschrieb und positionierte ihn vor
einem Schild mit der Aufschrift »Closed Set«.

April 15, 1973: Steve McQueen off the set of *Papillon* in Jamaica.
The shot I wanted and requested was Steve and Ali MacGraw—a hot
romance that started with *The Getaway*. Steve said "No." I asked if
I could get pictures of him alone. He agreed to give me 10 minutes
provided I sign an agreement to take the next plane out of Jamaica.
I signed and posed him in front of a sign that read "Closed Set."

CLOSED SET
NO ADMITTANCE

Photography with the PAPARAZZI *approach*

FELIX

RON

MATTHIAS

POSING REALITY

Felix Hoffmann

Bei einem Feuergefecht während eines Einsatzes der US-amerikanischen Truppen in Afghanistan im Juni 2011 wurde der amerikanische Marineinfanterist Blas Trevino in den Bauch geschossen und rettete sich schließlich in einen Hubschrauber. Auf dem Foto der Pulitzer-Preisträgerin Anja Niedringhaus, das später in vielen deutschen Tageszeitungen veröffentlicht wurde, schreit der Soldat in die Linse der Kamera, kurz bevor er ins Krankenhaus geflogen wird. Der zum Schrei in die Kamera aufgerissene Mund kann als Ausdruck des physischen Schmerzes verstanden werden, als Wut über den Hergang des Feuergefechtes und der kriegerischen Auseinandersetzung, als Erleichterung über die Rettung, oder aber auch als Protest gegen eine Öffentlichkeit, die die Fotojournalistin mit ihrer Kameralinse vertritt.

Wie nahe muss man an einer Sache dran sein, um die Frage nach der Authentizität eines fotografischen Bildes beantworten zu können? Muss man neben den Gewehren an den Frontlinien der Kriegs- und Krisengebiete stehen, damit die Bilder den Eindruck erwecken, am Ort des Geschehens dabei gewesen zu sein? Und welchen Anteil am Bild haben jeweils die Erwartungen der Konsumenten und die Absichten der Produzenten? Die Vorstellung, dass ein unmittelbares Bild, die Aufzeichnung einer Situation möglich sei, verbindet

die Kriegsfotografie mit der Herangehensweise der Paparazzi: Scheinbar nichts steht zwischen Fotograf und Fotografierten und damit auch nichts zwischen dem voyeuristischen Blick eines Yellow-Press-Publikums und den Objekten seiner Begierde. Echt, posenfrei und direkt scheint das Verhältnis – unabhängig von der unterschiedlich gefährlichen, angespannten oder aggressiven Umgebung. Die jeweilige Motivation des Fotografen mag eine grundsätzlich andere sein – zeigen die Kriegsreportagen jene entfernten Konfliktgebiete der Welt, deren Gewalt uns in der Regel unvertraut bleibt, so machen Paparazzi Dinge öffentlich, die sonst im sorgsam gehüteten Geheimnis oder der banalen Unsichtbarkeit des Alltags verborgen blieben.

Die Lippen und der Schmollmund des Rolling-Stones-Sängers Mick Jagger haben sich über Jahrzehnte im öffentlichen Bewusstsein eingeprägt. Als Ron Galella 1977 Mick Jagger im Fond einer Limousine neben Jerry Hall ablichtete, ist der Schrei in Richtung Kamera keiner des physischen Schmerzes, sondern der Wut angesichts einer Meute von Fotografen, die noch die unwesentlichsten und intimsten Momente eines prominenten Lebens zur Nachricht machen. Das Foto zerrt das ans Licht, was eigentlich privat bleiben soll: Jagger hatte sich zu jenem Zeitpunkt noch nicht offiziell von seiner Frau Bianca

getrennt, aber offensichtlich schon das Model Jerry Hall zur neuen Partnerin an seiner Seite erkoren. Die Öffentlichkeit erfuhr davon über die Bilder in den Klatschblättern, was die Trennung von Bianca Jagger beschleunigte. Der aufgerissene Mund zeigt aber nicht nur Wut, sondern auch Anklage – gegen das Bild und die gerade stattfindende Enthüllung. Nur scheint dieses Bild eigenartig kalkuliert, und die abwehrende Geste und der Schrei geraten zur Pose für und nicht gegen die Öffentlichkeit.

Diese Dialektik der Prominenz, deren Protagonisten stets zwischen Zeigen und Verbergen oszillieren und deren Gegenspieler und gleichzeitig Komplizen die Paparazzi sind, zieht sich als Grundthema durch viele Bilder Ron Galellas. Als er 1978 Greta Garbo in New York auf der Straße fotografierte, schreit diese eben nicht in die Kamera, sondern hält sich ein Taschentuch vors Gesicht: Die Verhüllung wird zur Waffe gegen die Entblößung der Privatsphäre, zum Widerstand gegenüber dem Paparazzo und doch auch zum Zeichen der Fügung ins offenbar Unvermeidliche.

Wie die Kriegsfotografie hat die Fotografie der Paparazzi bestimmte Körpergesten kultiviert: »Das Objekt der Begierde weiß sich im Rampenlicht. Es weiß, dass es von Teleobjektiven beobachtet, dass jeder seiner Schritte verfolgt wird. Es weiß, dass die wenigen,

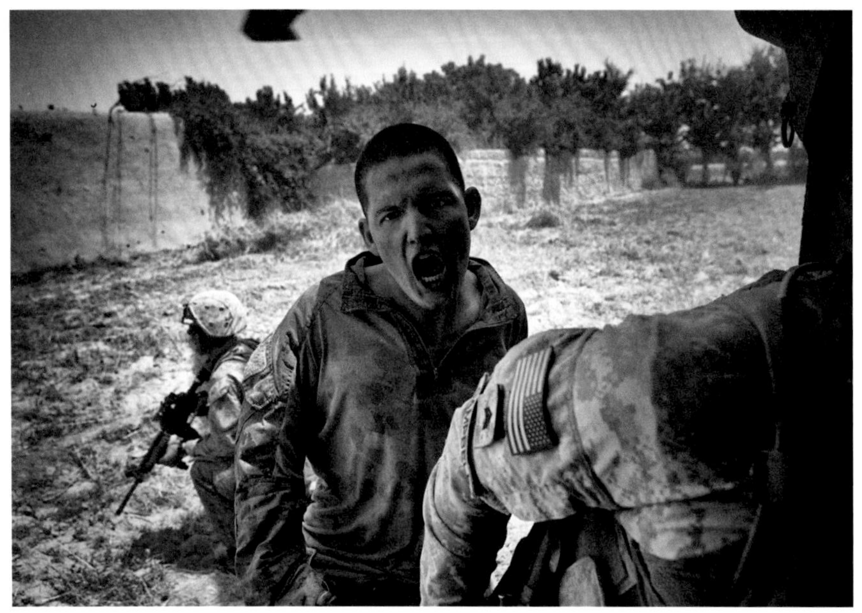

In a gunfight during the deployment of U.S. troops in Afghanistan in June 2011, the U.S. Marine Lance Corporal Blas Trevino was shot in the stomach and eventually managed to rescue himself in a helicopter. On the photograph taken by the winner of the Pulitzer Prize, Anja Niedringhaus, which was later published in several German daily papers, the soldier screams into the camera lens just before he is flown to hospital. The torn open mouth, screaming into the camera, can be read as an expression of physical pain, of anger over the events of the gunfight and the military conflict, as relief about being rescued or also as protest against the public represented by the photojournalist with her camera lens.

How close must one be to something before one can answer the question of how authentic a photographic image is? Does one have to stand next to the weapons on the front-line of an area of war or conflict for the images to evoke the feeling of having been at the scene of action? And how much of the image is influenced by the expectations of the consumer and the intentions of the producer? The notion that it is possible to take a picture that is immediate, to record a situation, links war photography to the approach of the paparazzi: it seems that nothing stands between the photographer and the person photographed and as a result nothing between the voyeuristic gaze of the yellow press readers and the object of their desire. The relationship seems real, unpretentious and direct—independent of an environment that is dangerous, tense or aggressive to differing degrees. The respective motivation of the photographer may in principle be completely different—while the war reporters generally depict distant areas of conflict around the world, whose violence remains unfamiliar to us as a rule, the paparazzi make things public that would otherwise remain hidden as carefully kept secrets or simply because they are invisible in everyday life.

The lips and the pouting mouth of the Rolling Stone singer Mick Jagger has imprinted itself in the public consciousness over the course of decades. When Ron Galella photographed Mick Jagger in 1977 in the back of a limousine next to Jerry Hall, the scream in the direction of the camera is not one of physical pain but one of rage in the face of the pack of photographers who were making news of what was still a very insignificant yet extremely intimate moment in the celebrity's life. The photo drags something to light that should actually have remained private: at that time Jagger had not officially split up from his wife Bianca, however he had obviously already chosen the model Jerry Hall as the new partner at his side. The public learned about it through the pictures in the gossip rags, which speeded up the breakup from Bianca Jagger. The wide open mouth not only depicts rage but also denunciation—of the picture and the act of exposure. Only this picture seems oddly calculated and the dismissive gesture and scream become a pose for and not against the public.

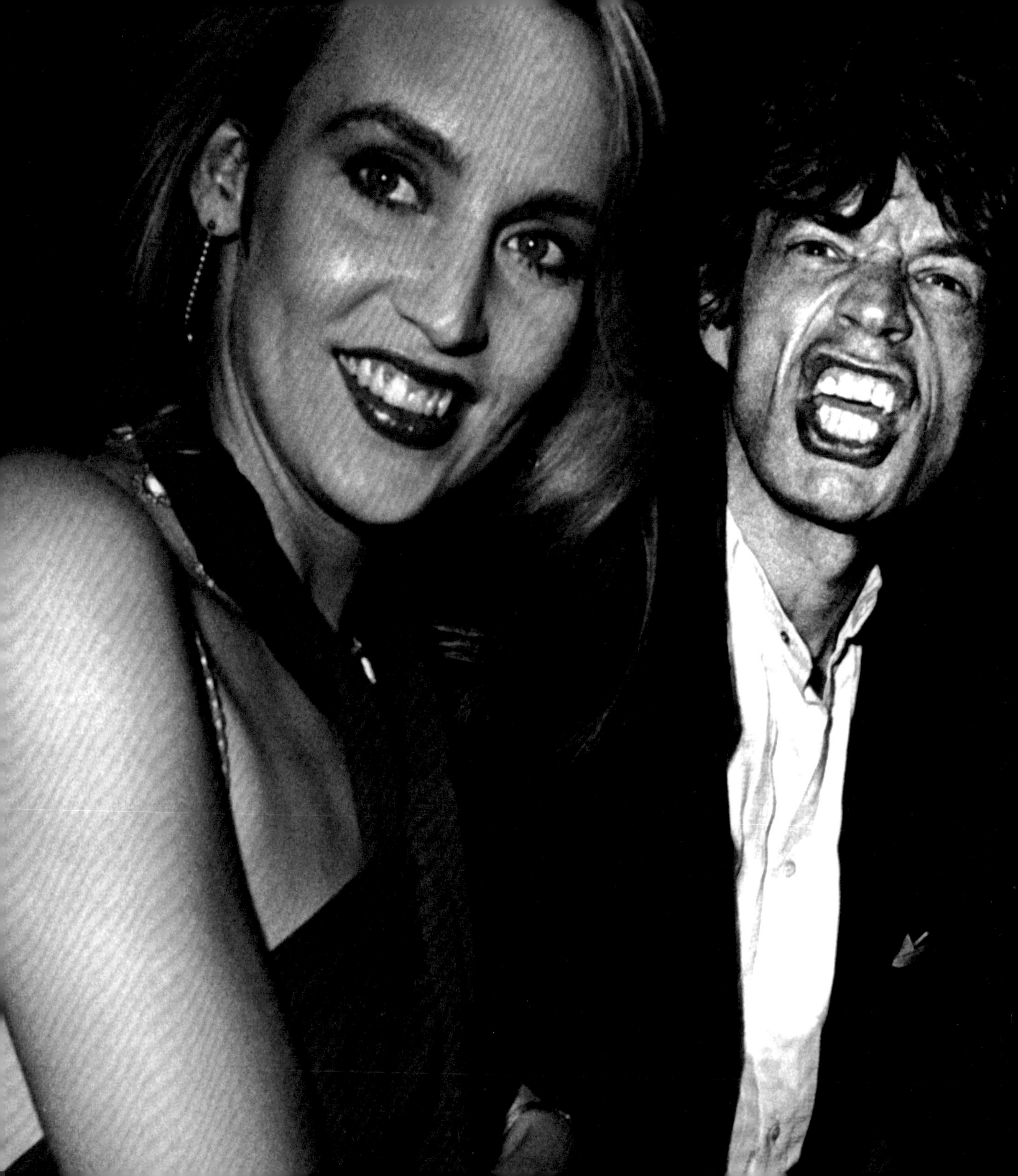

19. September 1984: New York – Ein Schnappschuss von
Mick Jagger und seiner Freundin, dem Model Jerry Hall, beim
Verlassen des Nachtclubs The Limelight nach einer Party
für den Produzenten der Rolling-Stones-Videos, Reid Rogers.
September 19, 1984: New York—Mick Jagger and his girlfriend,
model Jerry Hall were snapped as they departed The Limelight
where they attended a party for Reid Rogers who produced the
Rolling Stones videos.

kalkulierten Bilder in den kommenden Wochen um die Welt gehen werden [...].«[1] Der fragil scheinende Moment vor der Kamera, der sich als Pose in die Fotografiegeschichte eingeschrieben hat wird zu einem kalkulierten Moment, bei dem beide Seiten – Fotograf und Objekt – genau wissen, wie sie sich zu verhalten haben.

»Vor dem Objektiv bin ich zugleich der, für den ich mich halte, der, für den ich gehalten werden möchte, der für den der Photograph mich hält, und der, dessen er sich bedient, um sein können vorzuzeigen«, schreibt Roland Barthes zum fotografischen Porträt. »In anderen Worten, ein bizarrer Vorgang: ich ahme mich unablässig nach, und aus diesem Grund streift mich jedesmal, wenn ich photographiert werde (mich photographieren lasse), unfehlbar ein Gefühl des Unechten [...].«[2] Was Barthes als unablässige Selbstnachahmung beschreibt, findet auch dann statt, wenn dem Fotografierten augenscheinlich nicht passt, dass er fotografiert wird: Mehr als 170 Jahre Fotografiegeschichte haben zur Zu- und Ausrichtung der Körper für die Kamera geführt – sie haben die Fotografie zu einem so gewöhnlichen Bestandteil des Alltages werden lassen, dass der Blick des anderen durch die Kamera antizipiert wird und zu Bildern führt, die anderen Bildern auch dann noch gleichen, wenn sie in Extremsituationen aufgenommen wurden: In seiner Reaktion auf die Kamera entspricht der schreiende Soldat nicht nur Modellen aus Action- und Kriegsfilmen, sondern wendet – wie auch Mick Jagger und Greta Garbo – Strategien der Bildabwehr durch Verzerrung oder Verhüllung an, die sich spätestens in dem Moment etablierten, als in der kriminalistischen Fotografie gegen den Willen der Täter oder Verdächtigen Porträts erzwungen wurden. Die Pose dient auch hier als ein Spielfeld, dessen Seiten durch die von Barthes genannten Parameter begrenzt werden, auf die die Akteure in unterschiedlicher Weise Zugriff haben. Sie produziert Bilder, in denen die Absichten der Fotografierten und der Fotografierenden sich gegenseitig überlagern, auslöschen, verstärken. Der Fotografie – zumal der digitalen – allein ihr manipulatives Potenzial vorzuwerfen, vernachlässigt daher ihr emanzipatives: Sie lässt den Körper nicht nur zu einem wahrgenommenen und aufgezeichneten werden, sondern als Medium der Massenkultur befähigt sie diesen selben Körper auch, seine Wahrnehmungs- und Erscheinungsmöglichkeiten zu potenzieren. Die Fotografie macht ihre Paradoxie gegenwärtig und die Pose als Geste der Ohnmacht wie der Selbstermächtigung sichtbar.

1 Thomas Seelig, »Look-Alikes«, in: G.R.A.M., *Paparazzi*, Salzburg 2009, S. 34 ff.

2 Roland Barthes, *Die helle Kammer*, Frankfurt am Main 1985, S. 22.

Felix Hoffmann (geb. 1972) ist Kunsthistoriker und Kulturwissenschaftler. Als Hauptkurator bei C/O Berlin hat er seit 2004 Ausstellungen unter anderen mit Nan Goldin, Robert Frank, Peter Lindbergh oder Robert Mapplethorpe verantwortet. Darüber hinaus ist er Autor und Herausgeber zahlreicher Texte und Bücher.

This dialectic response of the celebrities, whose protagonists constantly oscillate between exhibition and concealment and for whom the paparazzi are also accomplices, is a basic theme in many of Ron Galella's pictures. When he photographed Greta Garbo in 1978 in New York she did not scream into the camera but held a handkerchief in front of her face: here, the act of veiling becomes a weapon against the exposure of privacy, resistance to the paparazzo yet at the same time a symbol of surrendering to one's destiny.

In a similar way to war photography, the photography of the paparazzi has cultivated specific bodily gestures: "The object of desire knows he is in the limelight. He knows he is being observed through the telephoto lens and that someone is following every step he makes. He knows that the few, calculated pictures will go round the world in the coming weeks . . ."[1] The seemingly fragile moment in front of the camera, which has engraved itself in the history of photography becomes a calculated moment, in which both parties—photographer and object—know exactly how to behave.

"In front of the lens I am who I think I am and also who I would like people to think I am, who the photographer thinks I am and the person he uses in order to present his skill," Roland Barthes writes about the photographic portrait. "In other words a bizarre process: I am incessantly imitating myself, and for this reason I continually have the unerring feeling when I am being photographed (allow myself to be photographed) that things are not real . . ."[2] What Barthes describes as ceaseless self-imitation also occurs when the person depicted evidently does not feel at ease with being photographed: More than 170 years of photographic history have led to the body being arranged/adjusted for the camera—they have allowed photography to become such a normal component of everyday life that the gaze of the other through the camera lens is anticipated and leads to pictures that are the same as the other pictures even when they have been taken in extreme situations: in his response to the camera the screaming soldier does not only correspond to models from action and war films but uses—as do Mick Jagger and Greta Garbo—strategies of defense against pictures by means of distorting or veiling. These strategies were established at the latest when criminological photography coerced a portrait against the will of the offender or the suspect. Here the pose serves as a playing field, on which the sides of the pitch are limited by the parameters named by Barthes and to which the protagonists have access in different ways. It produces images, in which the intentions of the photographer and the person photographed mutually superimpose, delete and enhance one another. To accuse photography—above all digital photography—only of manipulative potential, hence neglects its emancipatory capabilities: it not only allows the body to be perceived and recorded but as a medium of mass culture it also enables the same body to increase its potential for perception and manifestation. Photography reveals its paradox nature and shows a pose to be a gesture of impotence as well as self-empowerment.

1   Thomas Seelig, "Look-Alikes," in: G.R.A.M., *Paparazzi* (Salzburg, 2009), pp. 34 ff.

2   Roland Barthes, *Die helle Kammer* (Frankfurt am Main, 1985), p. 22.

Felix Hoffmann (born 1972) studied Art History and Cultural Science. Since 2004, as chief curator of C/O Berlin, he has been responsible for exhibitions with Nan Goldin, Robert Mapplethorpe, Robert Frank, Peter Lindbergh, and others. He is also author and editor of numerous articles and books.

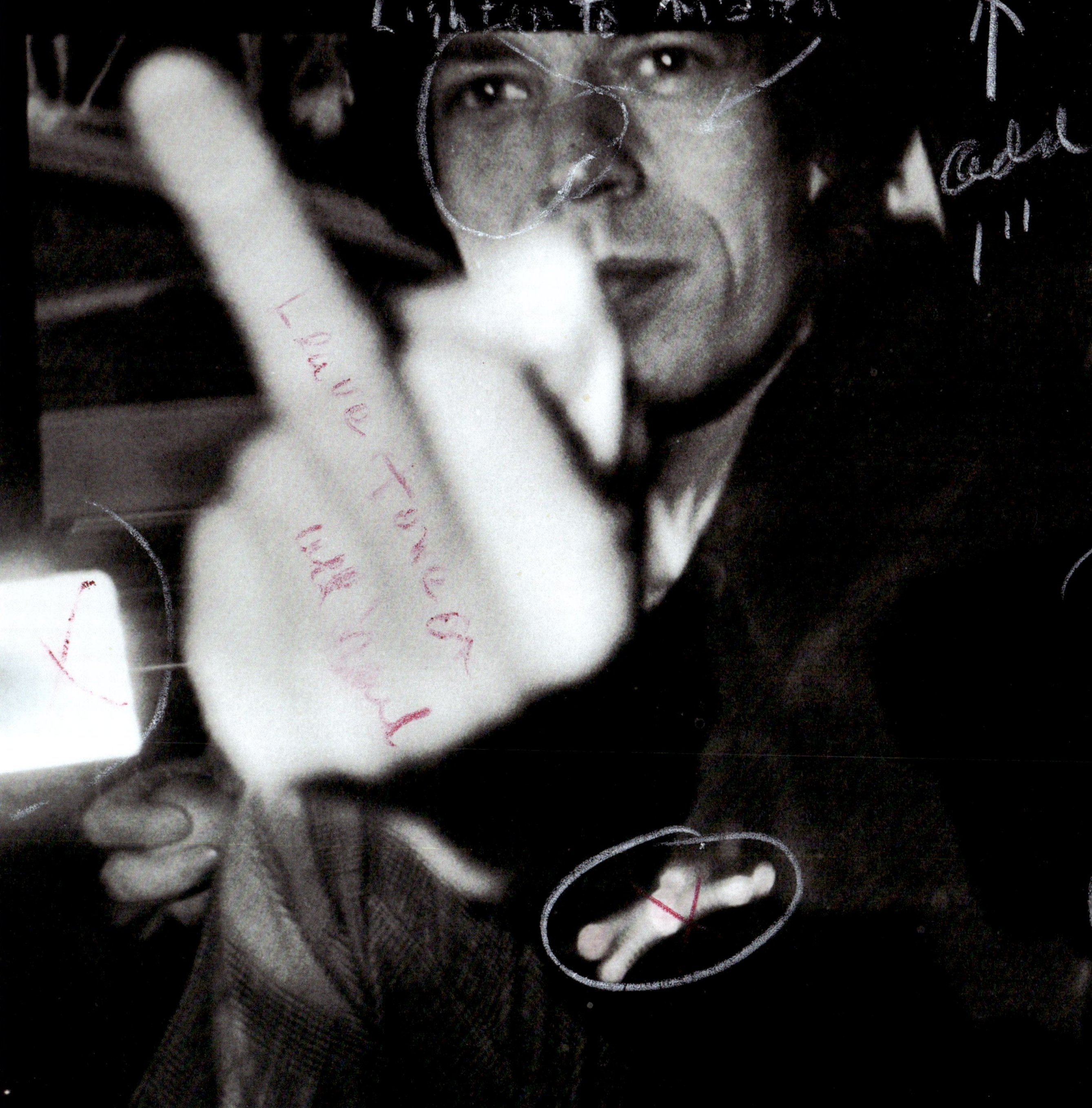
Lighten to moth
add
!!
Leave tone or

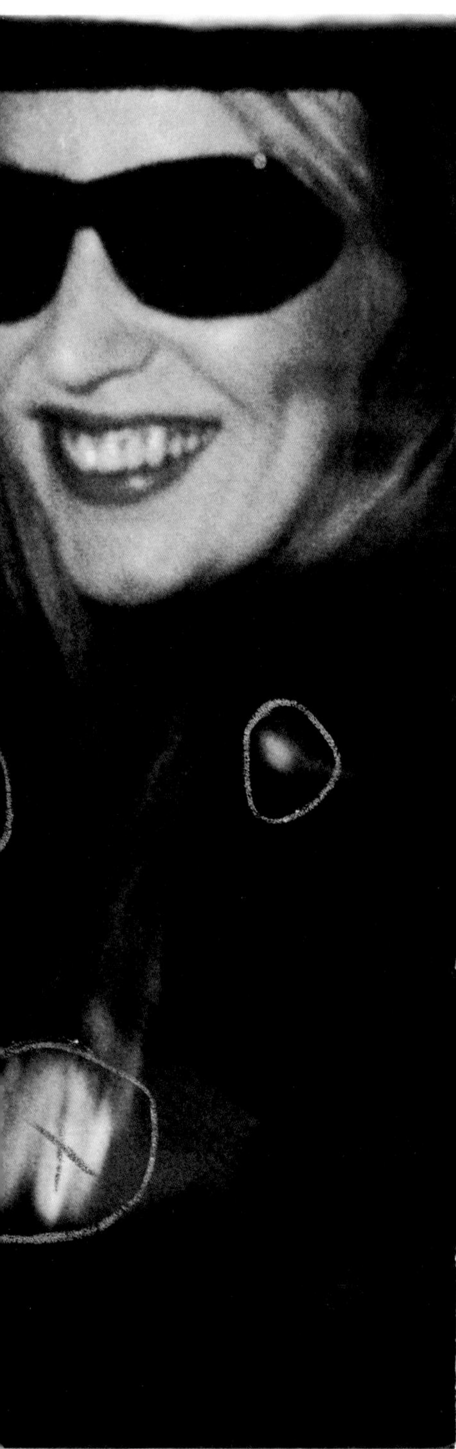

Bildkorrekturen auf einem Probeabzug
16. Januar 1983: Los Angeles, Kalifornien – Mick Jagger und
Jerry Hall bei einem Essen anlässlich einer Ausstellungseröffnung
in der Mizuno Gallery.
Pre-print corrections
January 16, 1983: Los Angeles, California—Mick Jagger and
Jerry Hall attending an opening luncheon at Mizuno Gallery.

PERFORMERS

Ron Galella

ALFRED

29. April 1974: New York – Alfred Hitchcock bei der
Film-Society-Gala zu seinen Ehren im Lincoln Center.
April 29, 1974: New York—Alfred Hitchcock attends the
Film Society Tribute to Alfred Hitchcock at Lincoln Center.

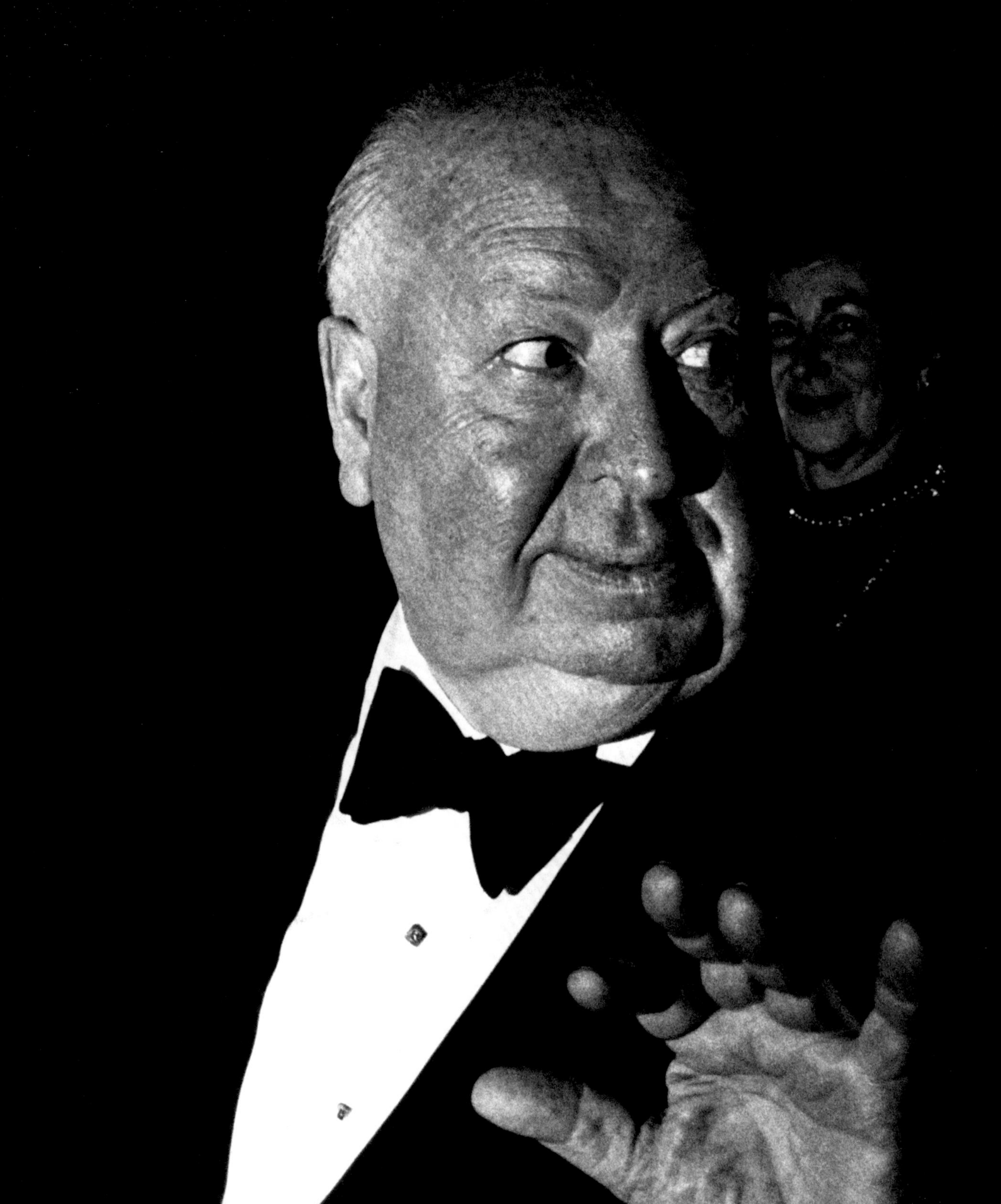

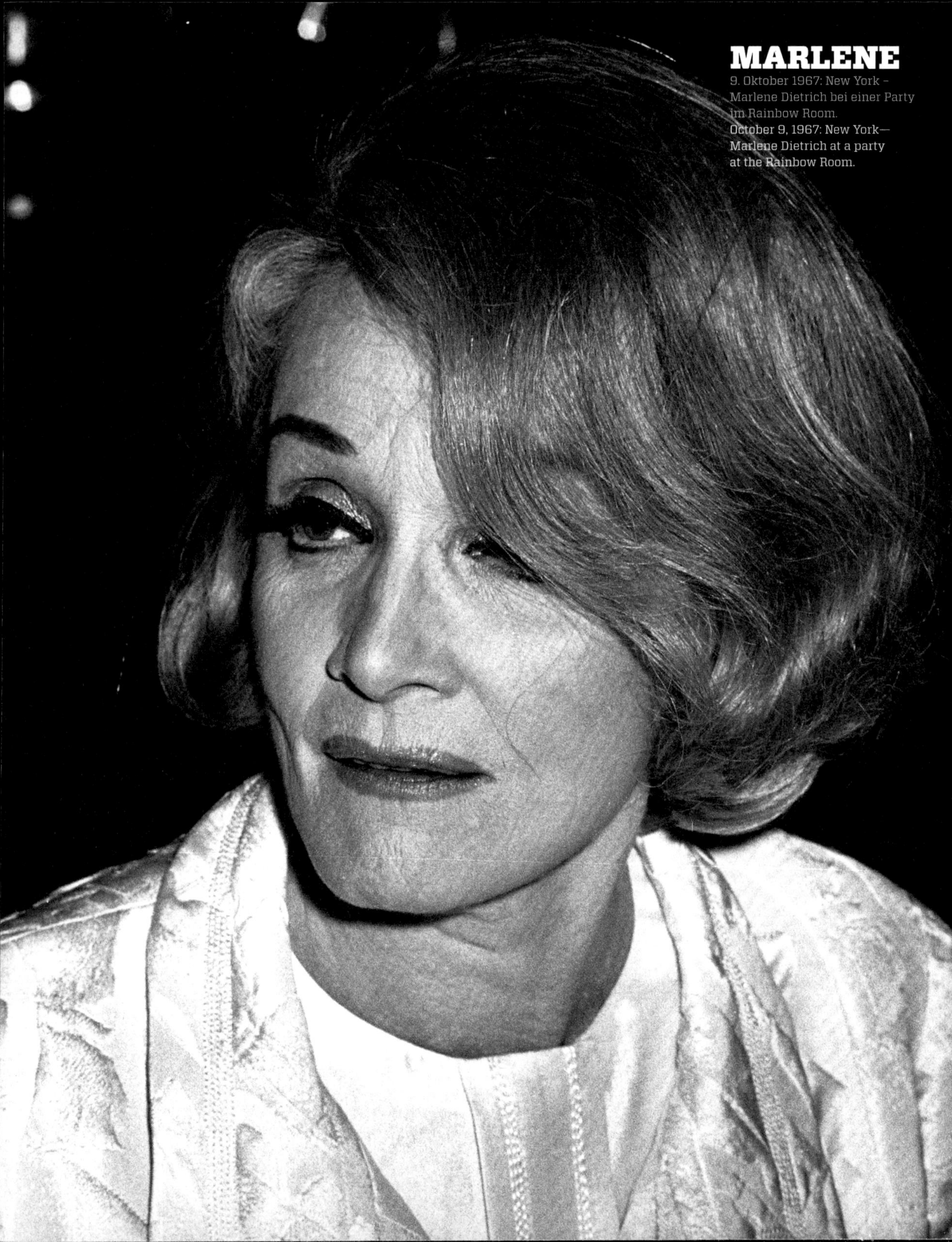

9. Oktober 1967: New York –
Marlene Dietrich bei einer Party
im Rainbow Room.
October 9, 1967: New York—
Marlene Dietrich at a party
at the Rainbow Room.

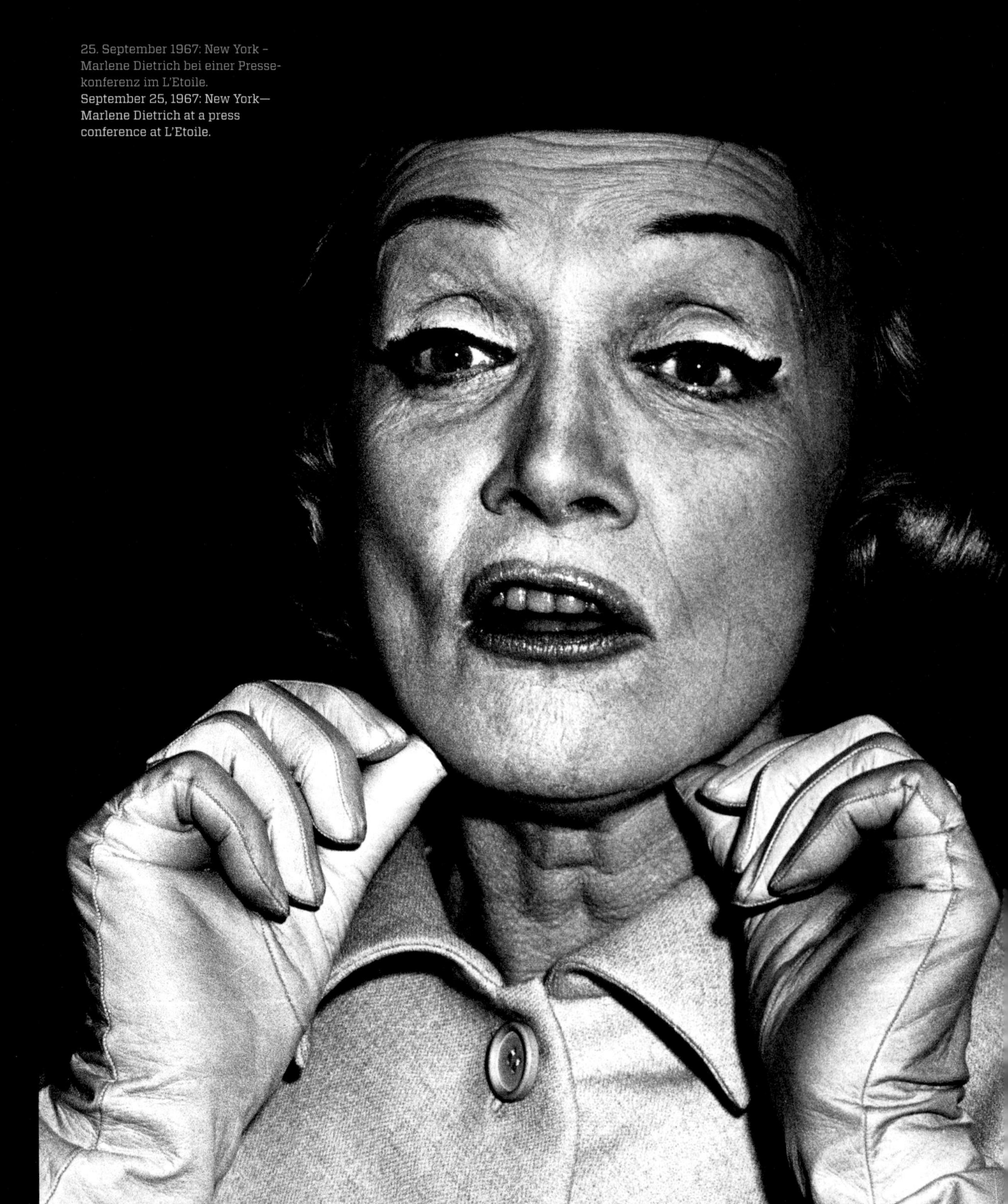

25. September 1967: New York –
Marlene Dietrich bei einer Presse-
konferenz im L'Etoile.
September 25, 1967: New York—
Marlene Dietrich at a press
conference at L'Etoile.

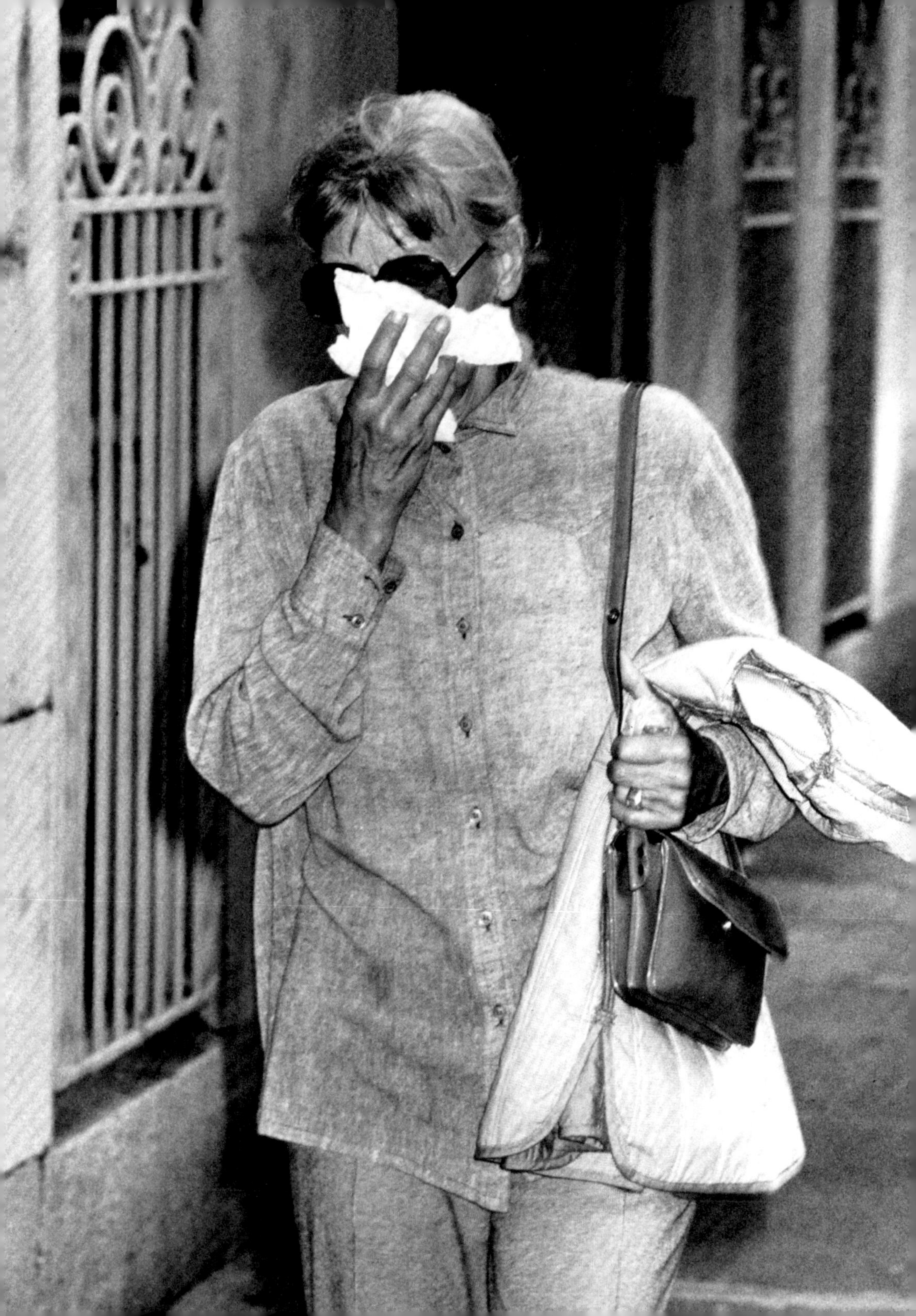

GRETA

1. Juni 1978: New York – Greta Garbo
in der Nähe der East 52nd Street.
June 1, 1978: New York—Greta Garbo
near East 52nd Street.

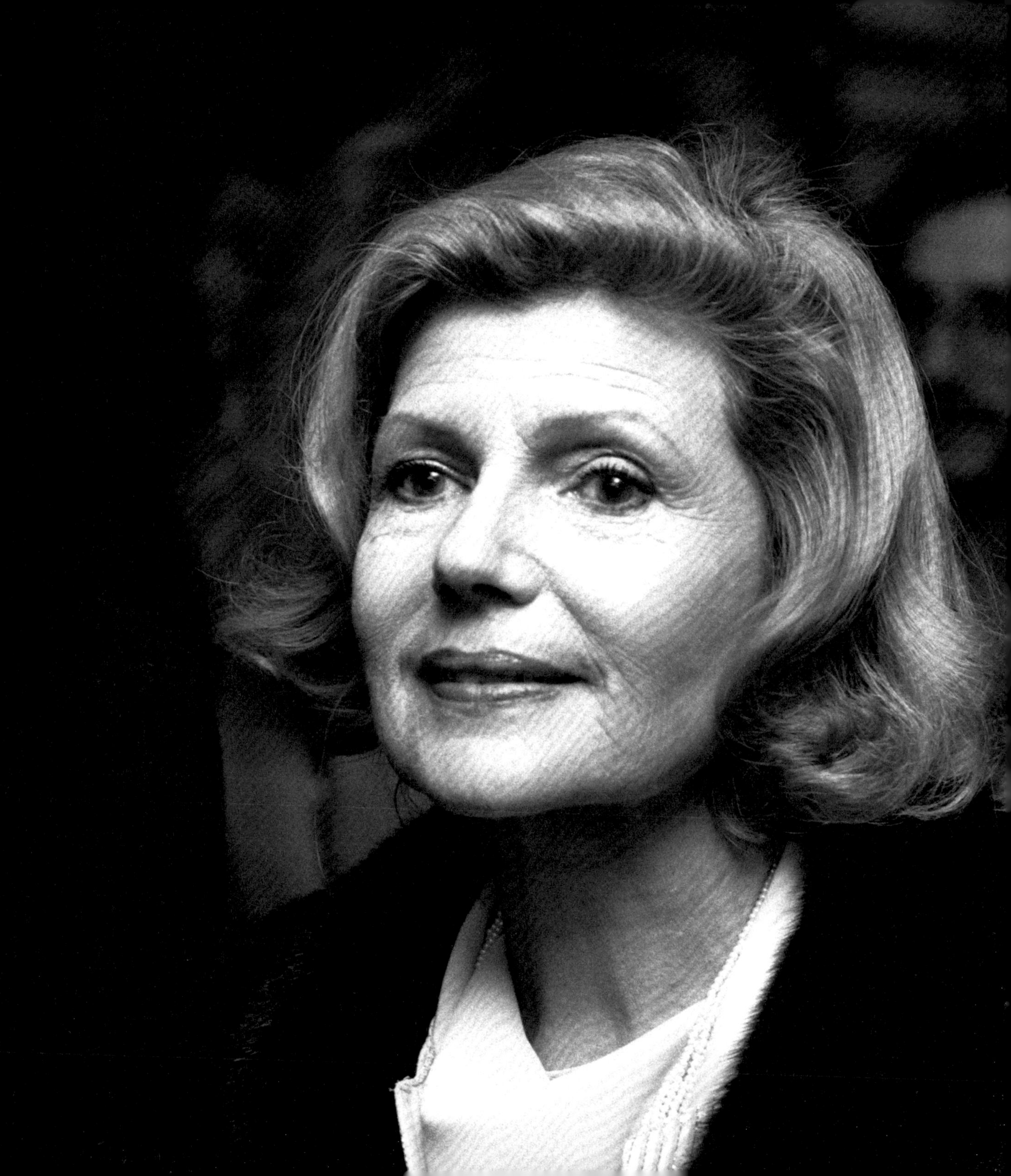

RITA

14. Februar 1979: Beverly Hills, Kalifornien – Rita Hayworth
auf der Party der Zeitschrift *Look* in Jimmy's Restaurant.

February 14, 1979: Beverly Hills, California—Rita Hayworth
attends the *Look* magazine party at Jimmy's Restaurant.

19. April 1970: New York - Cary Grant bei der 24. Verleihung
der »Annual Tony Awards« im Mark Hellinger Theater.
April 19, 1970: New York—Cary Grant attends the 24th Annual
Tony Awards at the Mark Hellinger Theater.

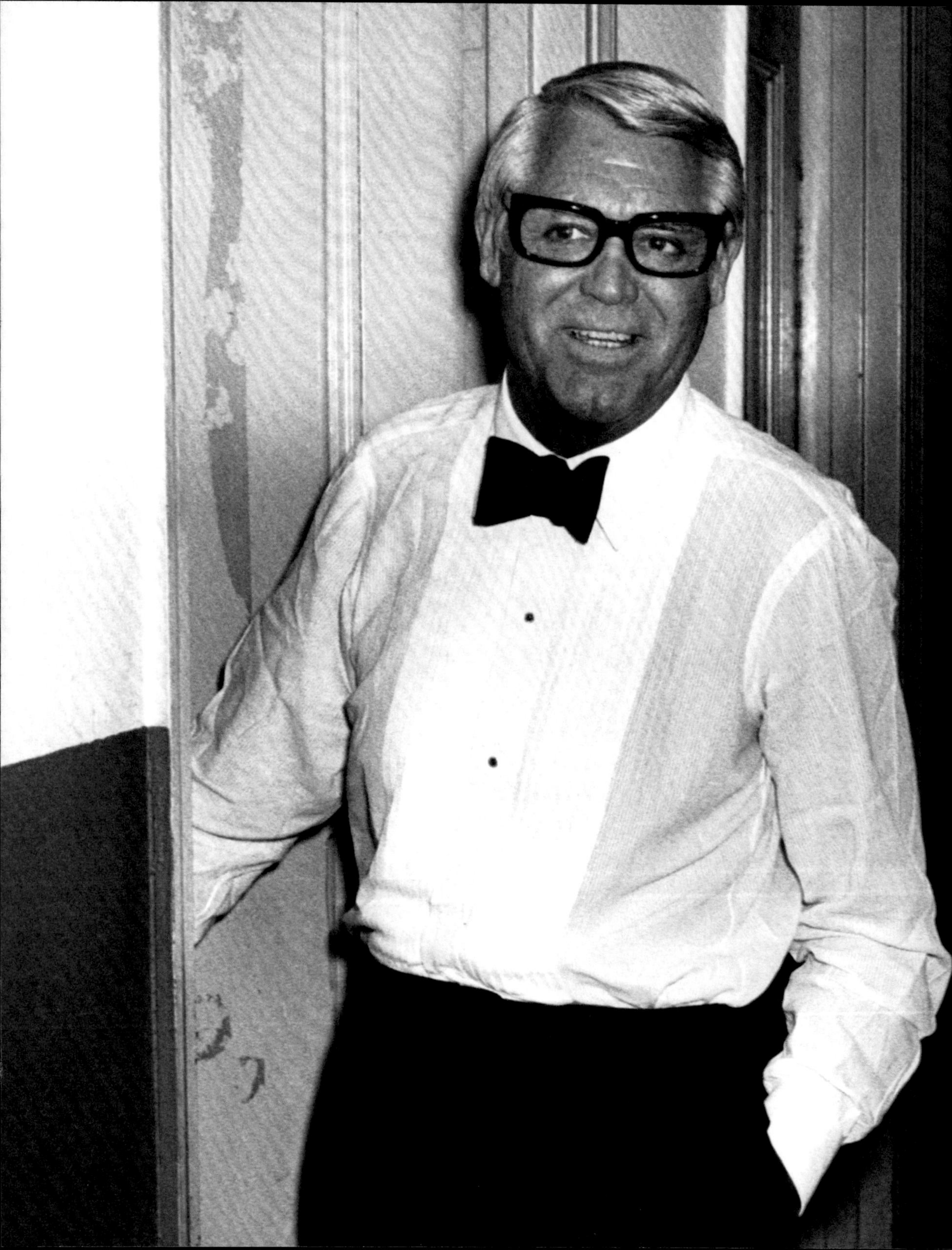

CHARLTON

15. Juli 1969: London, England – Charlton Heston
am Set von *Julius Caesar.*
July 15, 1969: London, England—Charlton Heston
on the set of *Julius Caesar.*

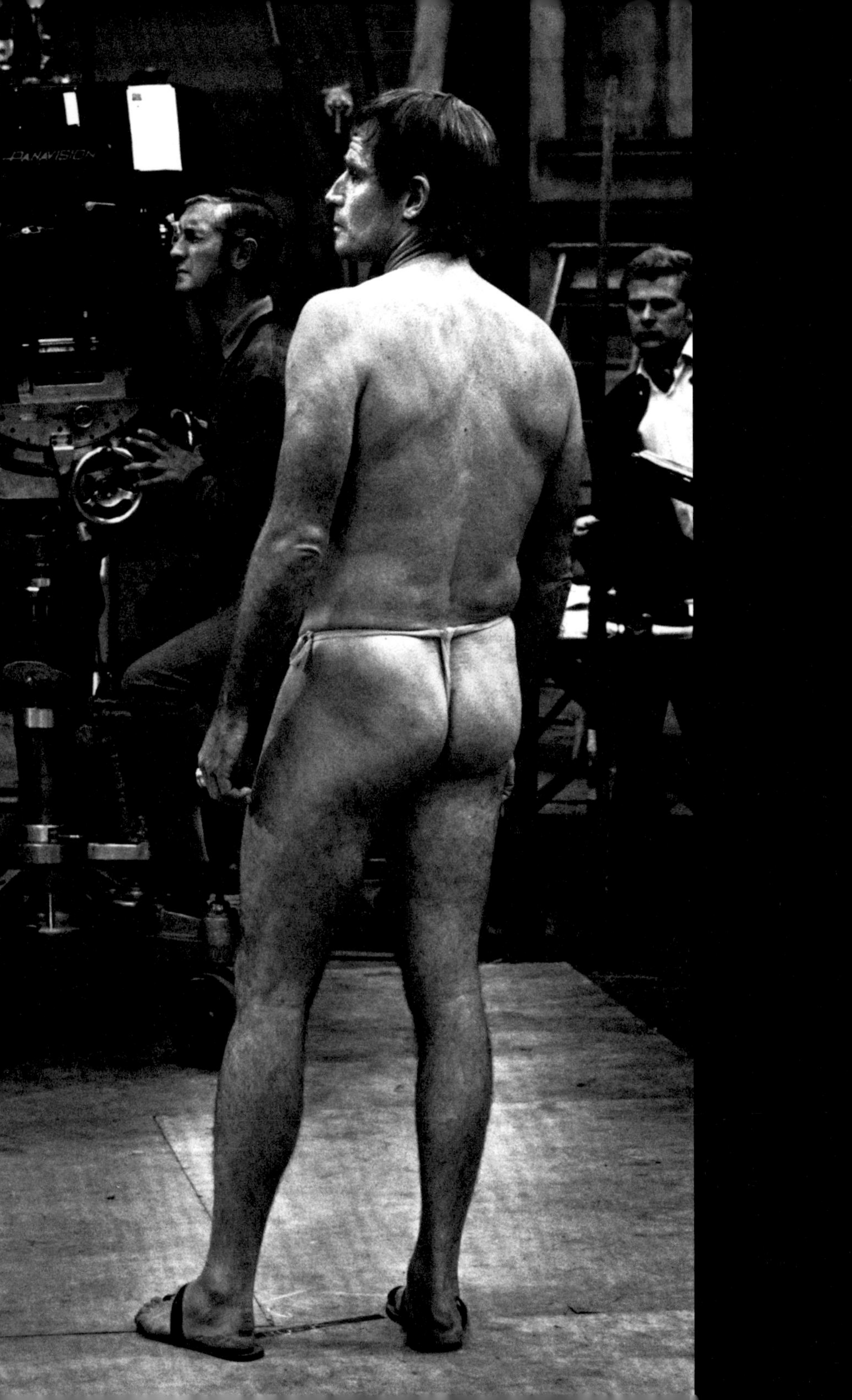

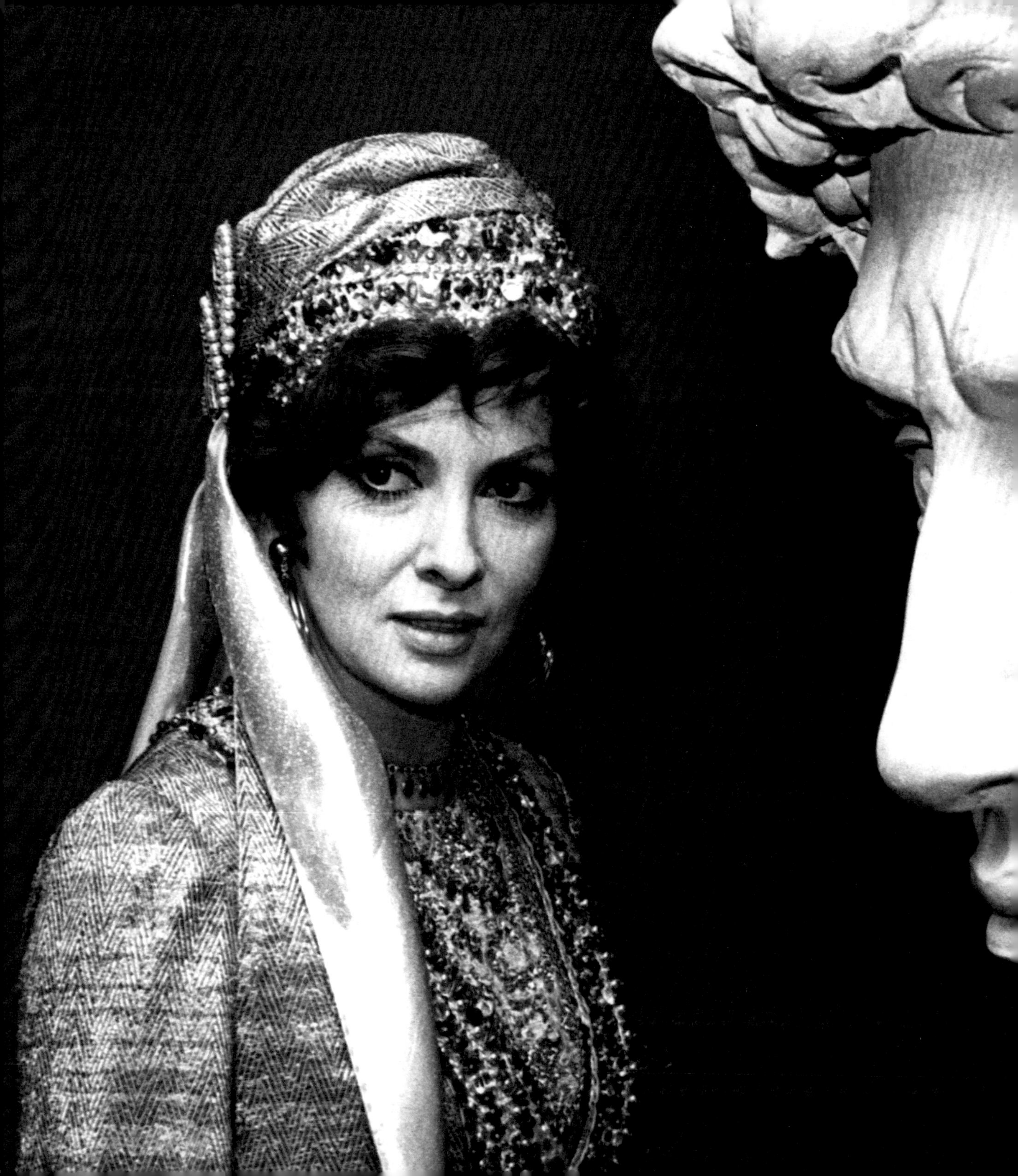

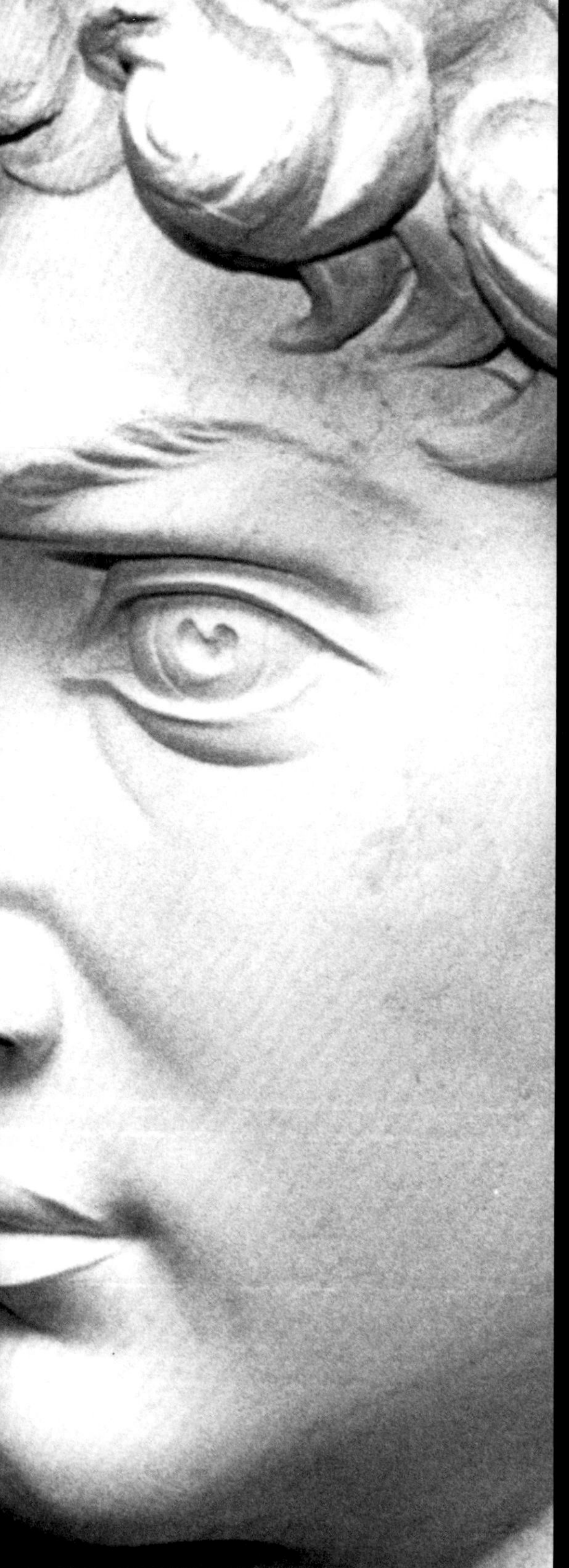

GINA

May 4, 1970: New York—Two Italian works of art,
Gina Lollobrigida and Michelangelo's David, at the
Million Dollar Extravaganza Art Exhibit in the Gran
Ballroom of the Waldorf-Astoria Hotel.

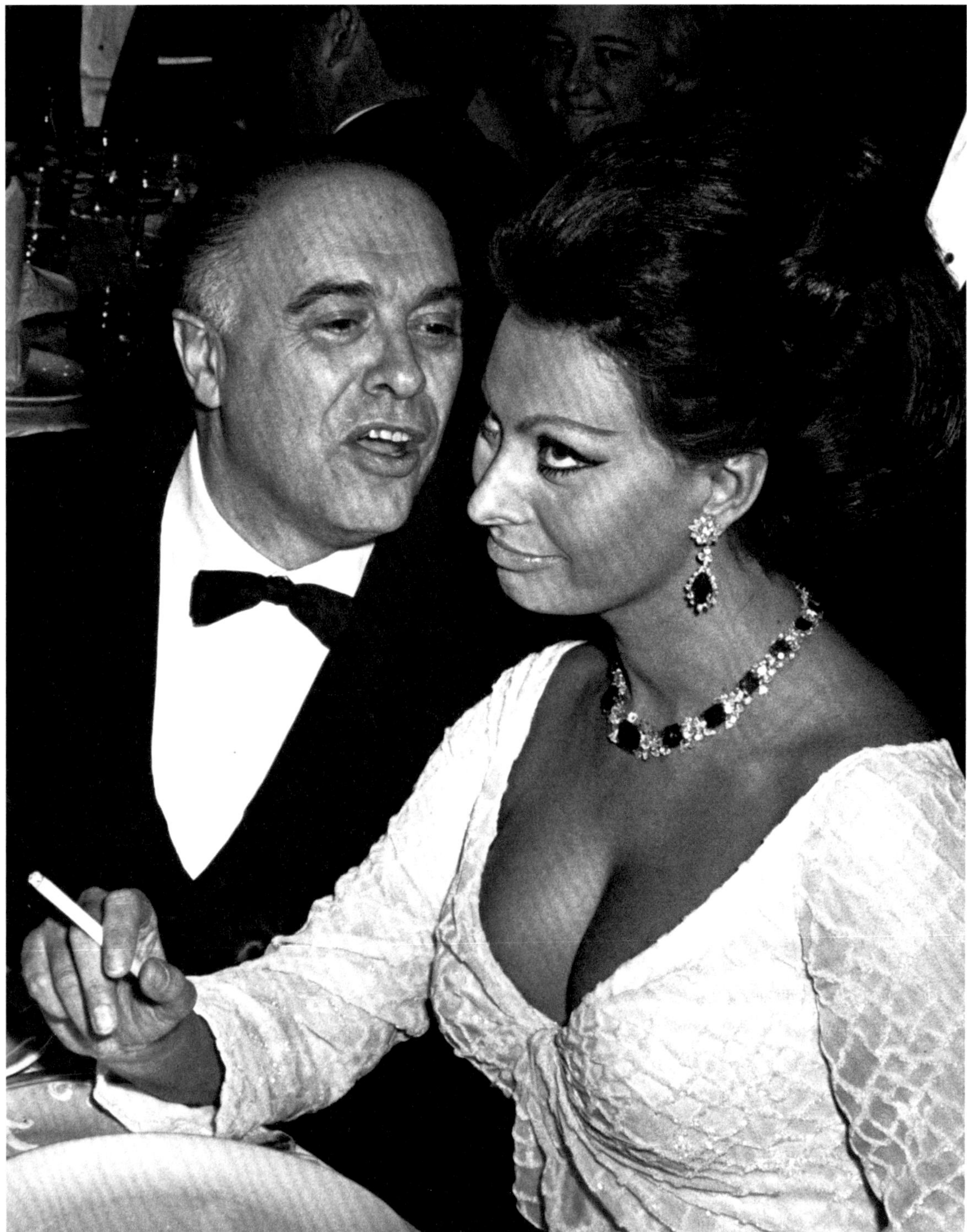

DECEMBER 22, 1965: ;DR. ZHIVAGO, directed by David Lean, produced by Carlo Ponti and starring Omar Sharif, Julie Christie, Rod Steiger, Alec Guinness, Ralph Richardson, Geraldine Chaplin premiered in New York City and was followed by a celebratory party at the Americana Hotel. Photographer Ron Galella asked SOPHIA LOREN what she found fascinating about the film's star, Omar Sharif. "His eyes!" she said making an expressive gesture. "I thought the Italians had the most beautiful eyes, now I think the Egyptians have!" She accompanied her husband CARLO PONTI to the unspooling. CREDIT: RON GALELLA / RON GALELLA, LTD.

THIS IS AN ORIGINAL PHOTOGRAPH BY RON GALELLA:

RON GALELLA

BRIGITTE

September 1968: St. Tropez, Frankreich –
Brigitte Bardot im Nachtclub Zoom.
September, 1968: St. Tropez, France—
Brigitte Bardot at Zoom Nightclub.

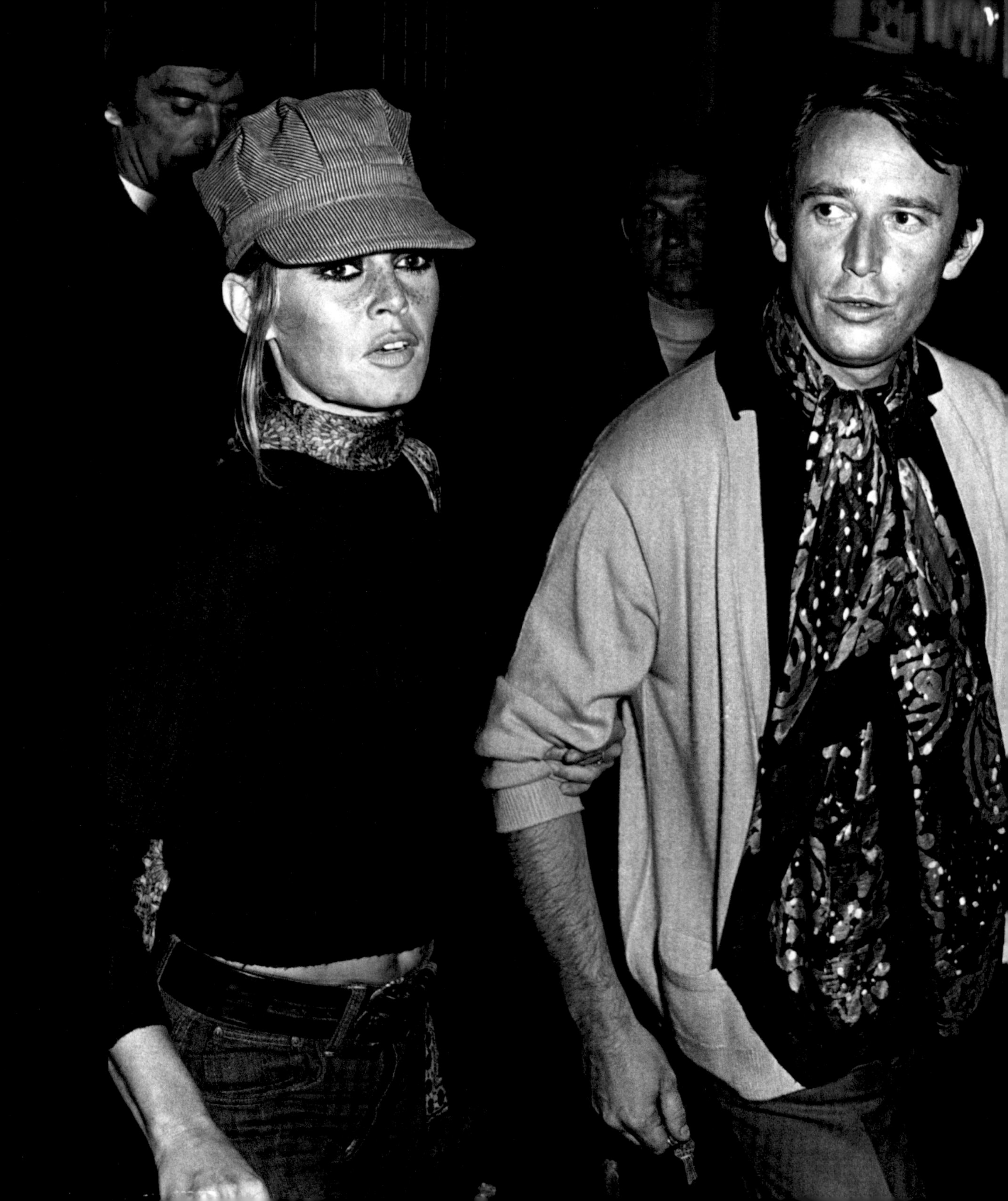

BRIGITTE

12. September 1968: St. Tropez, Frankreich – Brigitte Bardot.
Bei der Landung auf dem Flughafen von Nizza traf ich den Schau-
spieler George Sanders. Während ich ihn fotografierte, sagte er:
»Du solltest Brigitte Bardot verfolgen.« Ich bat einen Taxifahrer,
mich zu Brigitte Bardots Haus zu bringen. Er lehnte ab, weil ich
ein Fotograf war und er ihre Privatsphäre schützen wollte. Ich
versteckte die Kamera in meinem Lederbeutel und fragte einen
anderen Fahrer. Er hielt mich für einen Postboten und fuhr mich zu
Brigitte Bardots Haus an der Mittelmeerküste. Ich krempelte dann
meine Hosen hoch, watete durch das Wasser vor ihrem Grundstück
und beobachtete sie und ihren Freund beim Wasserski. Nachdem
ich ein Dutzend Fotos geschossen hatte, fing ihr Freund an, mich
mit Wasser zu bespritzen und ich rückte ab.

September 12, 1968: St. Tropez, France—Brigitte Bardot.
Upon landing at Nice Airport, I met actor George Sanders, and
while photographing him, he said, "You should be going after
Brigitte Bardot." I asked a taxi driver to take me to Brigitte Bardot's
house. He refused, as I was a photographer and he wanted to
protect her privacy. I then hid my camera in my leather mailbag
and asked another driver. He assumed I was a mailman and drove
me to Bardot's house on the Mediterranean shore. I then rolled
up my trousers and waded in the water adjacent to her property
to view her and her boyfriend water skiing. After taking a dozen
shots, her boyfriend began hosing me with water, and I departed.

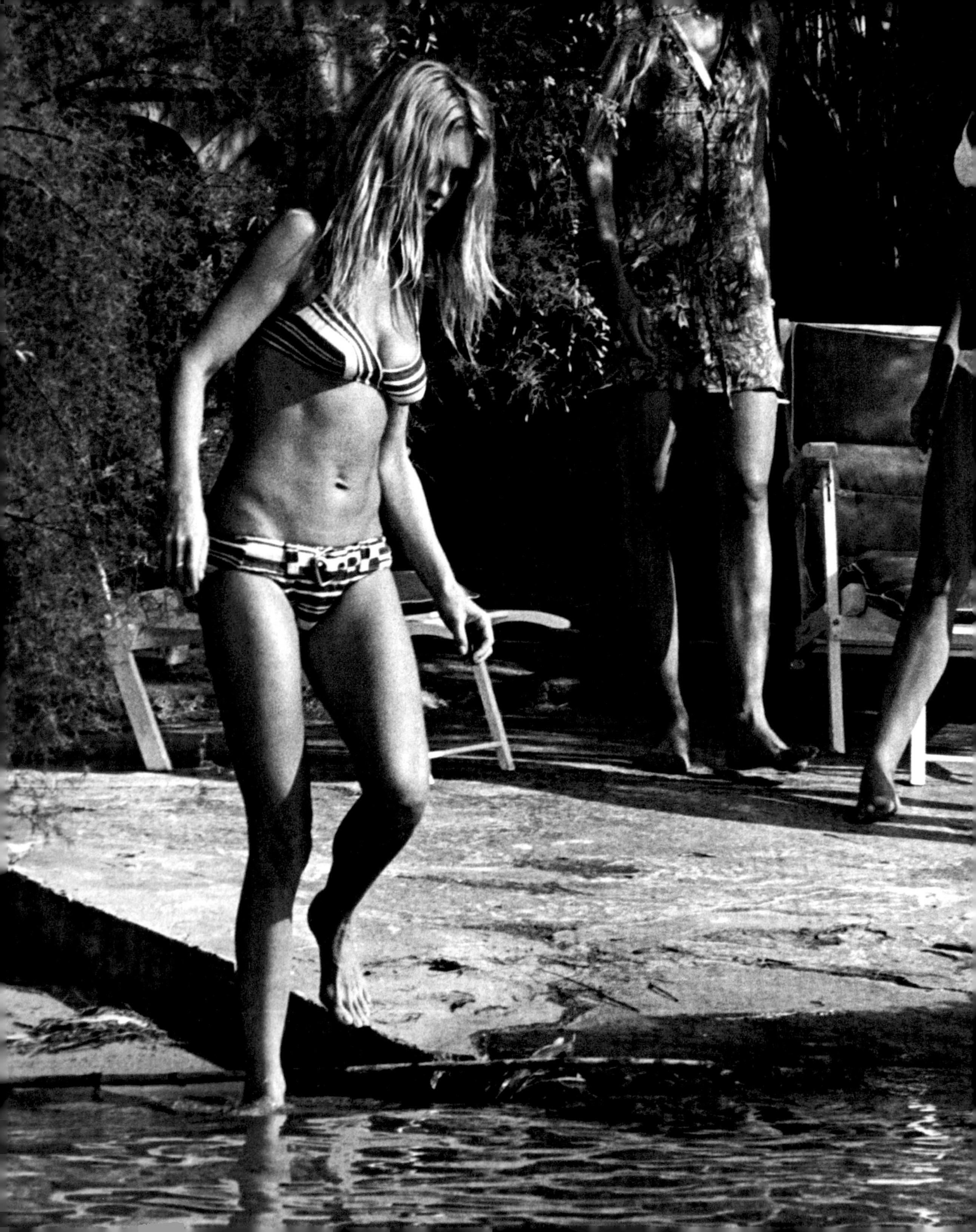

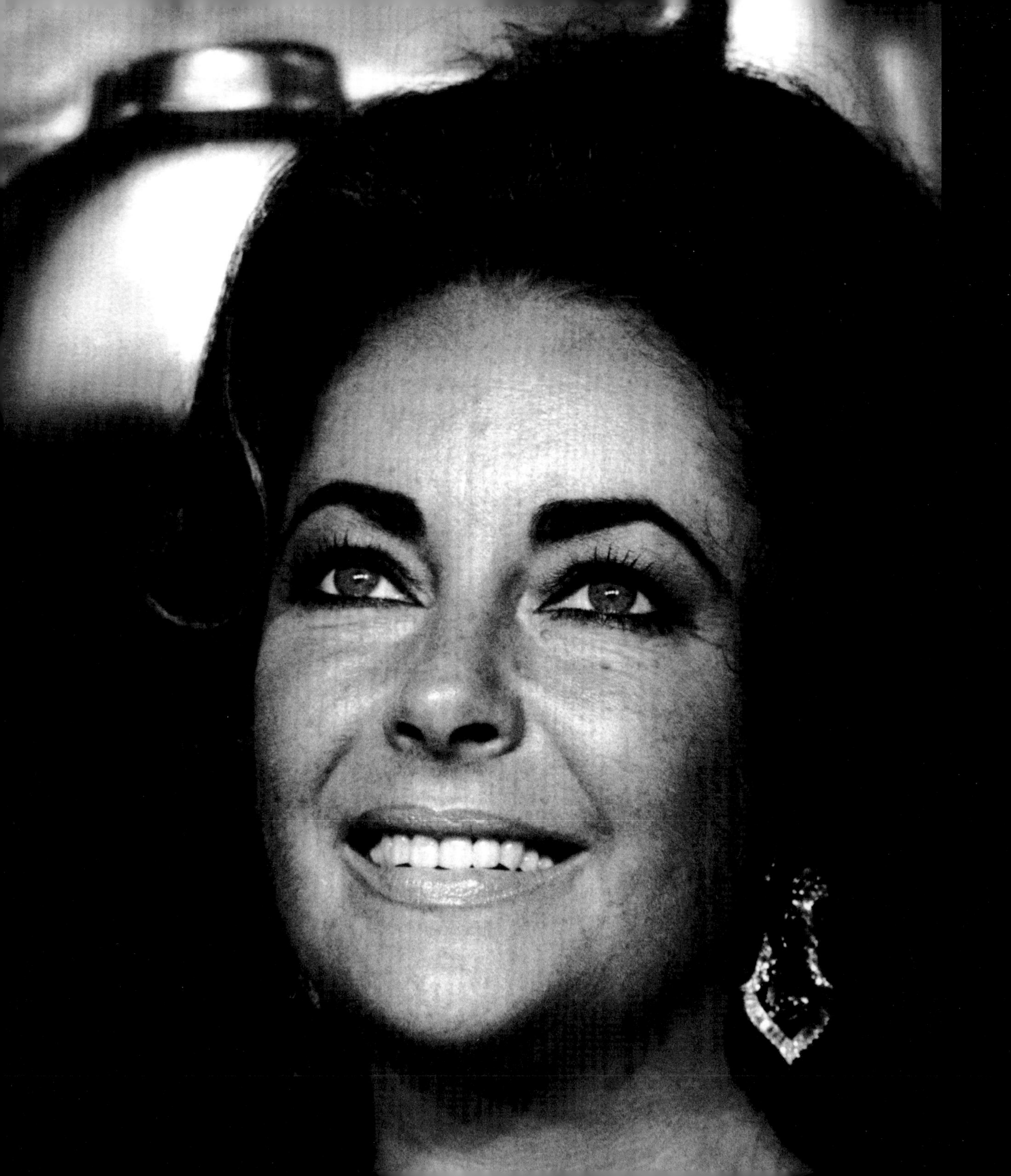

ELIZABETH

2. April 1974: Los Angeles, Kalifornien – Elizabeth Taylor
bei der 46. Verleihung der »Annual Academy Awards«
im Dorothy Chandler Pavilion.
April 2, 1974: Los Angeles, California—Elizabeth Taylor
attends the 46th Annual Academy Awards at Dorothy
Chandler Pavilion.

May 8, 1983: Her Majesty, The Queen!
Queen Elizabeth arrives at Rock
Hudson's New York City apartment-
that's where she's staying while
performing in "Private Lives"
starrin opposite her ex-husband
of two times Richard Burton at
the Lunt Fontane Theatre. Liz is
coming back from a party at Tavern on the Green in honor of
the opening of the new play, which
was produced by THE QUEEN herself
and Zev Bufman. The party wasn't
anything spectacular. Uniforned
cops and private Dick Tracy's num-
bered 280. 140 at the Theatre and
140 at Tavern on the Green. The city
agreed to block 46th Street between
Broadway and Eighth from 5to 9:30,
which they dont even do for the
real Queen Elizabeth. Liz sported
her own personal diamond tiara and
it was a sit down dinner for about
one thousand to be dressed in black
tie, dinner jackets and gowns
for the ladies. By the way Liz and
Rock starred in the "Giant" together which is being re-released.
Clives Barnes gave the play a
terrible review in the 5/9/83
New York Post.

SO-1363

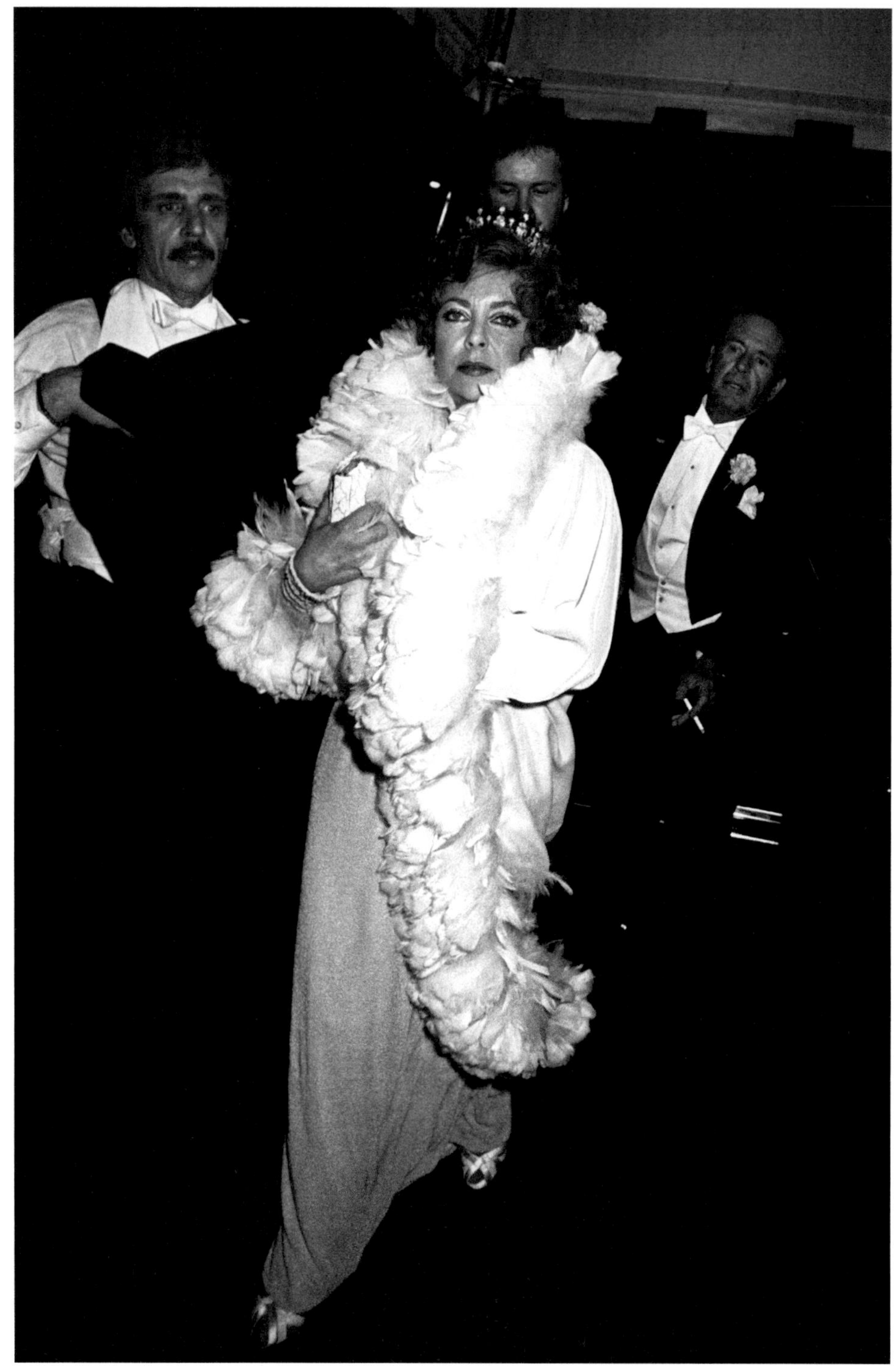

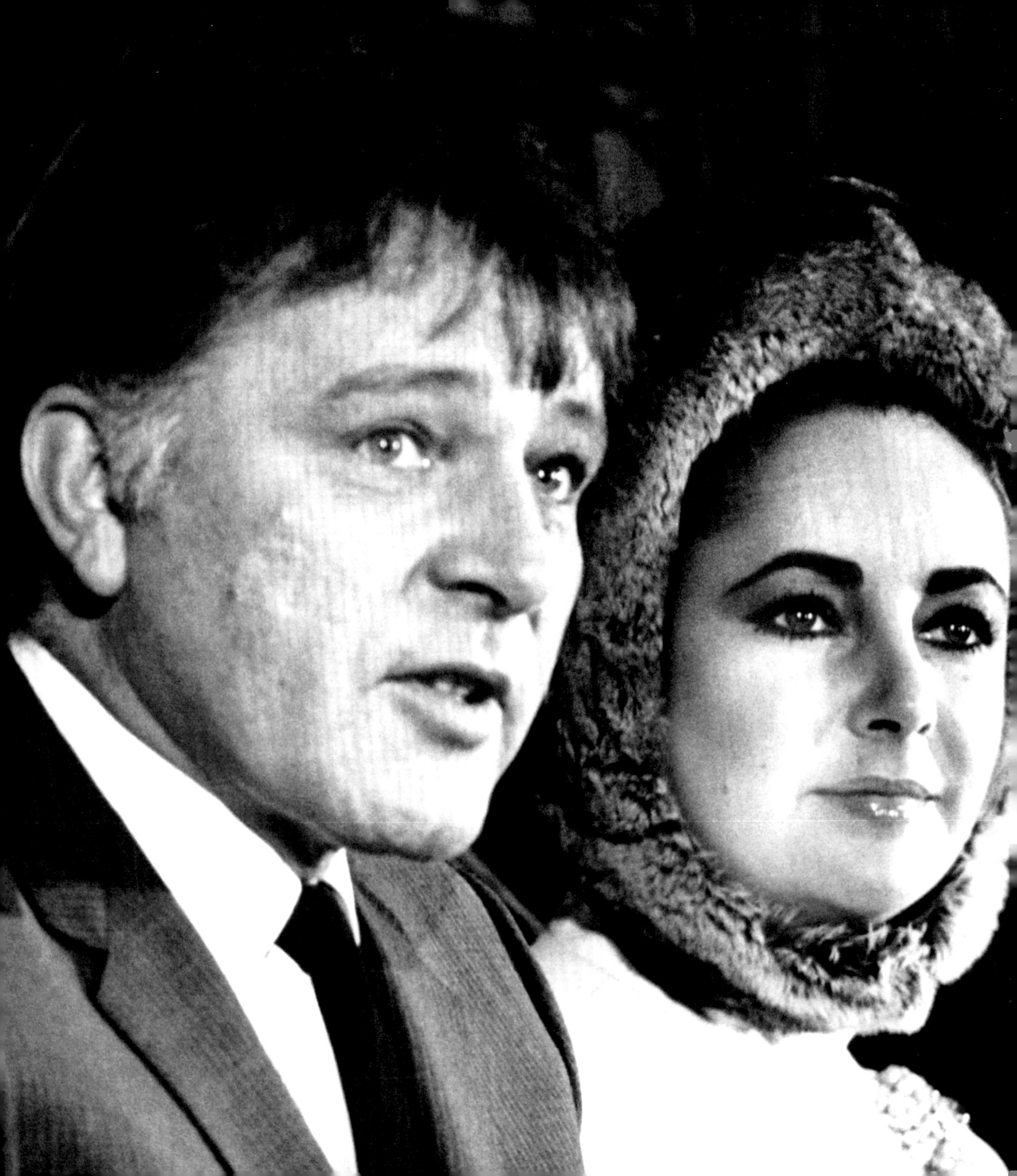

ELIZABETH & RICHARD

18. Oktober 1968: Paris, Frankreich – Elizabeth Taylor und
Richard Burton bei der Premiere von *Ein Floh im Ohr*.
October 18, 1968: Paris, France—Elizabeth Taylor and
Richard Burton at the premiere of *A Flea in Her Ear*.

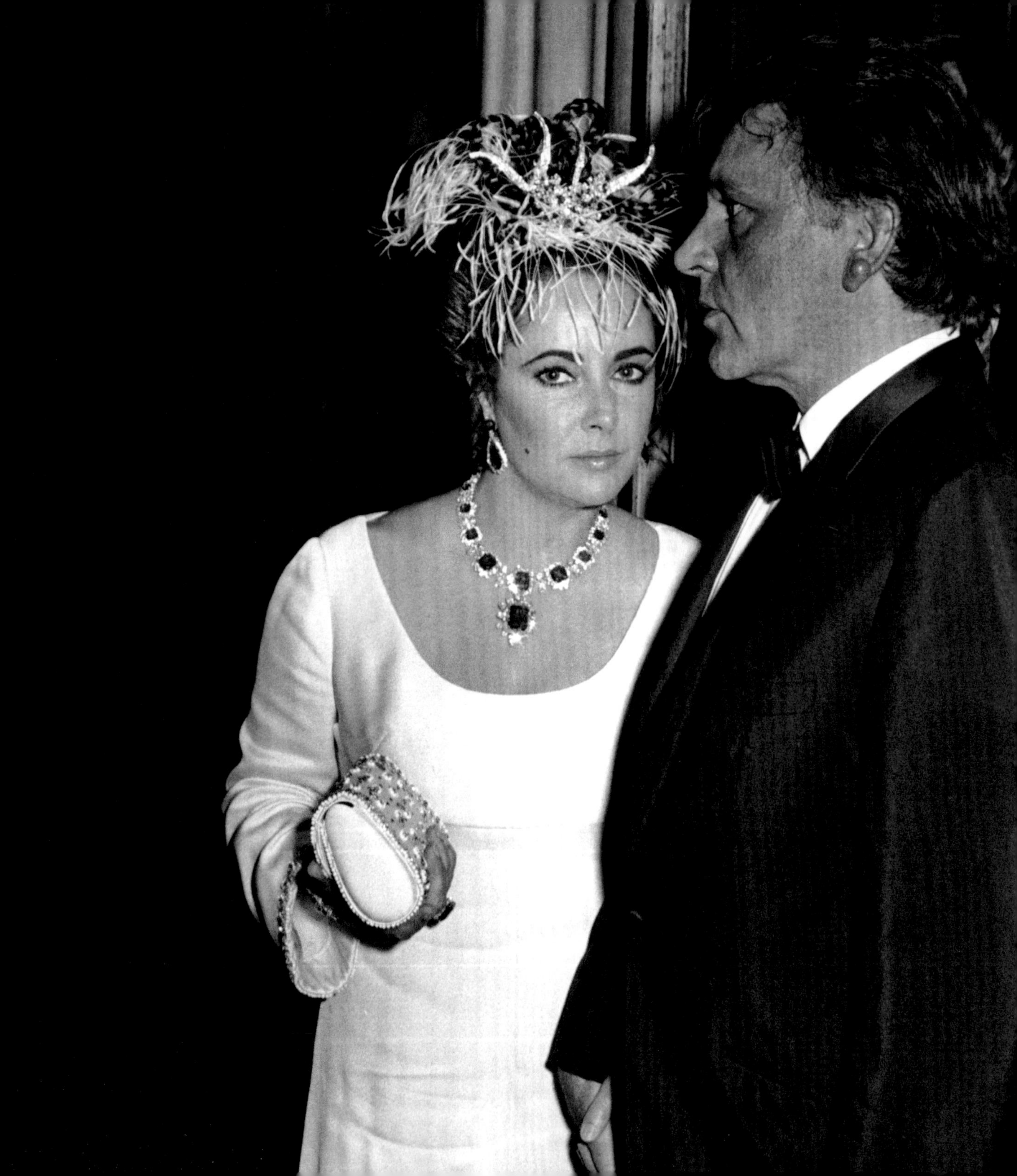

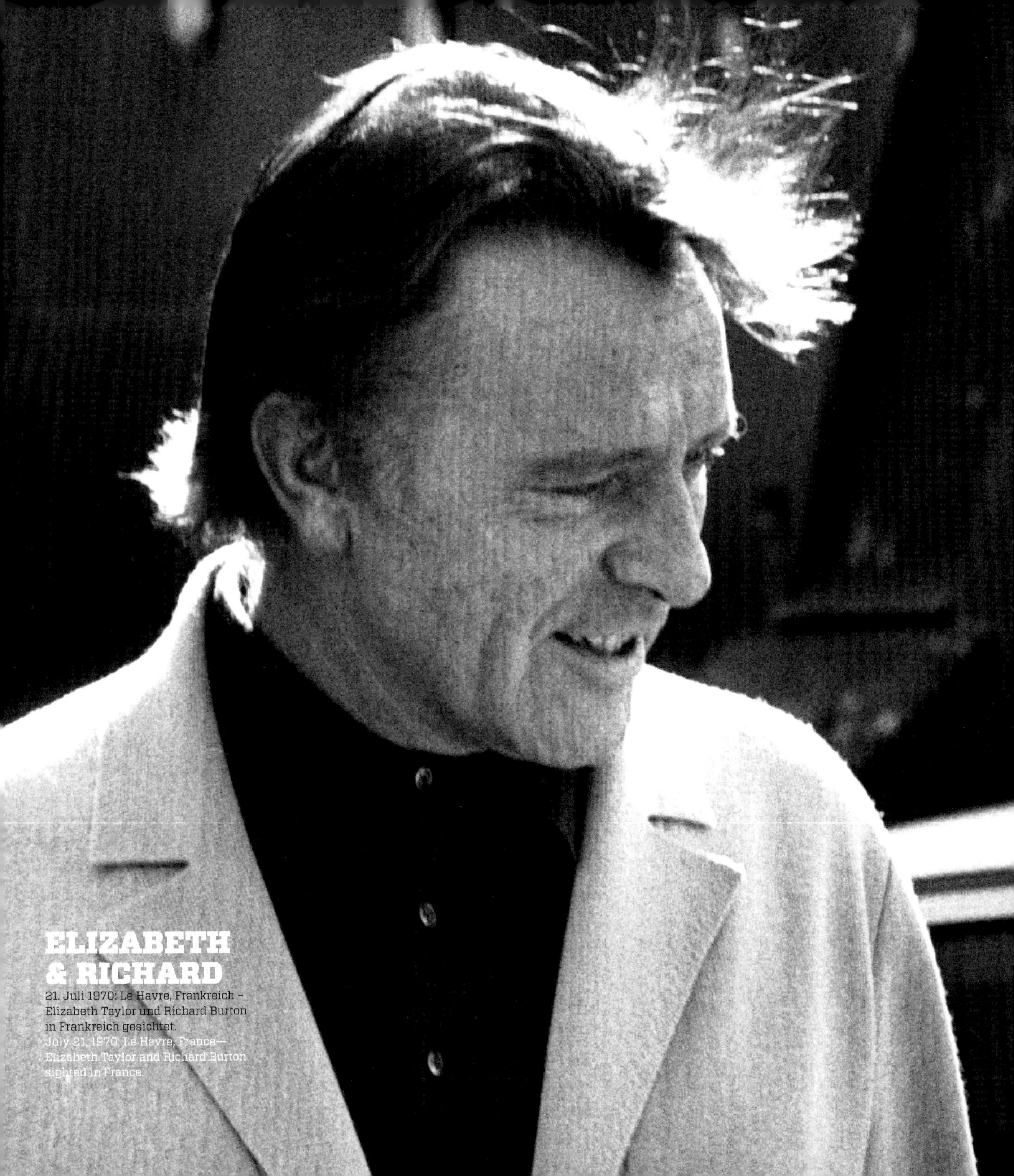ELIZABETH
& RICHARD
21. Juli 1970: Le Havre, Frankreich –
Elizabeth Taylor und Richard Burton
in Frankreich gesichtet.
July 21, 1970: Le Havre, France—
Elizabeth Taylor and Richard Burton
sighted in France.

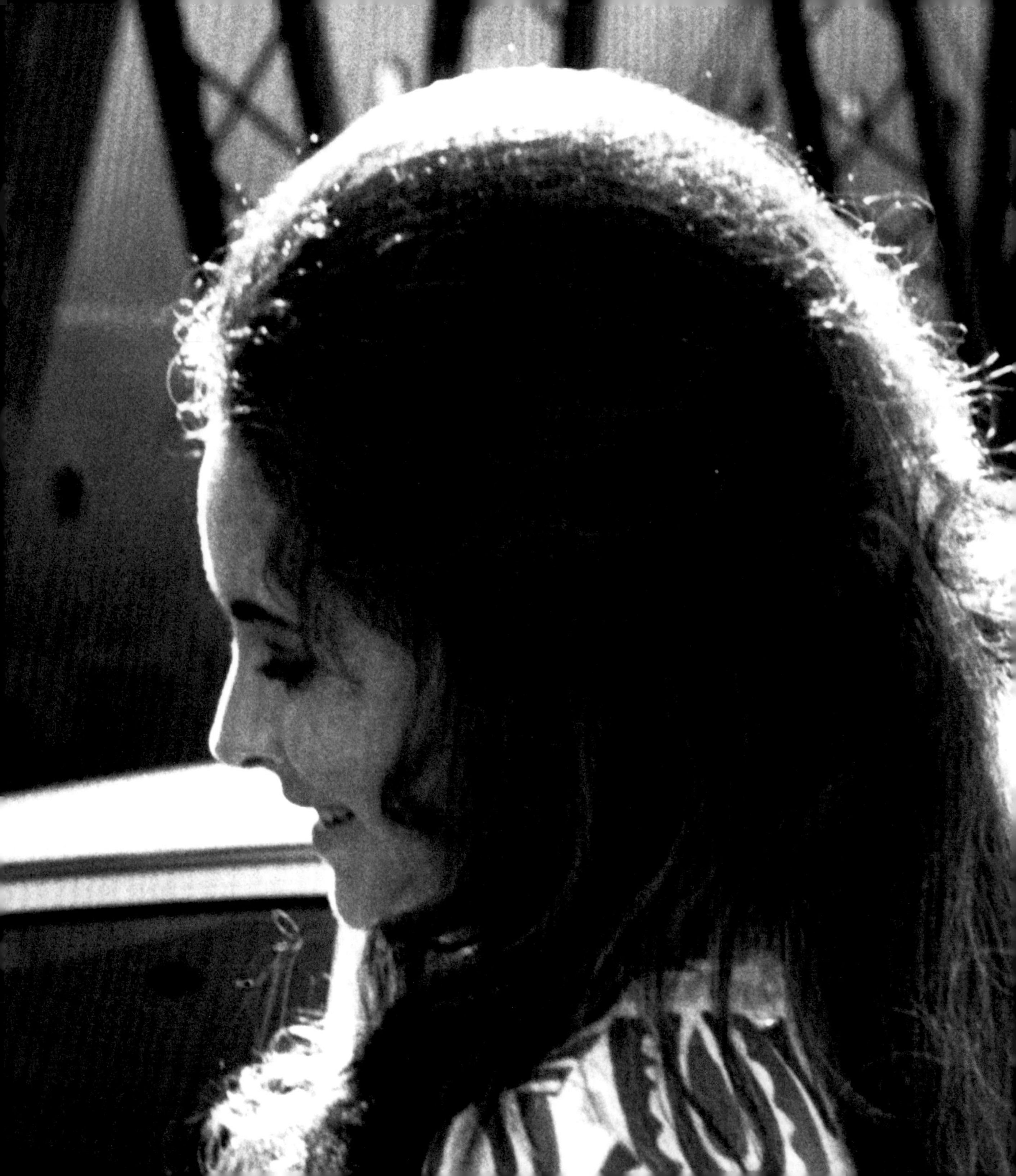

ELIZABETH & JOHN

7. Juni 1981: New York – Elizabeth Taylor und John Warner
tanzen auf der Party anlässlich der 35. Verleihung der
»Annual Tony Awards« im Hotel Waldorf-Astoria.
June 7, 1981: New York—Elizabeth Taylor and John Warner
dance at a 35th Annual Tony Awards party at the
Waldorf-Astoria Hotel.

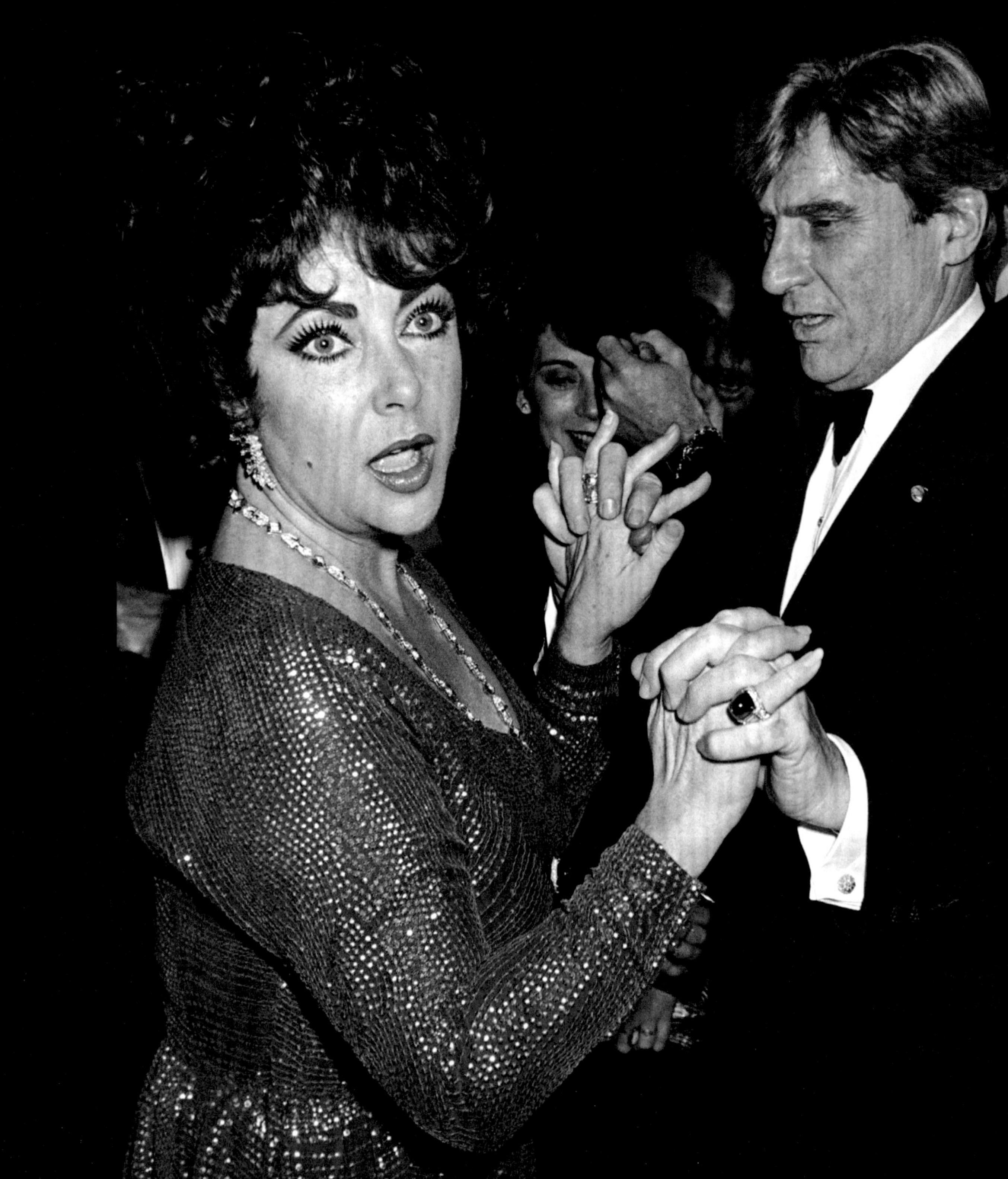

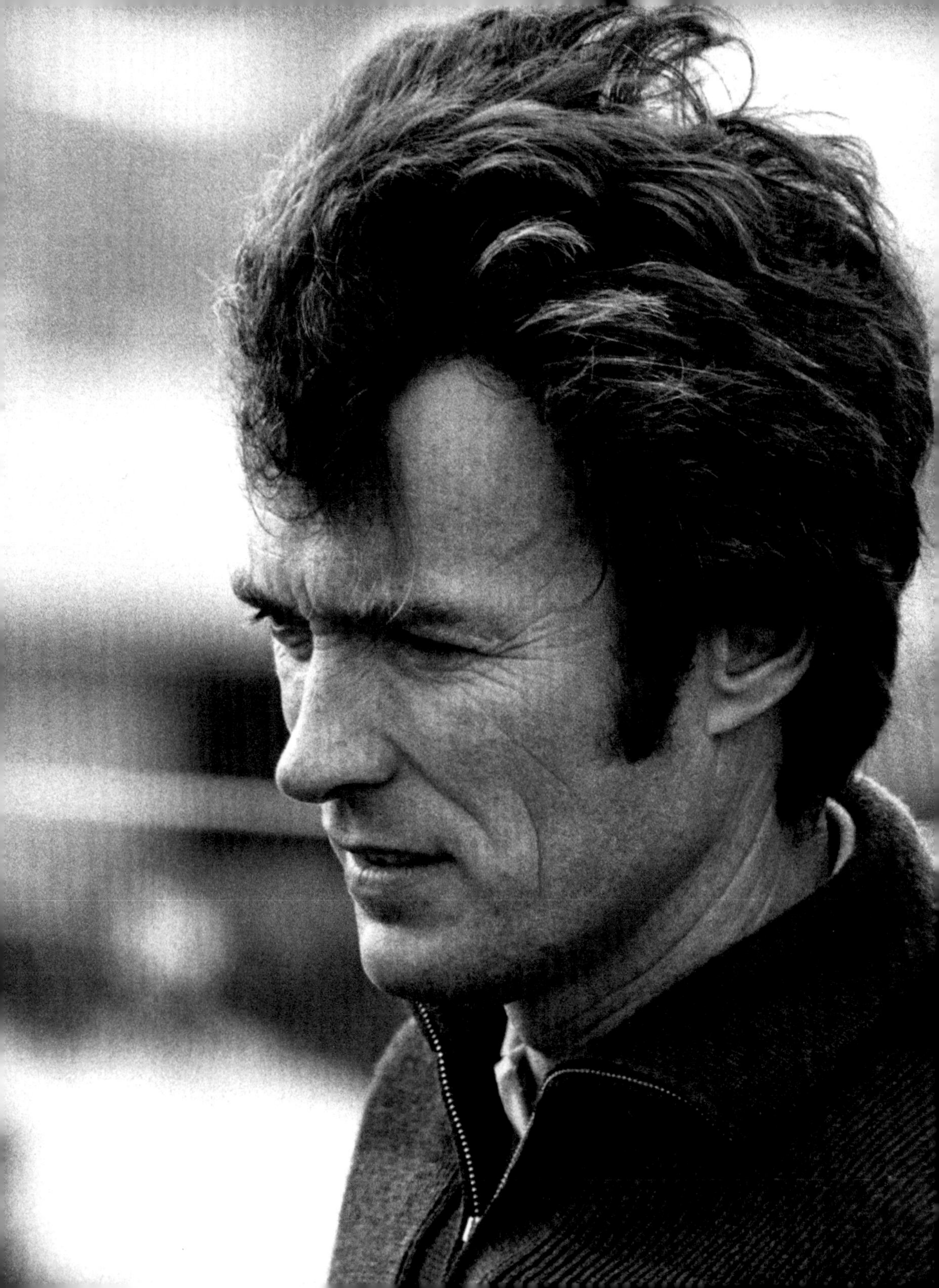

ROBERT

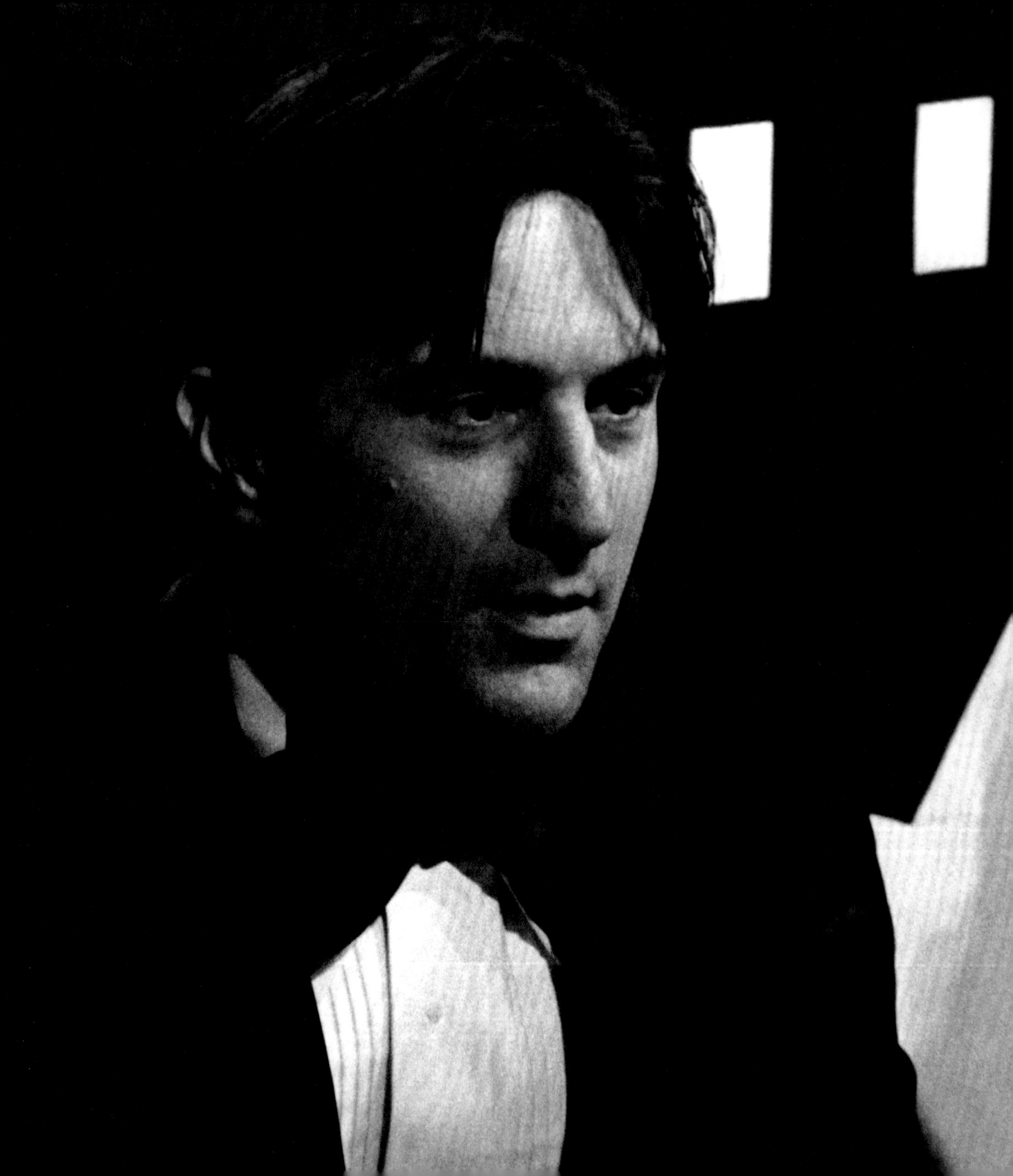

March 27, 1981: "Rocky III" press conference
LA Sports Arena. Sly Stallone introduces "Rocky's"
newest adversary "Mr. T" who will play Clubber
Lang. Mr. T who was born on the south side of
Chicago, is a boxer, bodyguard, wrestler & former
football player. "Rocky III marks his film acting
debut. Mr. T born Lawrence Tero.

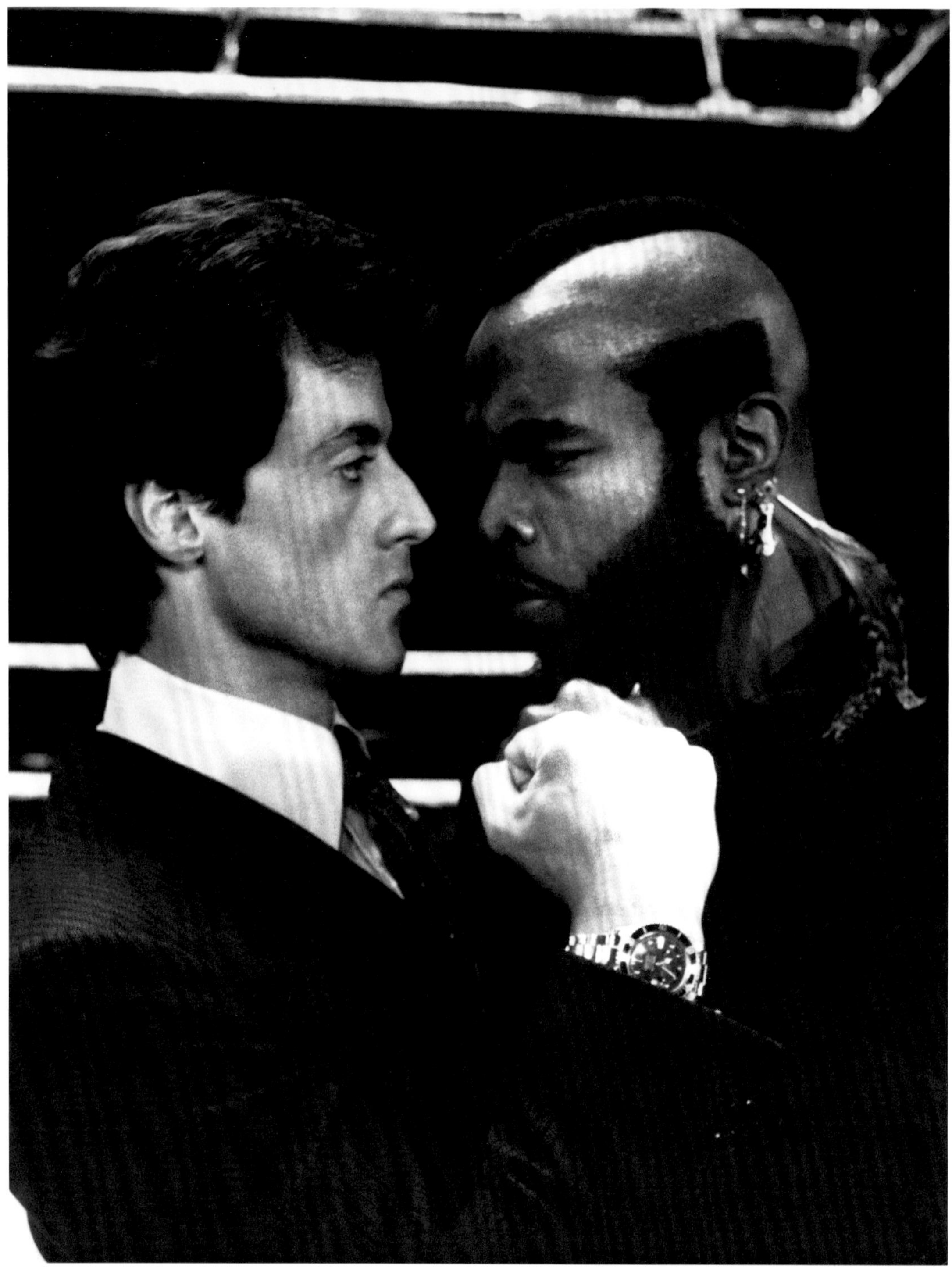

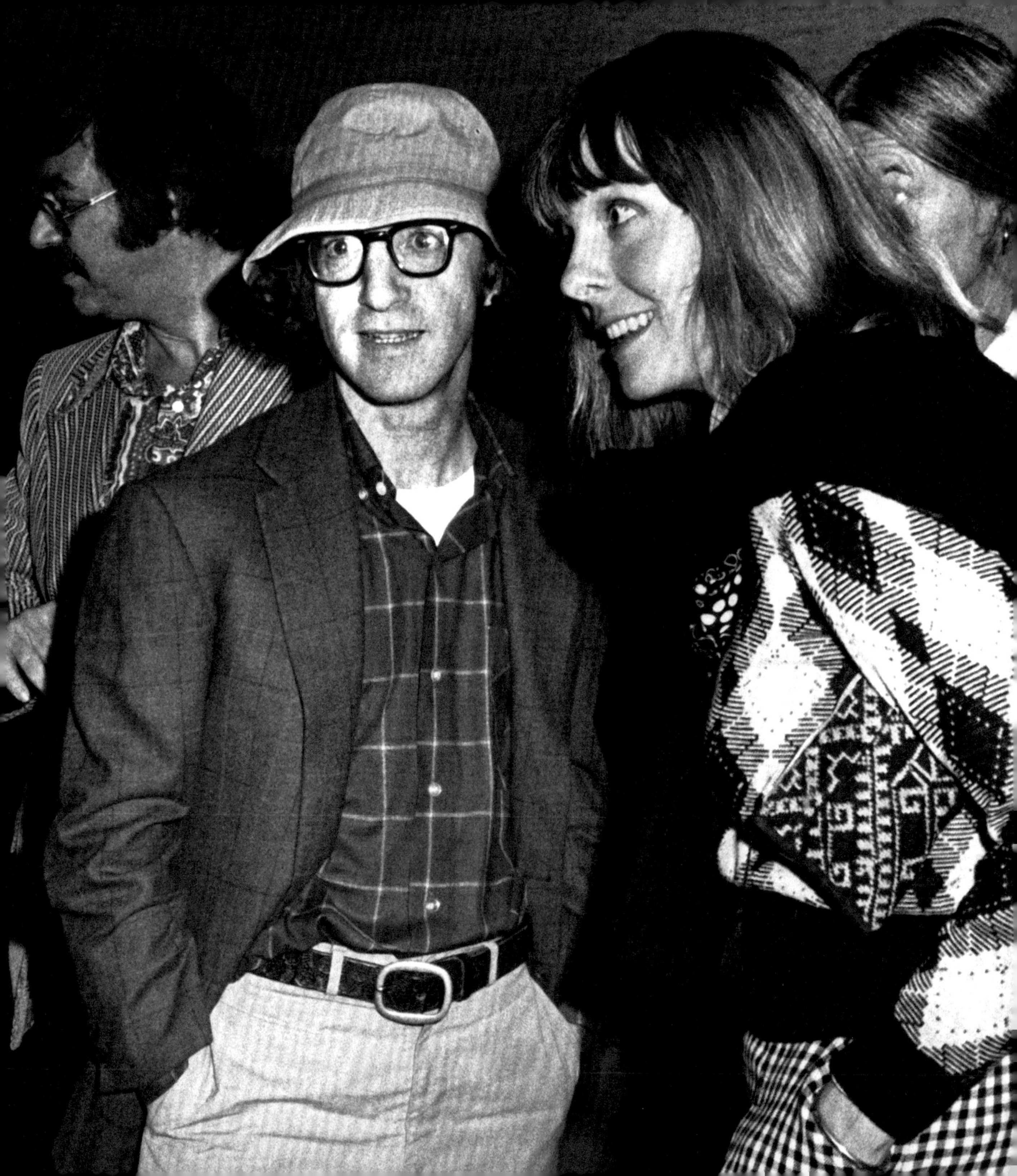

WOODY & DIANE

12. September 1972: New York – Woody Allen und Diane Keaton
bei der Buchvorstellung von *A Tracy and Hepburn Film Memoir*
im Lincoln Center.
September 12, 1972: New York—Woody Allen and Diane Keaton
attend a launch party for the book *A Tracy and Hepburn Film
Memoir* at Lincoln Center.

ALI & ROBERT

March, 1971: New York—Robert Evans and Ali MacGraw
arrive at JFK International Airport from Paris.

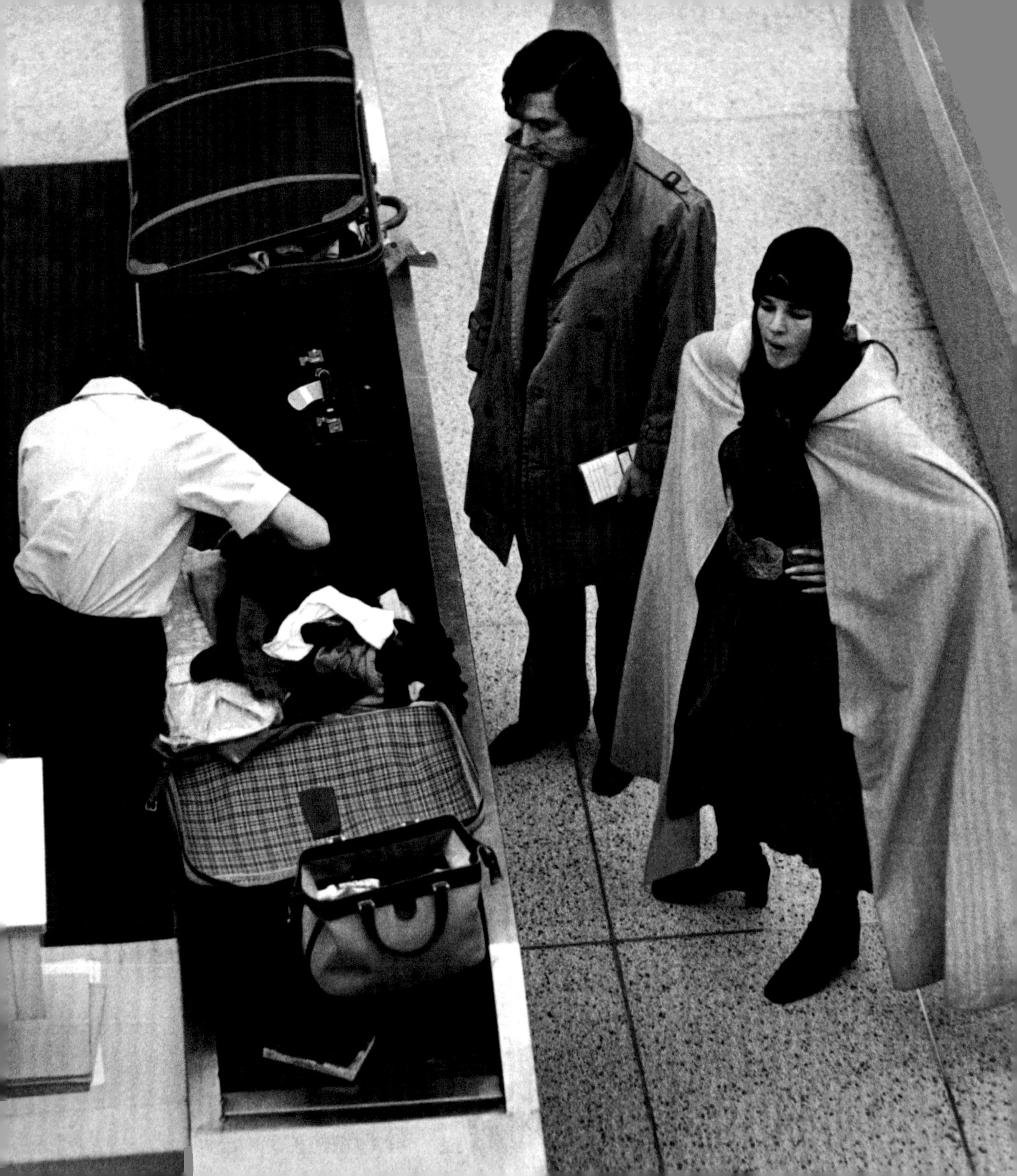

ROGER & SEAN

12. April 1982: Westwood, Kalifornien – Roger Moore
und Sean Connery im Hotel Westwood Marquis.
April 12, 1982: Westwood, California—Roger Moore
and Sean Connery at the Westwood Marquis Hotel.

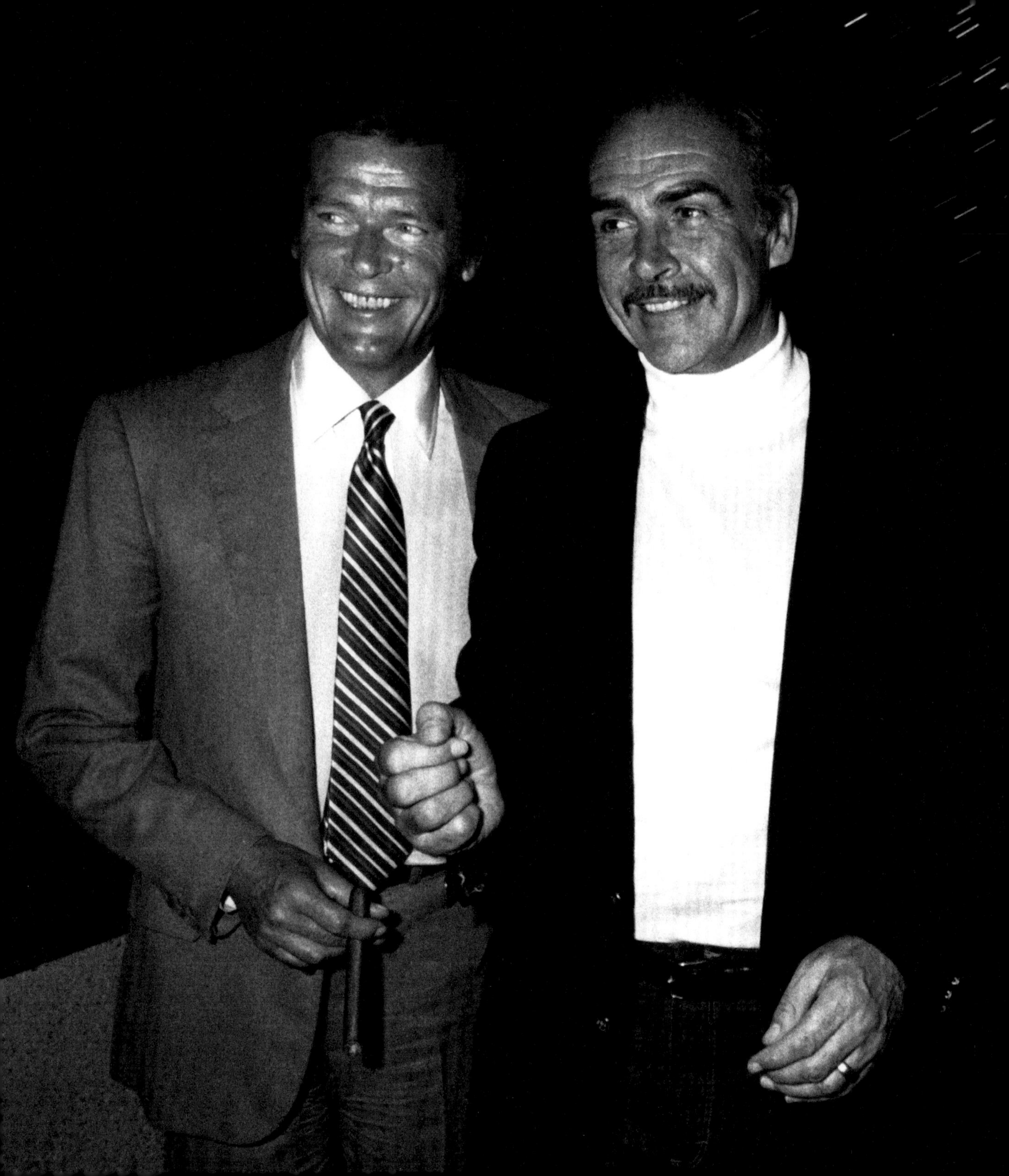

ROGER

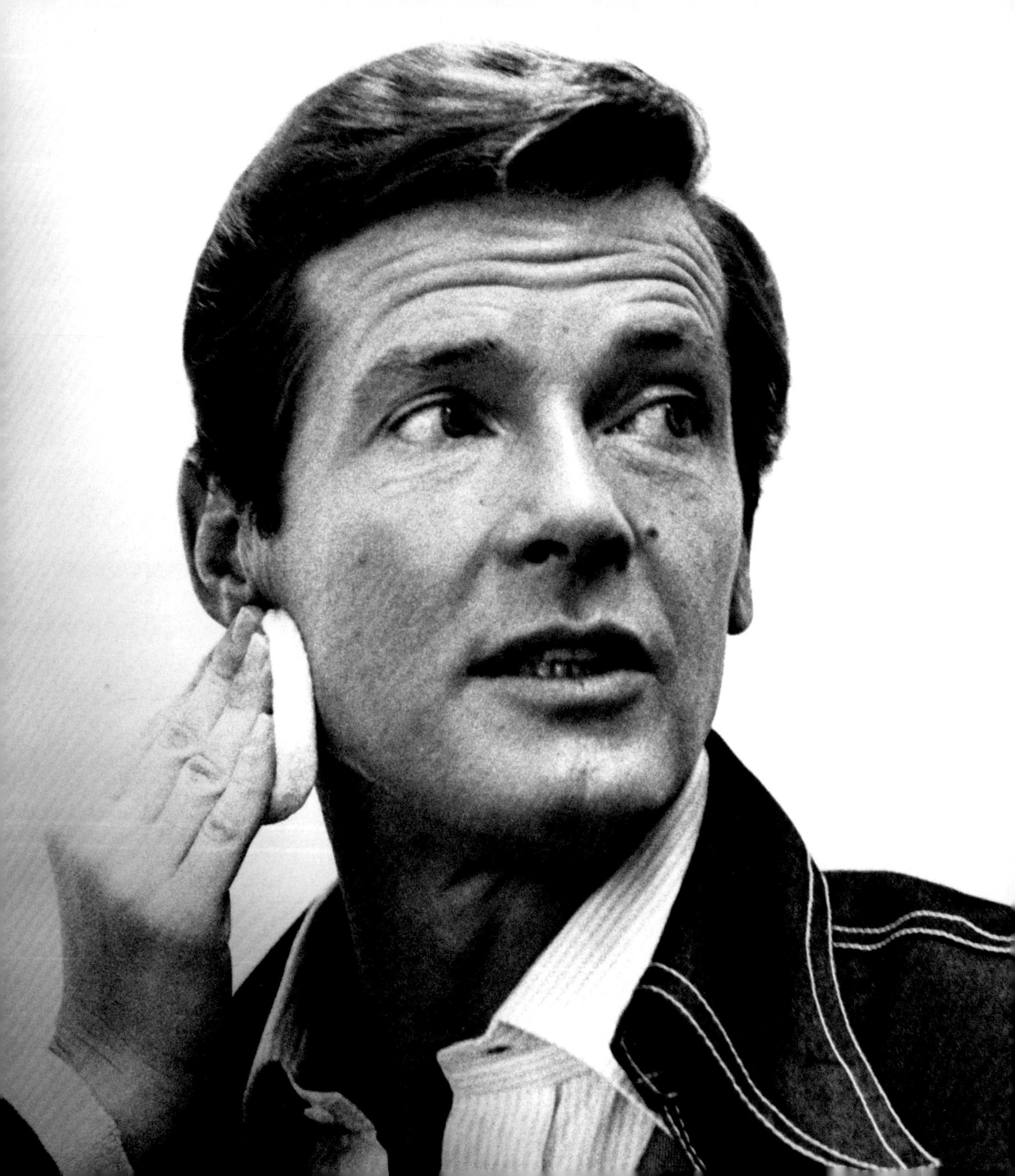

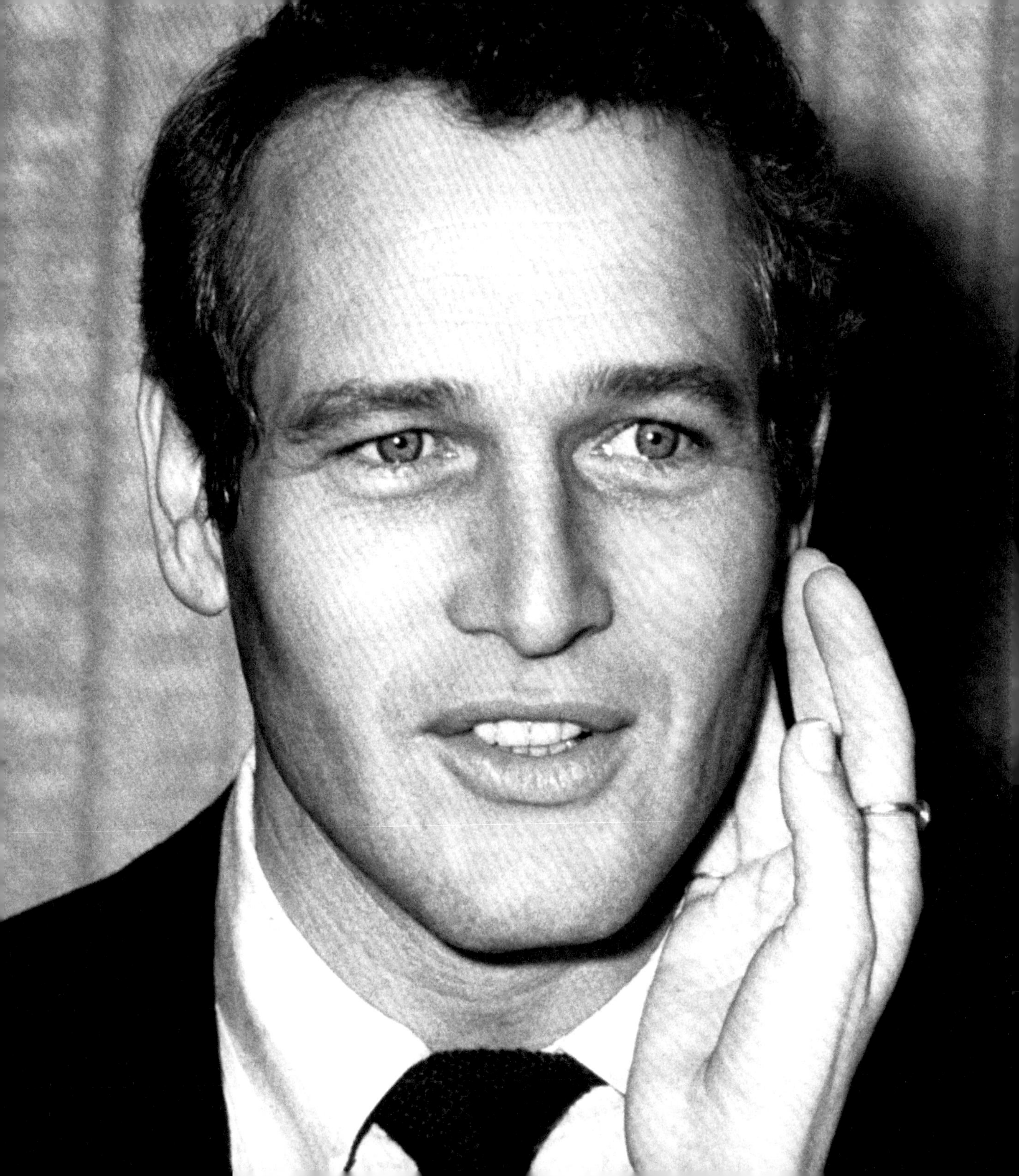

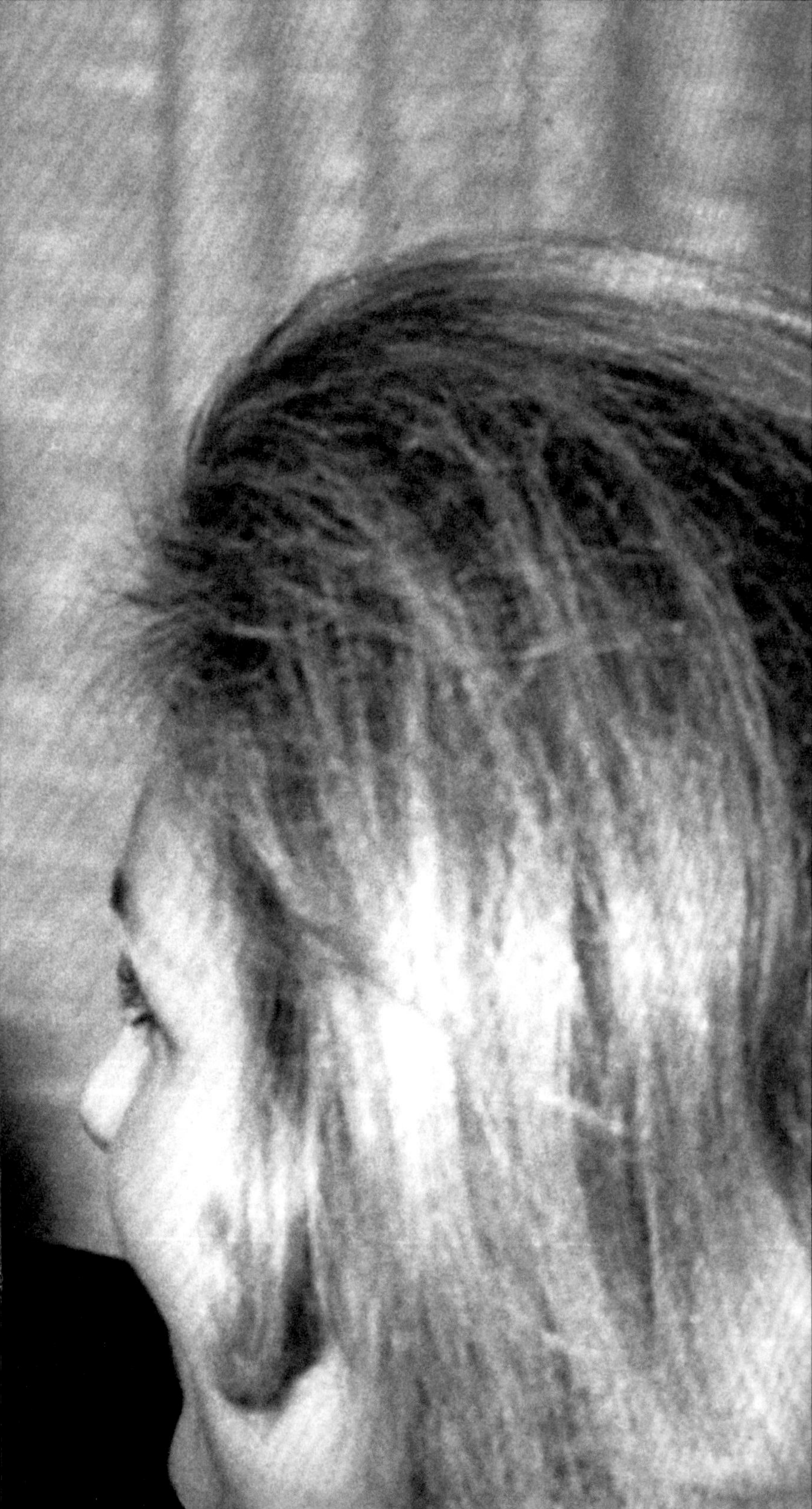

PAUL & JOANNE
26. Januar 1969: New York – Paul Newman und
Joanne Woodward nehmen 1969 an der Verleihun
der »New York Film Critics Circle Awards« im
Rainbow Room teil.
January 26, 1969: New York—Paul Newman and
Joanne Woodward attend the 1969 New York Film
Critics Circle Awards at The Rainbow Room.

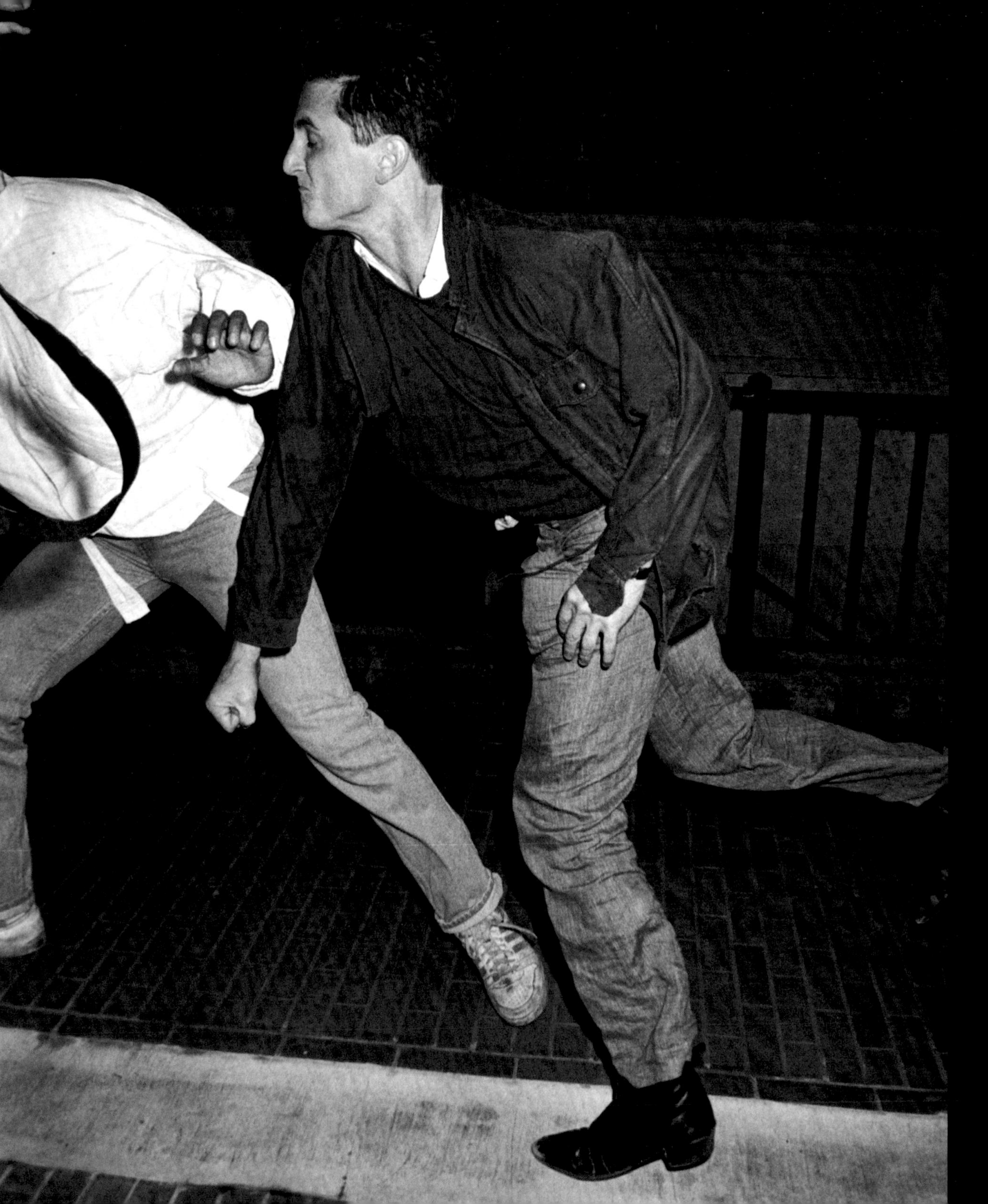

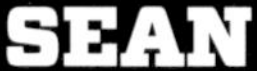

SEAN

Nach seinem Auftritt im Stück *Goose and Tomtom* im Mitzi Newhouse Theater, gingen der »böse Bube« Sean Penn und Madonna zum Essen ins Restaurant Gingerman. Nach dem Dinner liefen die beiden zu Fuß zu ihrer Wohnung in der West 64th Street. Als ich mit fünf weiteren fotografierenden Paparazzi über den Hintereingang ins Haus kam, wurde Penn wütend und schrie »Das war's, jetzt seid ihr auf einem Privatgrundstück, ihr seid tot!« Er begann seine Plastiktüten in Richtung meines Neffen, Anthony Savignano, zu schwingen und schlug ihm damit ins Gesicht. Anthony ist bei meiner Fotoagentur angestellt. Dann spuckte Penn Anthony an und versuchte ihn zu schlagen, was zu einem Boxkampf mit ein paar Treffern führte. Anthony spuckte zurück. Madonna schrie »Wie konntet ihr uns das nur antun, ihr habt hier nichts zu suchen. Hor auf, Sean, hör auf.« Dann holte ihr jähzorniger Mann nach Anthony aus, dieser wehrte seine Schläge ab, worauf Penn Anthony in den Schwitzkasten nahm und Anthony Penn am Hals packte. Schließlich kam ein Portier mit einem Besen heraus und alle Paparazzi suchten das Weite. Wir gingen gerade, als Penn sich umdrehte und Vinnie überraschend auf sein linkes Auge schlug. Vinnie war ein großer Madonna-Fan.

August 29, 1986: New York—Sean Penn.

After performing in the play *Goose and Tomtom* at the Mitzi Newhouse Theater, bad boy Sean Penn and Madonna walked to the Gingerman Restaurant. After dinner they walked to their West 64th Street apartment building. I was among five other paparazzi photographing when Penn got furious after we stepped into the courtyard entrance and screamed, "that's it, now you're on private property, you're dead!" He started swinging his plastic shopping bag at my nephew, Anthony Savignano, smacking him in the face. Anthony is a photographer employed by my agency. Penn then spat at Anthony and attempted to punch him, which led to a boxing match where few punches landed. Anthony spat back at Penn. Madonna screamed, "how could you do this to us, you have no business being here. Stop, Sean, Stop." As her hot-tempered husband lunged at Anthony, who blocked Penn's punches, Penn caught Anthony in a headlock and Anthony grabbed Penn by the throat. Finally a doorman came out with a broom and all the paparazzi fled. As we were leaving, Penn turned and punched Vinnie in his left eye by surprise. Vinnie was a big fan of Madonna.

MARLON

25. Mai 1968: Santa Monica, Kalifornien – Marlon Brando
in der Stadthalle von Santa Monica.
May 25, 1968: Santa Monica, California—Marlon Brando
at the Santa Monica Civic Auditorium.

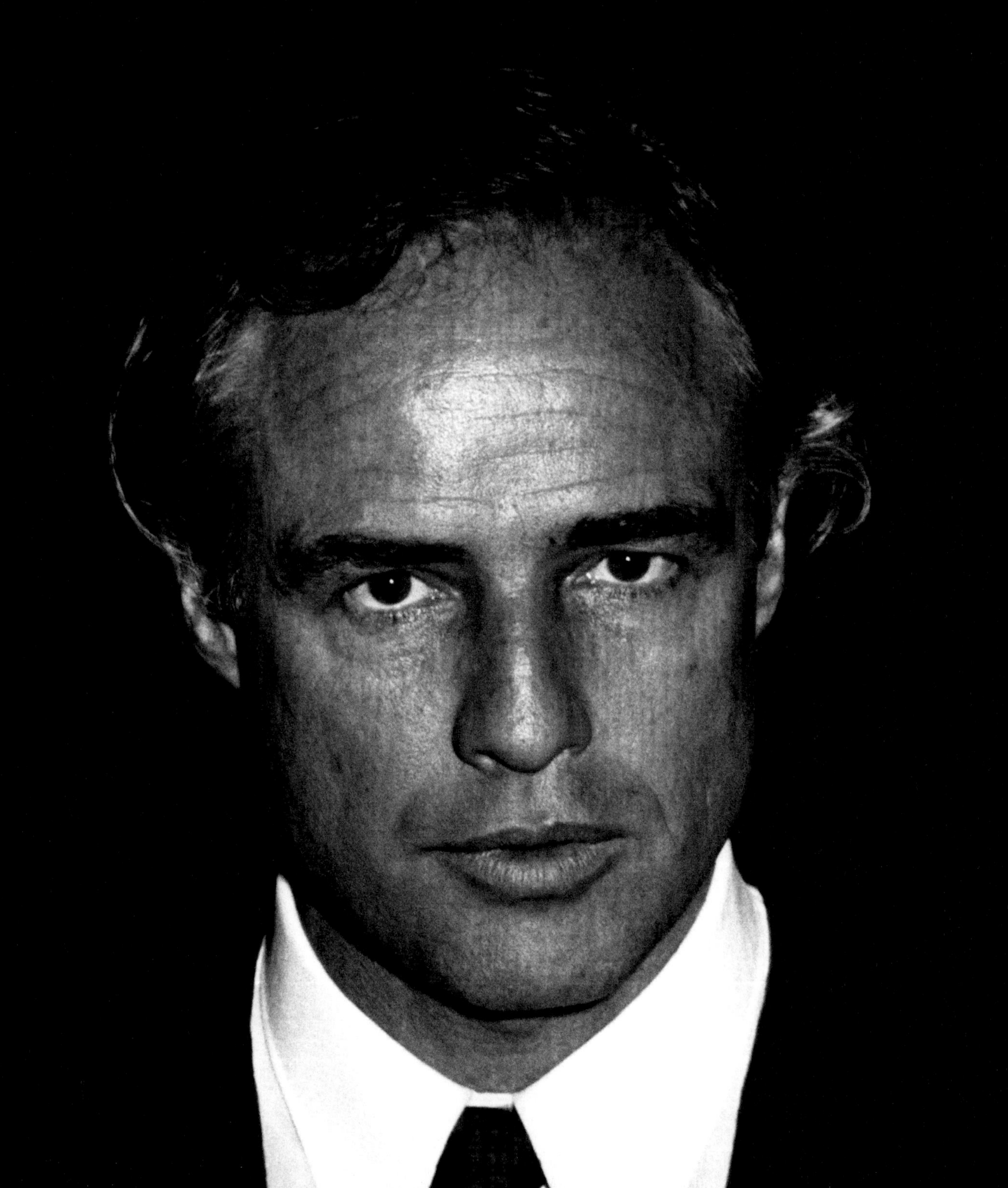

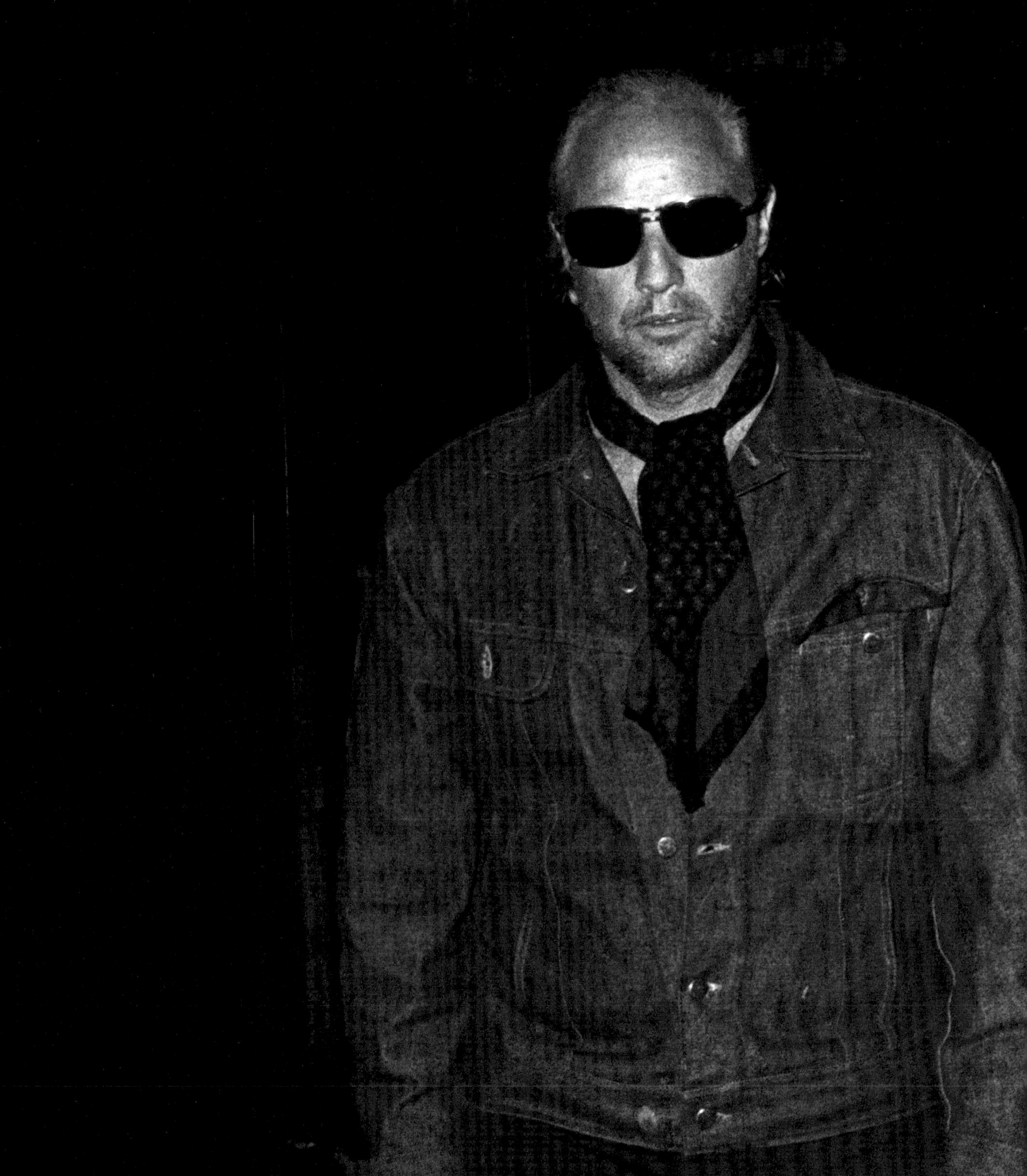

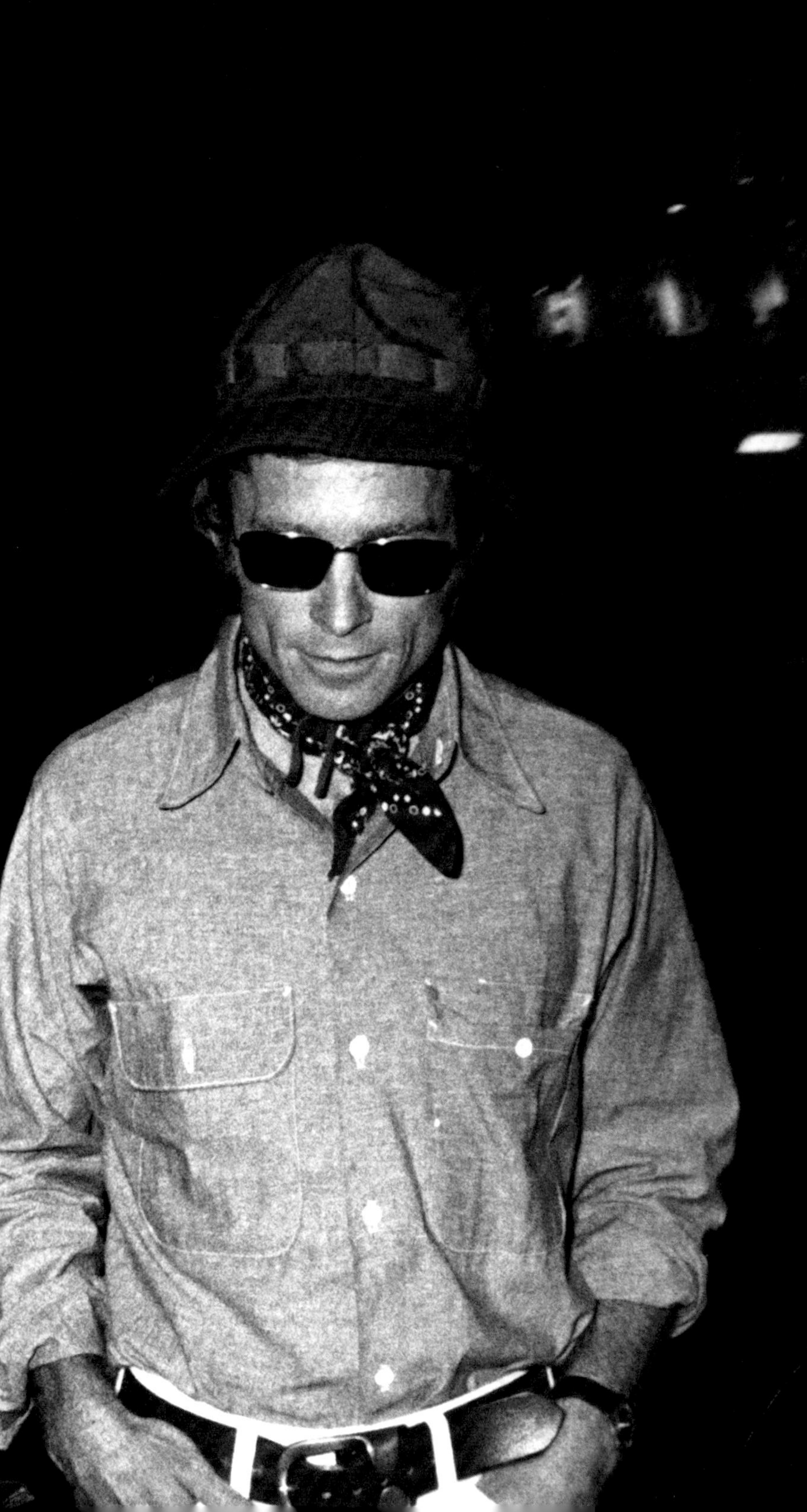

MARLON & DICK

12. Juni 1973: New York – Marlon Brando nahm die *Dick Cavett Show* in den ABC TV Studios auf. Ich folgte den beiden nach Chinatown, und nachdem ich dieses und ein Dutzend andere Fotos geschossen hatte, winkte mich Brando zu sich. »Was wollen Sie denn noch, was Sie nicht schon haben?« Ich bat ihn, seine Sonnenbrille abzusetzen. (Es war Nacht.) Er sagte »Nein« und dann Peng! Mit einem einzigen Schlag seiner Rechten brach mir Brando den Unterkiefer – mitsamt fünf Zähnen. Am nächsten Morgen brachte Cavett Brando mit einer entzündeten und geschwollenen rechten Hand in die New Yorker Klinik für Spezialchirurgie. Eine außergerichtliche Vereinbarung sprach mir später 40 000 Dollar zu, womit ich die aufwändige Zahnbrücke bezahlen konnte, die dreimal ersetzt werden musste.

June 12, 1973: New York—Marlon Brando taped the *Dick Cavett Show* at ABC TV studios. I followed the duo to Chinatown and after snapping this and a dozen other frames, Brando waved me over. "What else do you want that you don't already have?" I asked if he could please remove his sunglasses. (It was nighttime.) He said "No" and then wham! Brando threw a right punch to my lower jaw, breaking it along with 5 teeth. The next morning Cavett took Brando to NY Hospital of Special Surgery with an infected, swollen right hand. An out-of court settlement for $40,000 was reached later in my favor to help pay for the extensive dental bridge which has been replaced 3 times.

PAPARAZZO EXTRAORDINAIRE

Matthias Prinz

Paparazzi benutzen heute Kameras, die aussehen wie Waffen. Manche Objektive sind lang und klobig wie eine Panzerfaust. Mit diesen riesigen Geräten verfolgen Paparazzi ihr Jagdwild aus dem Hinterhalt. Wenn der Fotograf zu seinem Opfer blickt, sieht er jedes Haar und jede Falte. Blickt das Wild zurück zum Paparazzo, sieht es gar nichts. Das klingt harmlos. In der Realität ist es aber gespenstisch. Man wähnt sich unbeobachtet und allein. Beim Skifahren oder Tennis. Beim Sprung ins Mittelmeer. Niemand zu sehen, kein Fotograf weit und breit. Dennoch findet man später Fotos dieser Szenen in den Gazetten und merkt, dass man sich niemals unbeobachtet fühlen kann. Die Jagd der Paparazzi kann auch Furcht einflößen. Es ist schwer zu erahnen, ob die Autos, die einen verfolgen, von Fotografen gesteuert werden oder von Verbrechern. Manchmal verschwimmen die Grenzen. Als Prinzessin Caroline aufgrund einer Krankheit ihre Haare verloren hatte, wurde ihr Auto auf einer französischen Autobahn von Paparazzi brutal an den Straßenrand gedrängt, um ein Foto ihres kahlen Kopfes zu erzwingen. Das hätte zu einem tödlichen Unfall führen können, ebenso wie die Jagd auf Prinzessin Diana am 31.08.1997 in Paris. Paparazzi schleichen sich in Internate, um prominente Kinder zu fotografieren. Sie verstecken sich im Beichtstuhl, um eine prominente Hochzeit zu fotografieren. Paparazzi dringen gleich nach der Geburt mit einem Blumenstrauß auf der Entbindungsstation ein, um die ersten Fotos von Mutter und Kind zu erschleichen. Die Methoden sind schmutzig. Es geht nicht um Ethik oder journalistischen Anspruch sondern allein um Geld. Ob *Hello, Hola* oder *Novella:* viele zahlen Spitzenpreise für Paparazzi-Fotos. Der Markt ist groß. In Deutschland gibt es jede Woche dreißig Hefte der Regenbogenpresse, die Paparazzi-Fotos drucken. Dazu kommen die englischen, französischen, italienischen und spanischen Blätter. Die Fotografen verdienen und sind namenlos. Sie verpflichten ihre Abnehmer dazu, die Fotos ohne jeden Hinweis auf den Urheber zu veröffentlichen, damit sie nicht verklagt werden können. Denn bei einem Prozess müssten die Fotografen ihr Honorar offenlegen und an ihre Opfer auskehren. Da bleiben sie lieber anonym und verzichten auf Ruhm und Rampenlicht. Das gelingt ihnen auch deswegen so gut, weil ihre Werke keine besondere Handschrift haben. Ein Paparazzi-Foto ist heute wie das andere. Commodity, Produkt der technischen Entwicklung. Mit immer größeren Objektiven aus immer größerer Entfernung geschossen, belegen alle Fotos die überragende Technik der Kameras, nicht aber überragende Technik der Fotografen. Anders als bei den Werken von Ron Galella gibt es keine besonderen Merkmale, die auf die Qualität eines Fotografen hinweisen. Paparazzi-Fotografie ist heute Massenware und die Fotos sind denkbar langweilig. Im Winter sieht man Prominente in Skikleidung. Im Sommer liegen sie auf einer Yacht, schwimmen oder laufen am Strand entlang. Nichts besonderes. Ganz anders als die Fotos von Ron Galella in diesem Buch. Sind das eigentlich überhaupt Paparazzi-Fotos? Nicht jedenfalls im modernen Sinne. Die meisten Fotos sind aus nächster Nähe gemacht und offensichtlich mit Einverständnis der Abgebildeten. Man sieht kaum ahnungslose oder verfolgte, rennende und erschreckte Opfer. Stattdessen bereitwillige Pose der Abgebildeten. Das sieht nicht nach Verfolgungsjagd aus, sondern nach Gesellschaftsfotografie am roten Teppich. Aber Verfolgungsjagden gab es auch bei Ron Galella. Die Gerichtsprozesse mit Jackie O., die Prügel von Marlon Brando oder die Schlägerei mit den Bodyguards von Richard Burton beweisen, dass Galella auch Paparazzo war. Aber dennoch ein Fotograf von einer Qualität, die es heute in der anonymen Masse der Paparazzi nicht mehr gibt.

Matthias Prinz (geb. 1956) gehört zu den bekanntesten Rechtsanwälten auf dem Gebiet des Persönlichkeits- und Medienrechts in Deutschland. Für viele seiner prominenten Mandanten erwirkte Prinz wichtige Grundsatzurteile des Bundesgerichtshofs und des Europäischen Gerichtshofs für Menschenrechte, wie zum Beispiel für Prinzessin Caroline von Hannover.

Nowadays the paparazzi use cameras that look like weapons. Some lenses are long and chunky like a bazooka. With these huge pieces of equipment the paparazzi lie in ambush, hounding their game. When the photographer catches sight of his victim he sees every hair and every wrinkle. When the game looks back at the paparazzo, he sees nothing. That sounds harmless. However in reality it is spooky. One believes oneself to be unobserved and alone. While skiing or playing tennis. When jumping into the Mediterranean. There is no-one in sight, no photographer far and wide. Yet later one finds photos of these scenes in the gazettes and realizes that one can never feel unwatched. The paparazzi hunt can put fear into people. It is hard to tell whether the cars in pursuit are being driven by photographers or criminals. Sometimes the boundaries are blurred. When Princess Caroline lost her hair due to an illness, the paparazzi brutally forced her car onto the wayside on a French motorway in order to take a photograph of her bald head. This could have caused a deadly injury, like the pursuit of Princess Diana on 31.08.1997 in Paris. Paparazzi sneak into boarding schools to photograph the children of stars. They hide in the confessional booth in order to photograph a celebrity wedding. Armed with a bunch of flowers, paparazzi infiltrate the maternity ward immediately after a birth to surreptitiously take the first photos of the mother and child.

The methods are dirty. It is not about ethics or journalistic claims but about money alone. Whether *Hello, Hola* or *Novella,* many pay premium prices for paparazzi photos. The market is huge. In Germany, every week there are 30 tabloids that print paparazzi photos. They are joined by the English, French, Italian and Spanish newspapers and magazines. The photographers earn their money and remain nameless. They oblige their buyers to publish the photos without any reference to the author so that they cannot be sued. Because in a lawsuit the photographers have to reveal their royalties and pay these to their victims. So they prefer to remain anonymous and do without fame and glory. They are able to do this so well because their works do not have any special characteristics. Today, a paparazzi photo is just like any other. A commodity, a product of technical development. Taken with larger and larger lenses from an increasing distance, all the photos bear witness to the outstanding technique of the camera rather than the outstanding technique of the photographer. In contrast to the works by Ron Galella, there are no special characteristics that indicate the quality of a photographer. Nowadays, paparazzi photography is a bulk commodity and the photographs are conceivably boring. In winter one sees the celebrities in skiwear. In summer they lie on a yacht, swim, or walk along a beach. Nothing special, and very

different to Ron Galella's photos in this book. Are those paparazzi photos at all? Not in a contemporary sense anyway. Most of the photos have been taken at close range and obviously with the assent of the person pictured. One rarely sees unsuspecting or hunted, running or frightened victims. Instead one sees the willing poses of those portrayed. These pictures do not look like a pursuit but like society photographs on a red carpet. However, Ron Galella also pursued. The court case with Jackie O., his beating by Marlon Brando and his fight with Richard Burton's bodyguards prove that Galella was a paparazzo too. Yet he was also a photographer of a quality that no longer exists among the anonymous mass of the paparazzi today.

Matthias Prinz (born 1956) is one of the most renowned lawyers in the field of personal rights and media law in Germany. For many of his prominent clients Prinz was able to obtain significant leading decisions from the Federal Court of Justice and the European Court of Human Rights, for example for Princess Caroline of Hannover.

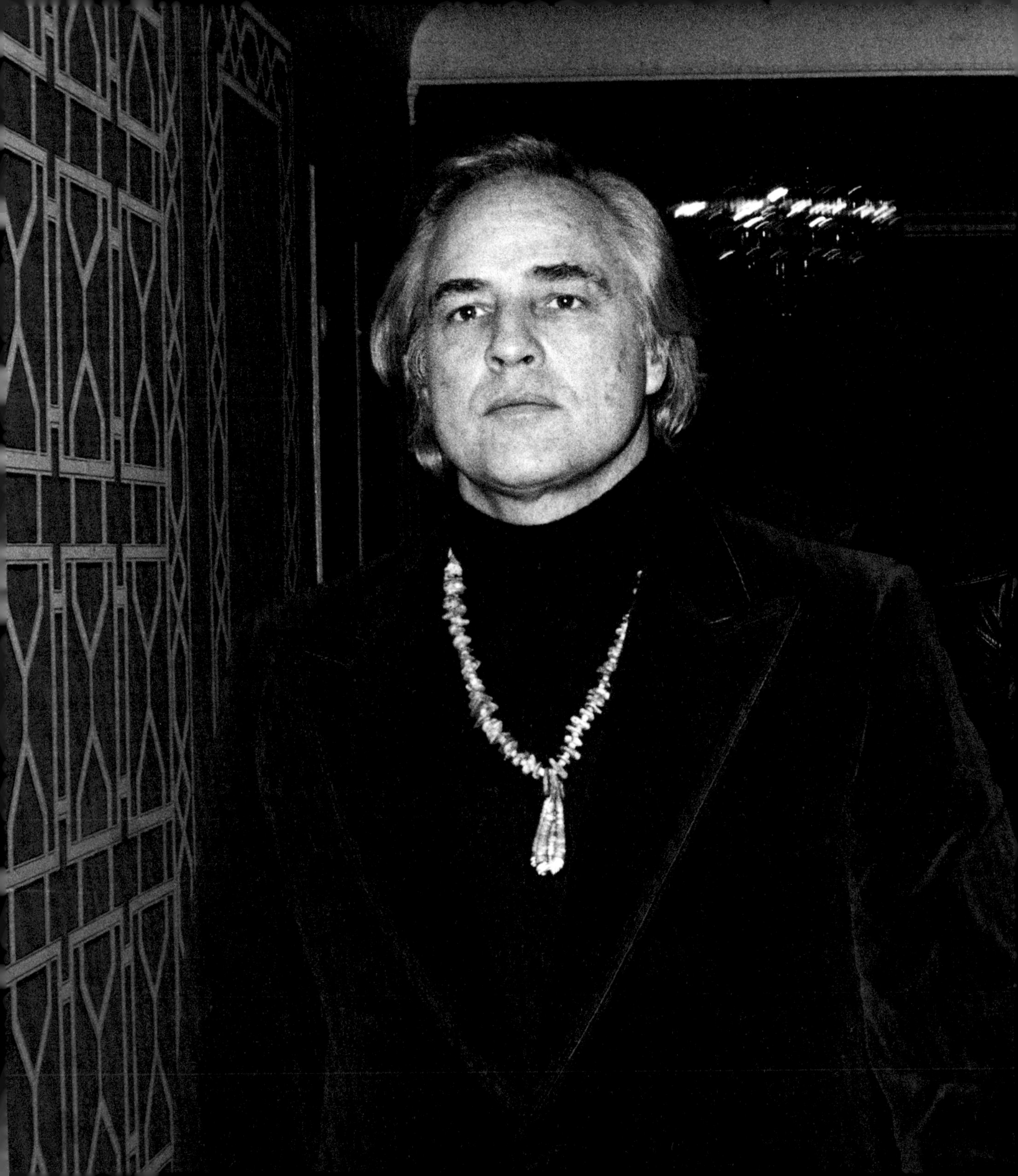

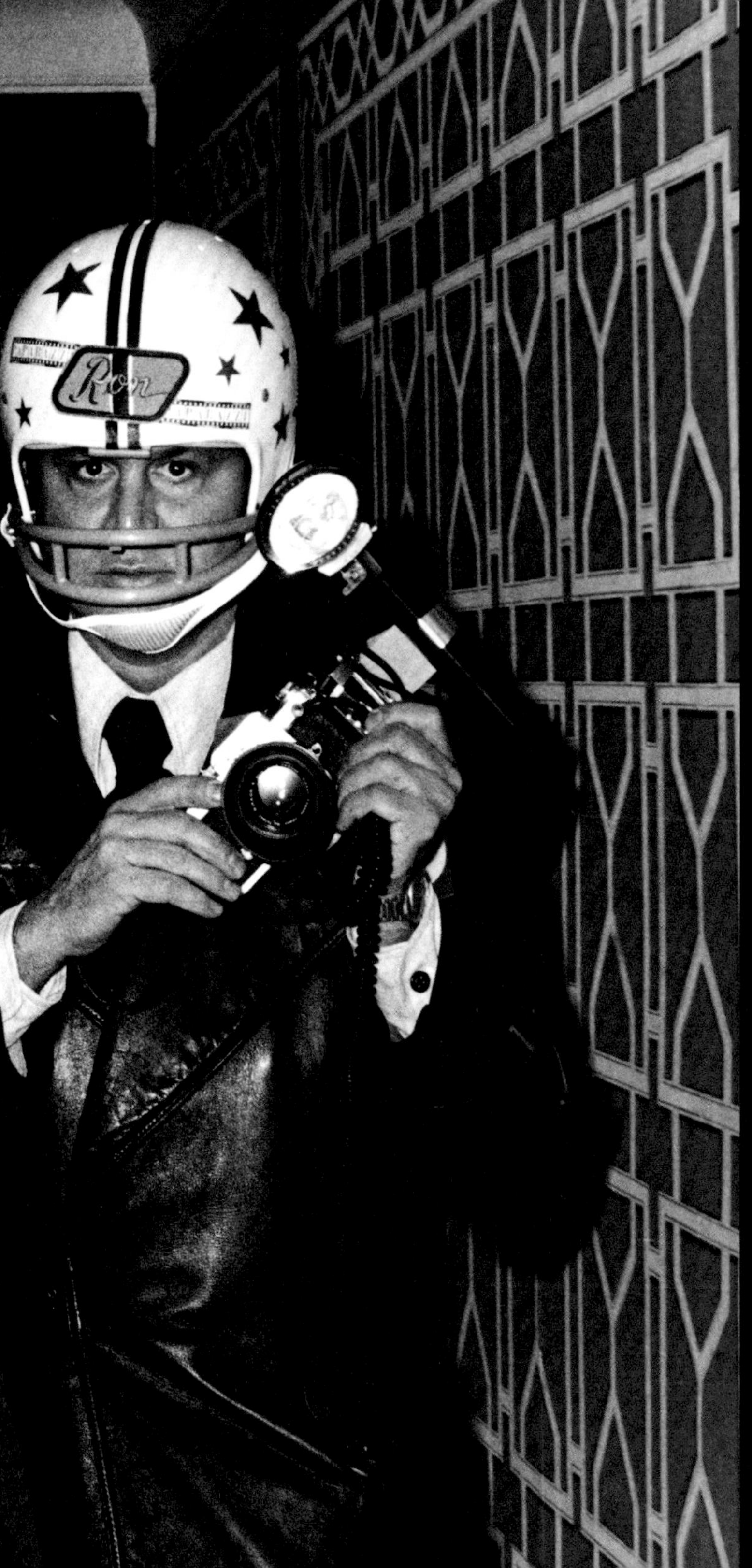

MARLON & RON

26. November 1974: New York, Hotel Waldorf-Astoria.
Die erste jährlich stattfindende Benefizgala der American Indian Development Association. Ich wurde von dieser Veranstaltung ausgeschlossen, daher wartete ich in der Lobby auf Marlon Brando. Dieses Mal war ich vorbereitet und trug einen Football-Helm. Ich musste den schüchternen Fotografen Paul Schmulbach regelrecht dazu drängen, das Foto zu machen. Dies wurde mein am häufigsten publiziertes Foto.
November 26, 1974: New York, Waldorf-Astoria Hotel.
First Annual Gala Benefit for the American Indian Development Association. I was barred from this event, so I waited in the lobby for Marlon Brando's arrival. This time I came prepared, wearing a football helmet. I had to physically push shy photographer Paul Schmulbach to take the picture. This has become the most published picture of me.

ARTISTS
Ron Galella

SALVADOR & ULTRA

13. Januar 1969: New York – Salvador Dalí bei der
Le-Bal-Blanc-Gala im Hotel St. Regis.
January 13, 1969: New York—Salvador Dalí at the
St. Regis hotel for the Le Bal Blanc Gala.

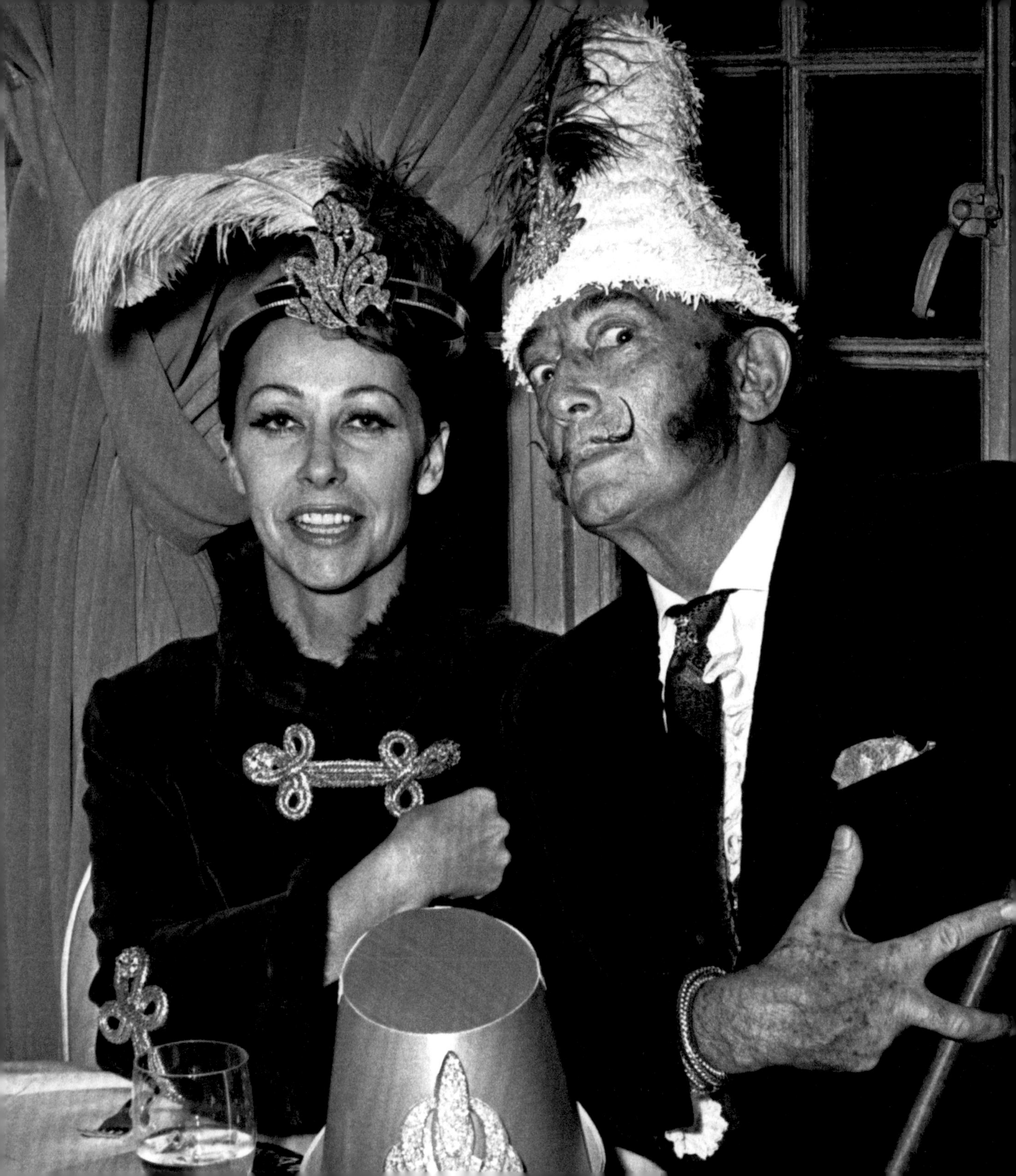

SALVADOR

7. März 1974: New York – Salvador Dalí und ein Modell bei
der Eröffnung seiner Ausstellung in der Madison Avenue.
March 7, 1974: New York—Salvador Dalí and model at the
opening of his exhibit on Madison Avenue.

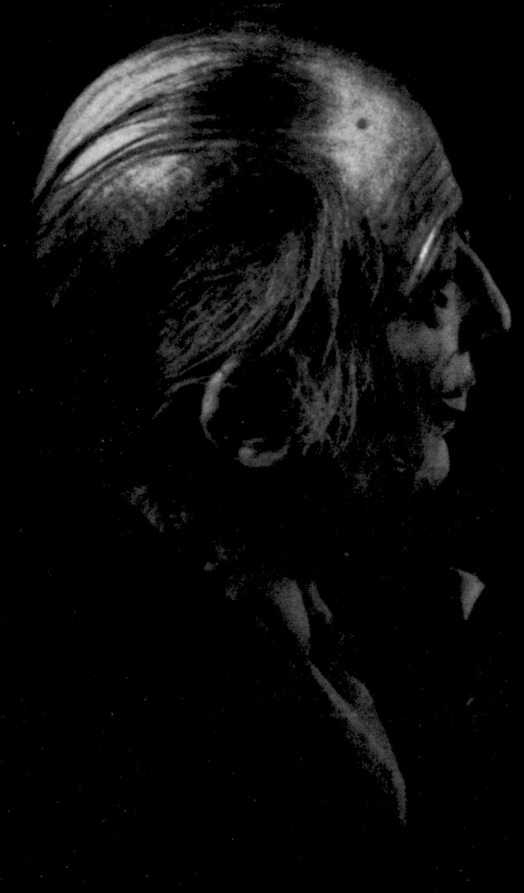

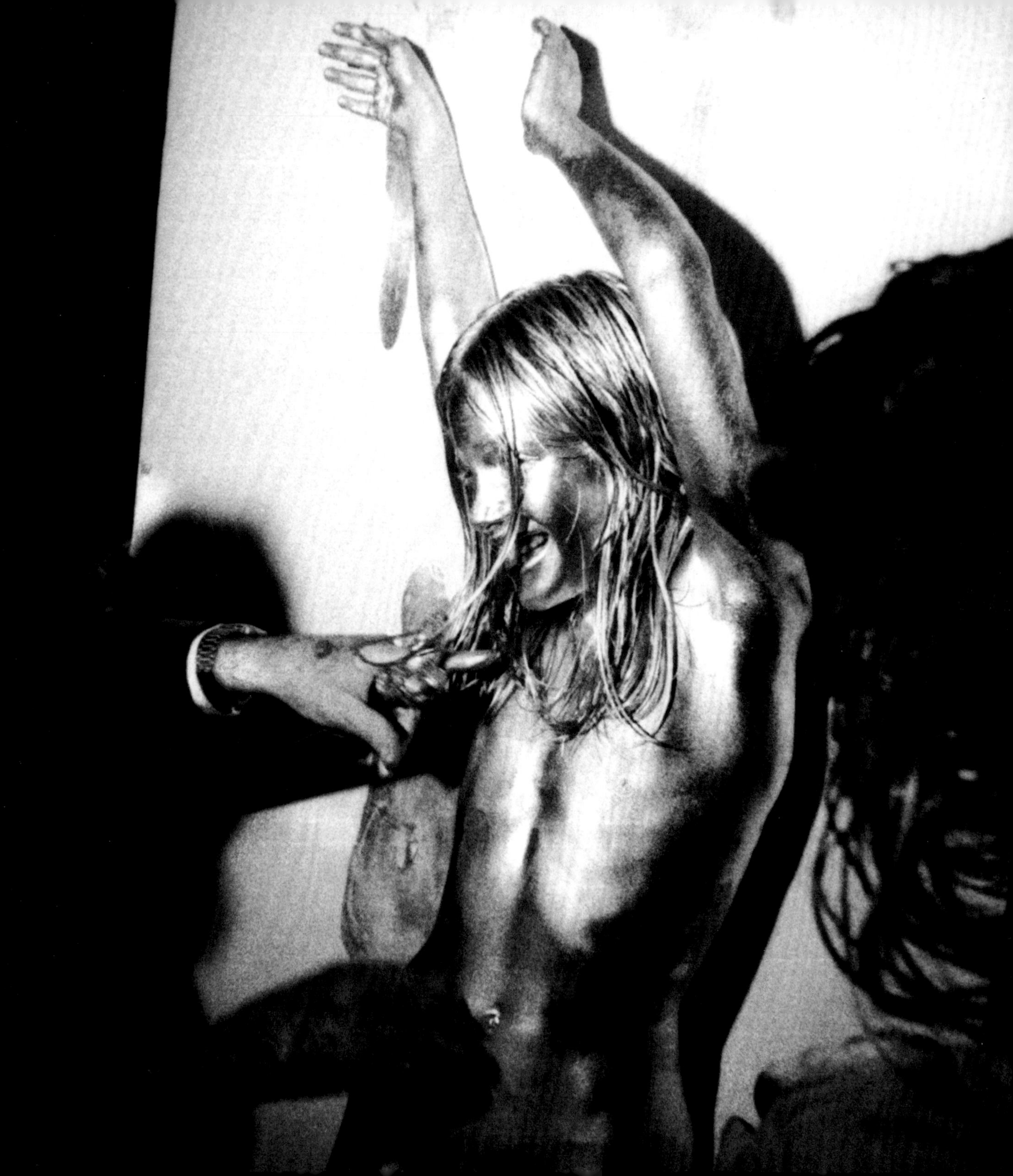

SALVADOR

7. März 1974: New York – Salvador Dalí bei der
Eröffnung seiner Ausstellung in der Madison Avenue.
March 7, 1974: New York—Salvador Dalí at the
opening of his exhibit on Madison Avenue.

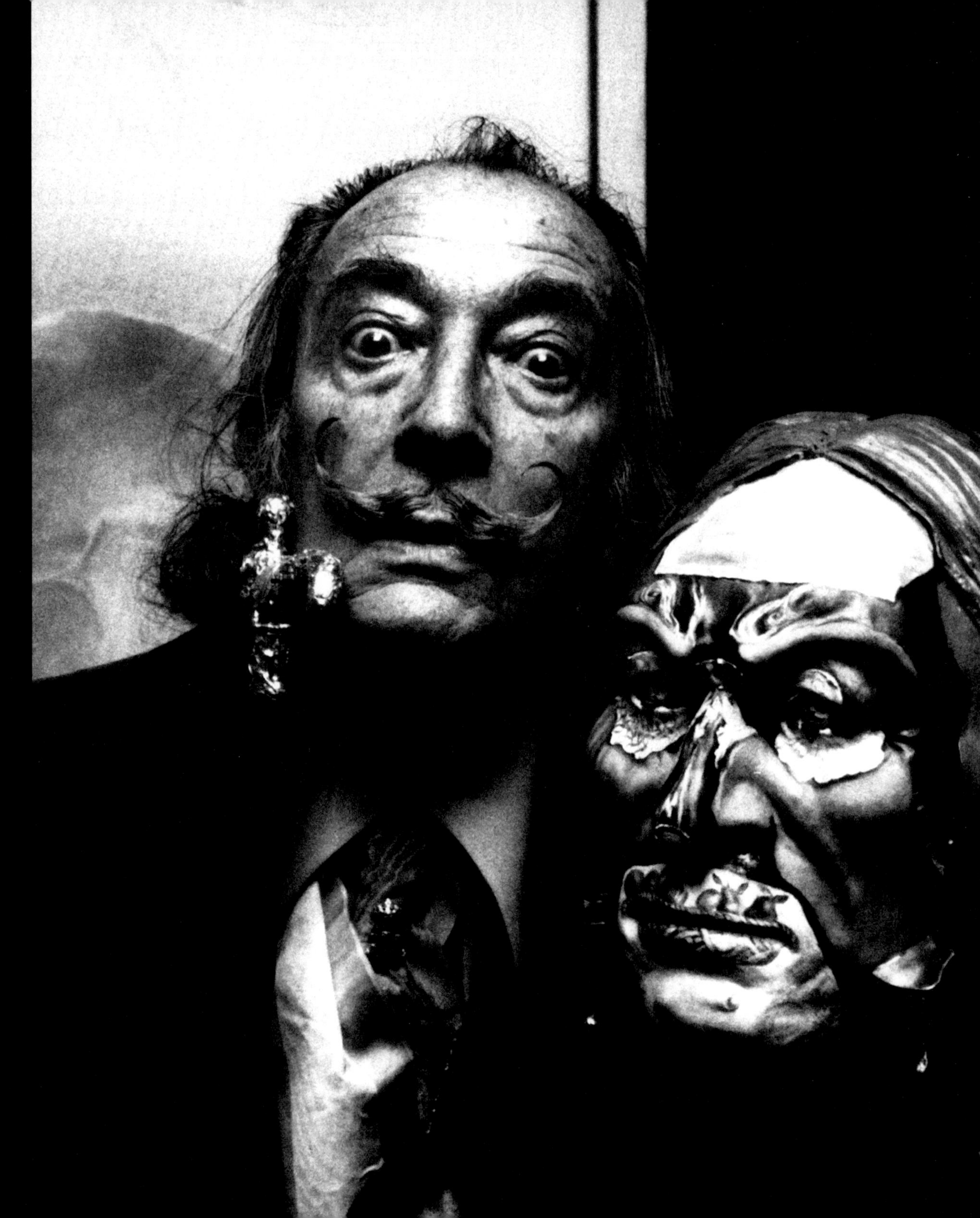

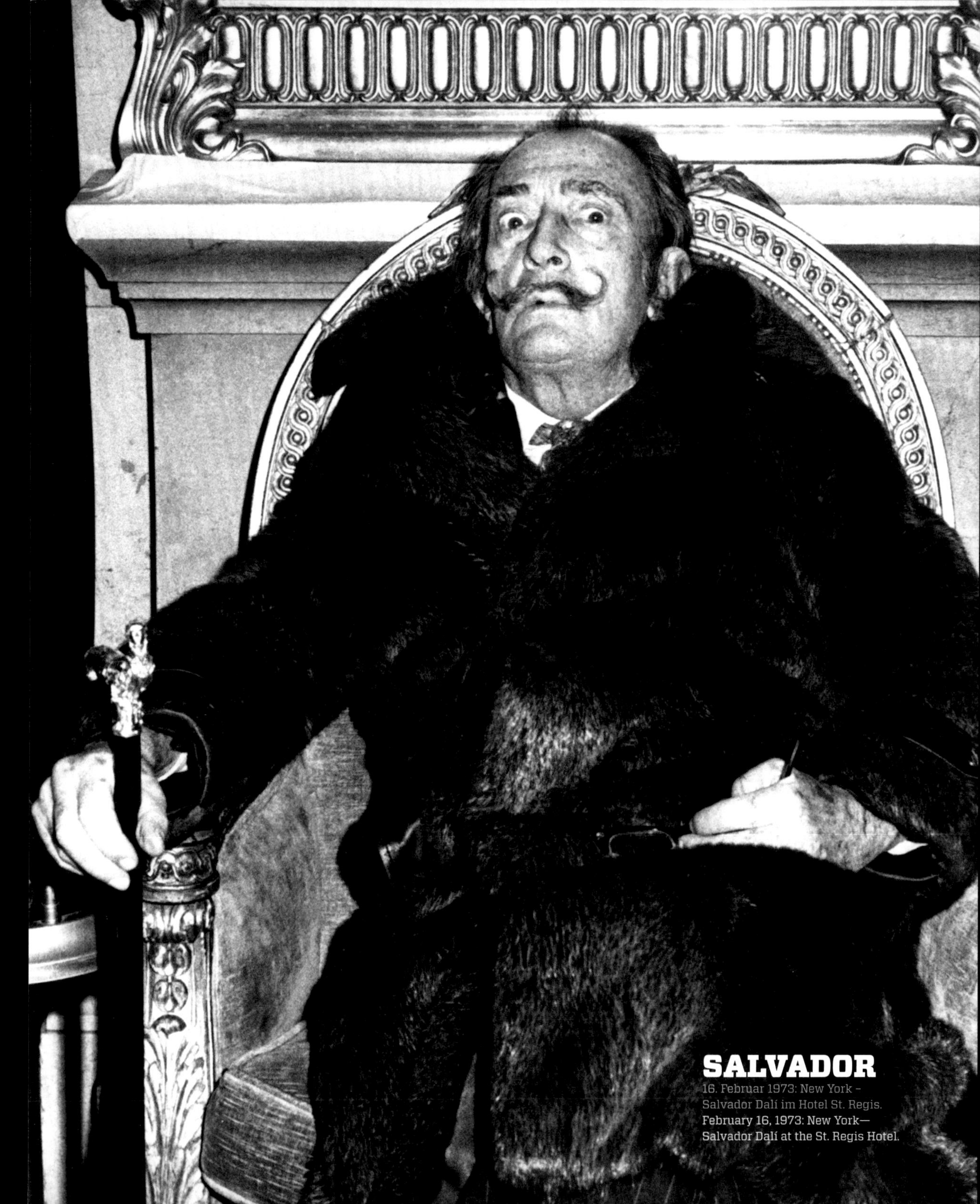

16. Februar 1973: New York –
Salvador Dalí im Hotel St. Regis.
February 16, 1973: New York—
Salvador Dalí at the St. Regis Hotel.

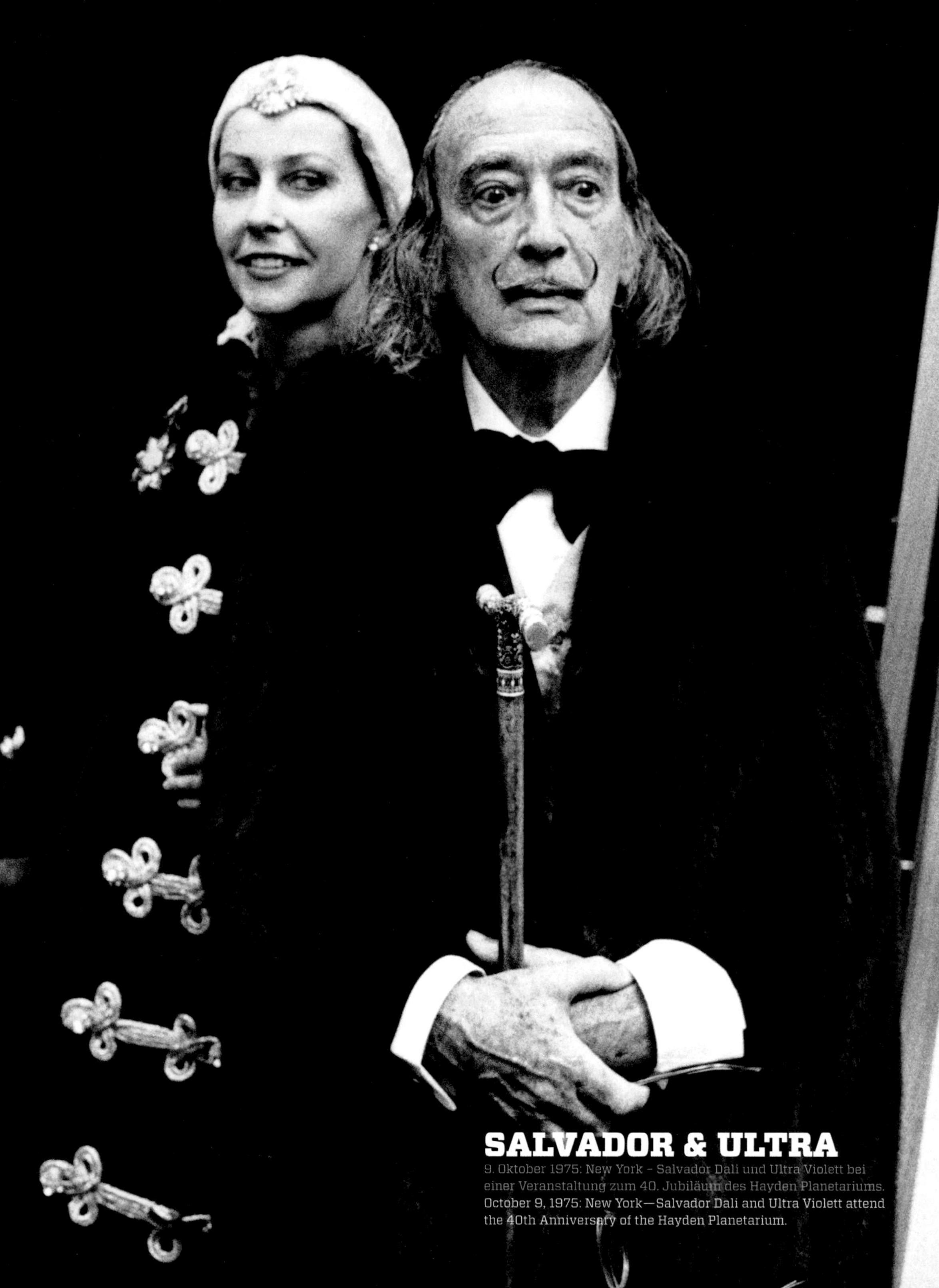

SALVADOR & ULTRA
9. Oktober 1975: New York – Salvador Dali und Ultra Violett bei
einer Veranstaltung zum 40. Jubiläum des Hayden Planetariums.
October 9, 1975: New York—Salvador Dali and Ultra Violett attend
the 40th Anniversary of the Hayden Planetarium.

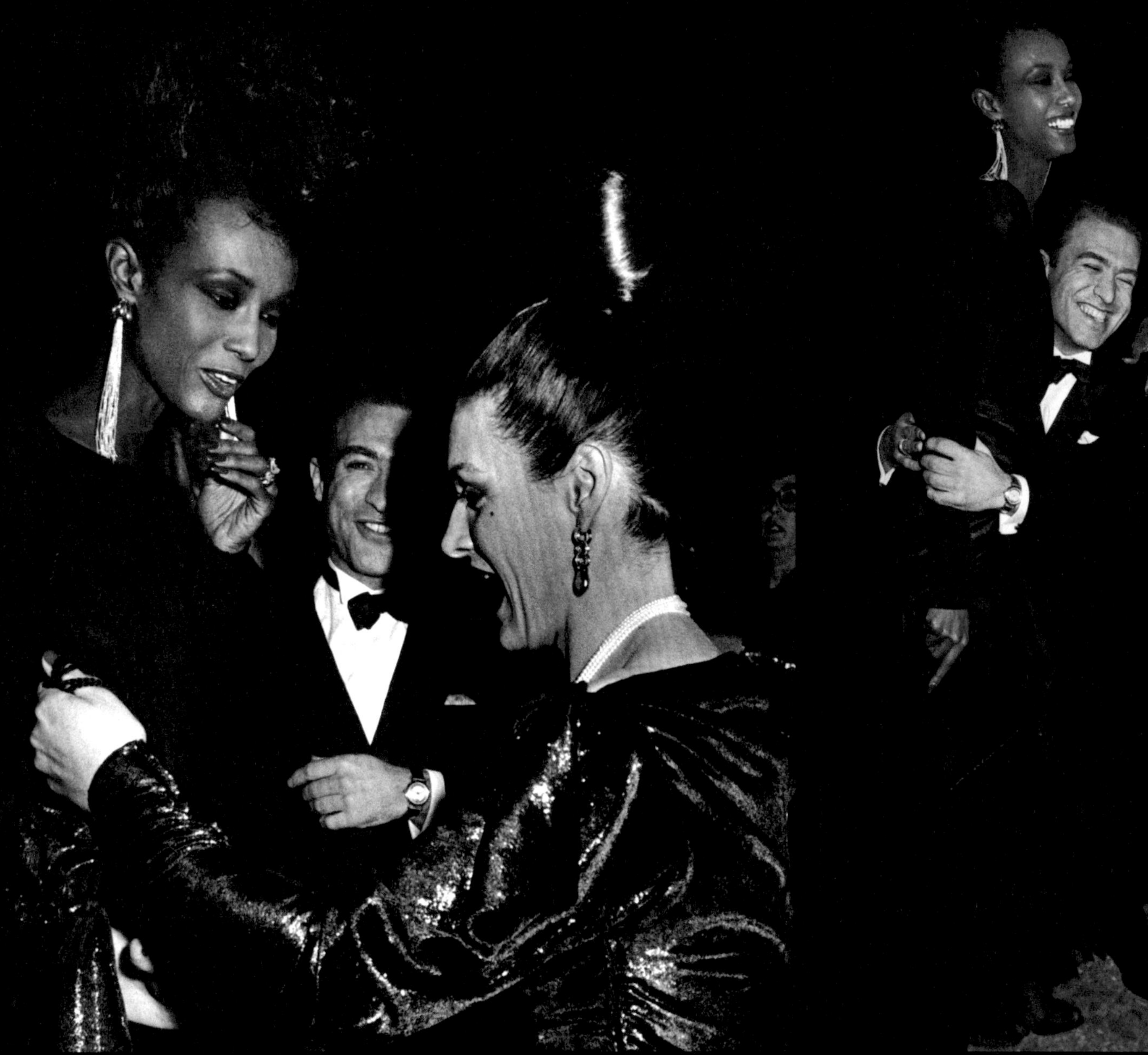

IMAN, RAFAEL & PALOMA

5. Dezember 1983: New York – Iman, Rafael Lopez-Sanchez und Paloma Picasso
besuchen die Yves-St.-Laurent-Retrospektive im Metropolitan Museum of Art.
December 5, 1983: New York—Iman, Rafael Lopez-Sanchez, and Paloma Picasso
attend the Yves St. Laurent retrospective at The Metropolitan Museum of Art.

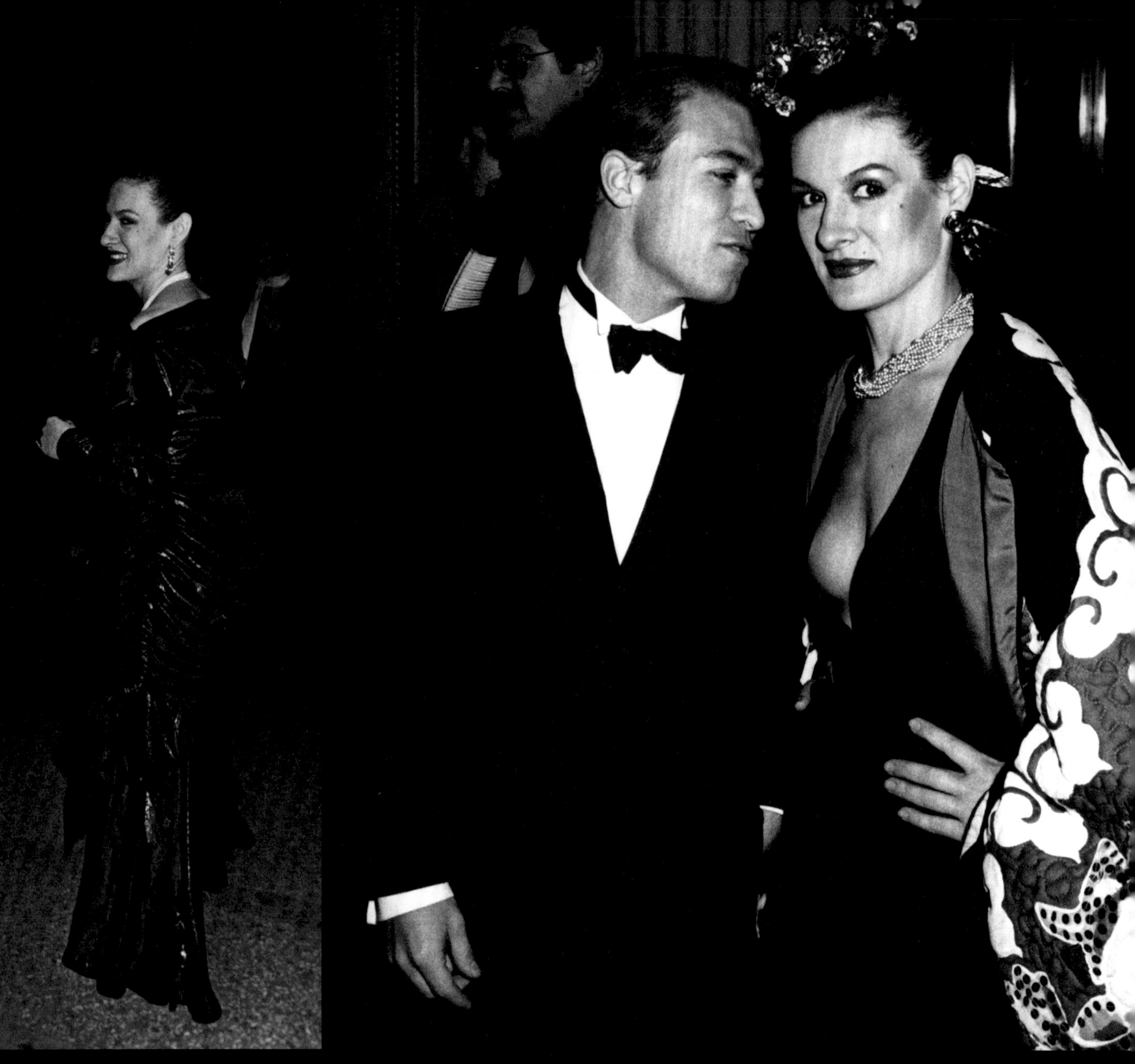

8. Dezember 1980: New York – Paloma Picasso und Rafael Lopez-Sanchez bei
Diana Vreelands »Annual Costume Exhibition« im Metropolitan Museum of Art.
December 8, 1980: New York—Paloma Picasso and Rafael Lopez-Sanchez attend
Diana Vreeland's Annual Costume Exhibition at the Metropolitan Museum of Art.

ANDY

13. Januar 1985: New York – Andy Warhol beim Dinner anlässlich
der Verleihung des »Council of Fashion Designers of America
Fashion Awards« sowie der Auszeichnung an James Galanos für
sein Lebenswerk in der New York Public Library. Der Popkünstler
Andy Warhol ging nirgendwo hin, ohne seine treue Autofokus-
kamera! Andys liebste Bemerkungen waren »Das ist großartig!«
oder »Das war toll« – immer wenn ihm ein Film gefallen hatte,
ein Foto oder ein Siebdruck, oder nach einer amüsanten Party.
Ich denke Andy war einfach großartig!

January 13, 1985: New York City—Andy Warhol at the Council of
Fashion Designers of America Fashion Awards Dinner and Lifetime
Achievement Tribute to James Galanos at the New York Public
Library. Pop Artist Andy Warhol never goes anywhere without his
trusty auto focus camera! Andy's favorite quip, "That's great!"
and "It was great"—he used this frequently after seeing a movie
he likes, a photo or silk screen print, or after a party he enjoyed.
I think Andy was just great!

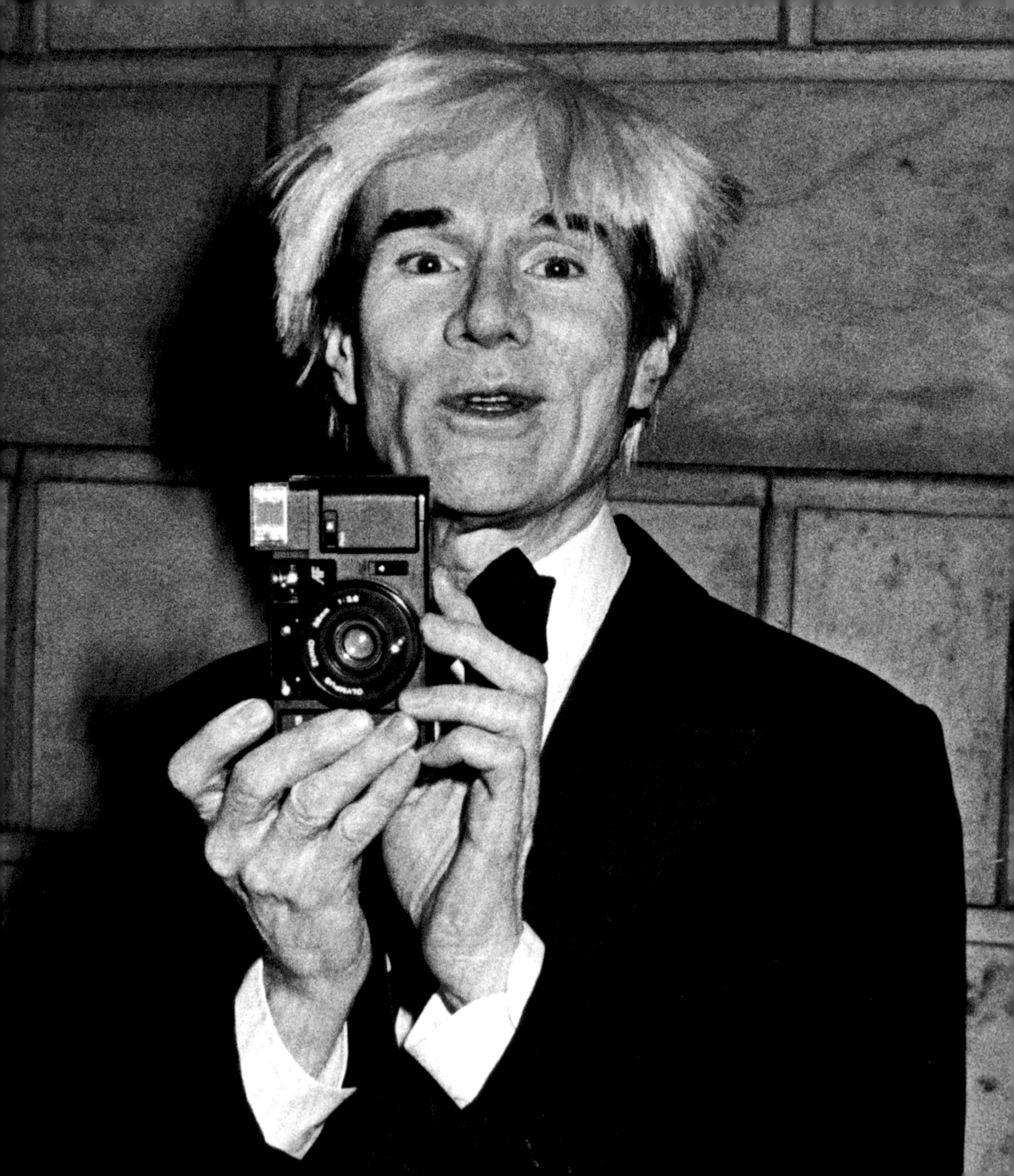

Elton John, Jerry Hall,
Ahmet Ertigun

6/12/78: Elton John, (Andy Warhol) Jerry
Hall and Ahmet Ertigun all attended ~~Grace~~ Roberta Clark
~~Jones Birthday~~ party at ~~Studio 54~~. ~~Xenon~~ Xenon
1987 Update: The man who turned soup cans and
commonplace objects into museum treasures
died of a heart attack at the age of 58.
One of the most famous artists for his
generation died in NY Hospital a day after
gall bladder surgery. (2/22/87)

@ Lefarfalle disco

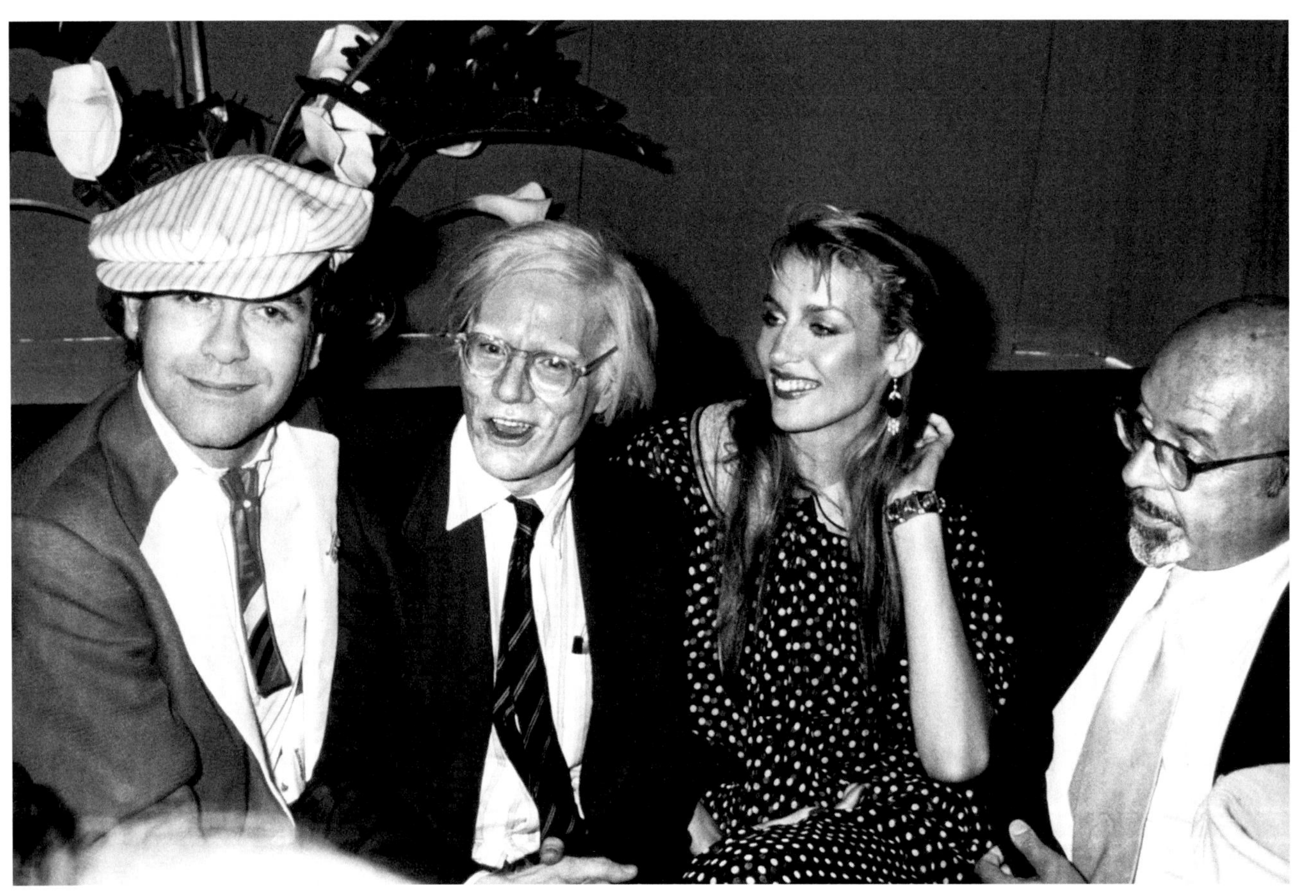

BIANCA

17. Februar 1977: Beverly Hills – Bianca Jagger bei einer
Party für Andy Warhol in Mr. Chow's Restaurant.
February 17, 1977: Beverly Hills—Bianca Jagger attends
a party for Andy Warhol at Mr. Chow's Restaurant.

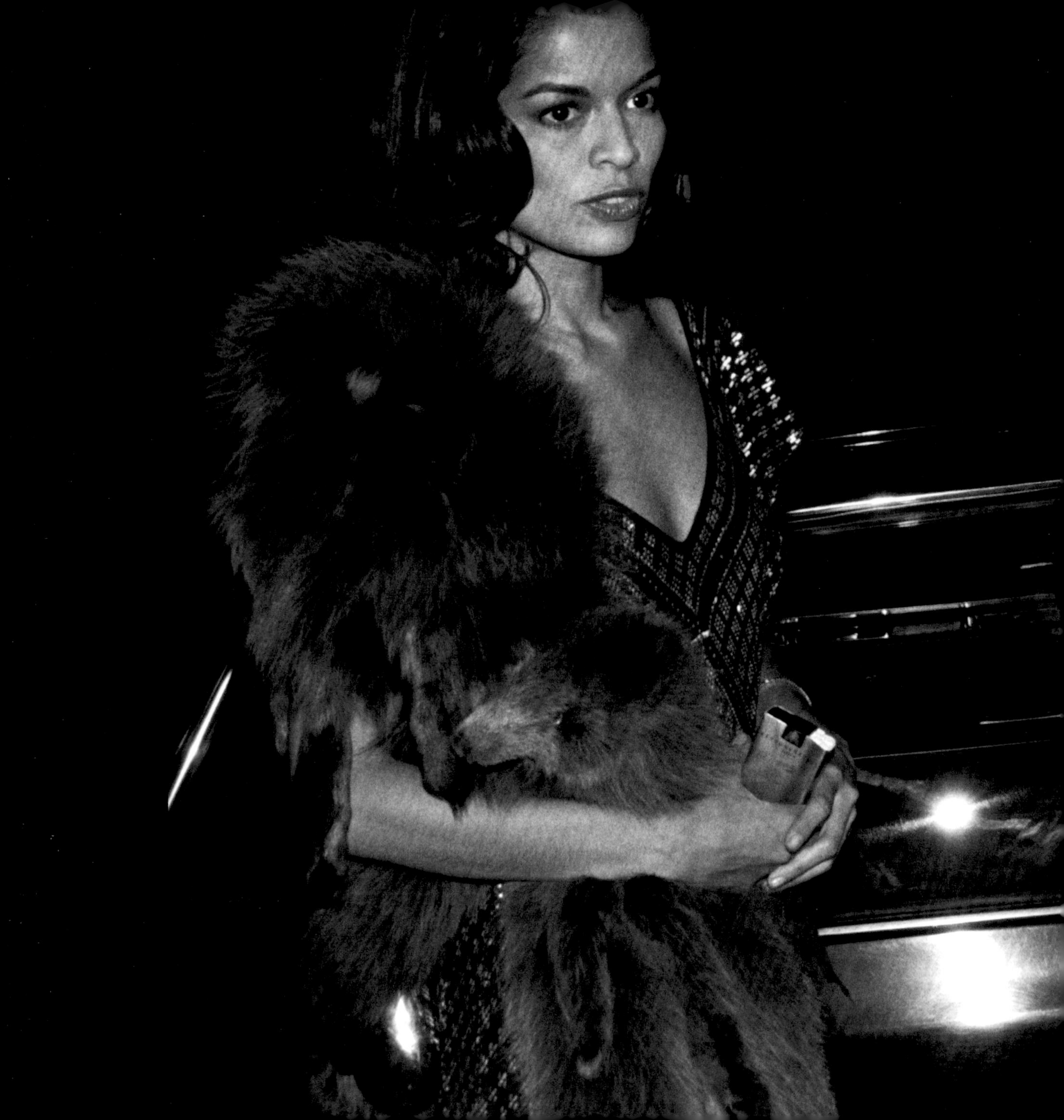

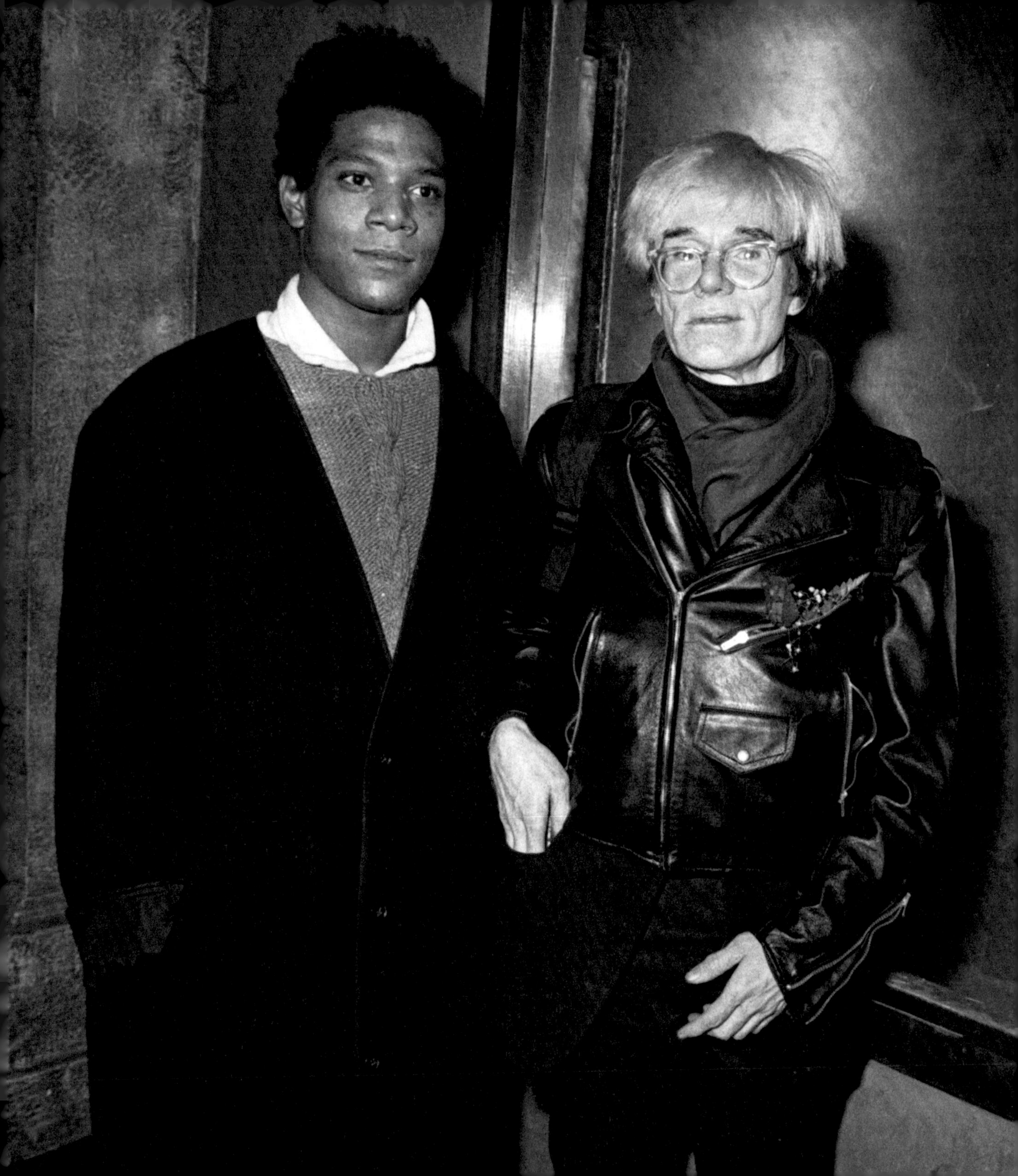

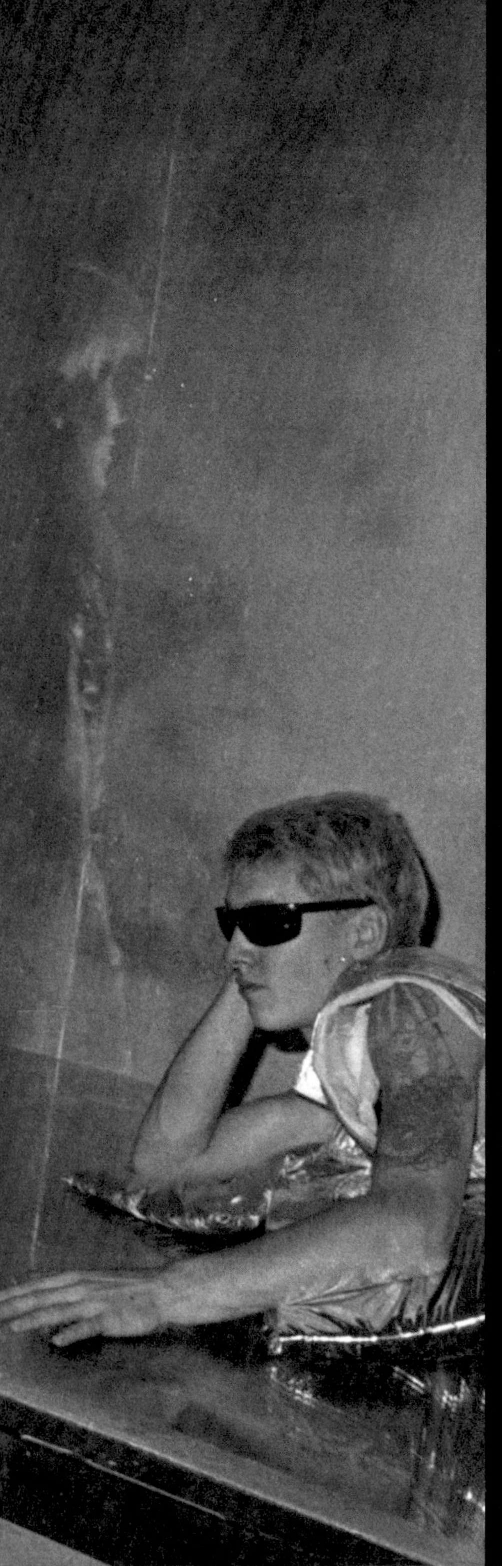

ANDY & JEAN-MICHEL

7. November 1984: New York – Andy Warhol und Jean-Michel Basquiat auf der Benefizveranstaltung »Gifts for the City of New York« im Area Nightclub.
November 7, 1984: New York—Andy Warhol and Jean-Michel Basquiat attend the "Gifts for the City of New York" benefit festival event at Area Nightclub.

GRACE

31. Dezember 1977: New York – Grace Jones bei
Steve Rubells Silvesterparty im Studio 54.
December 31, 1977: New York—Grace Jones at
Steve Rubell's New Year Party at Studio 54.

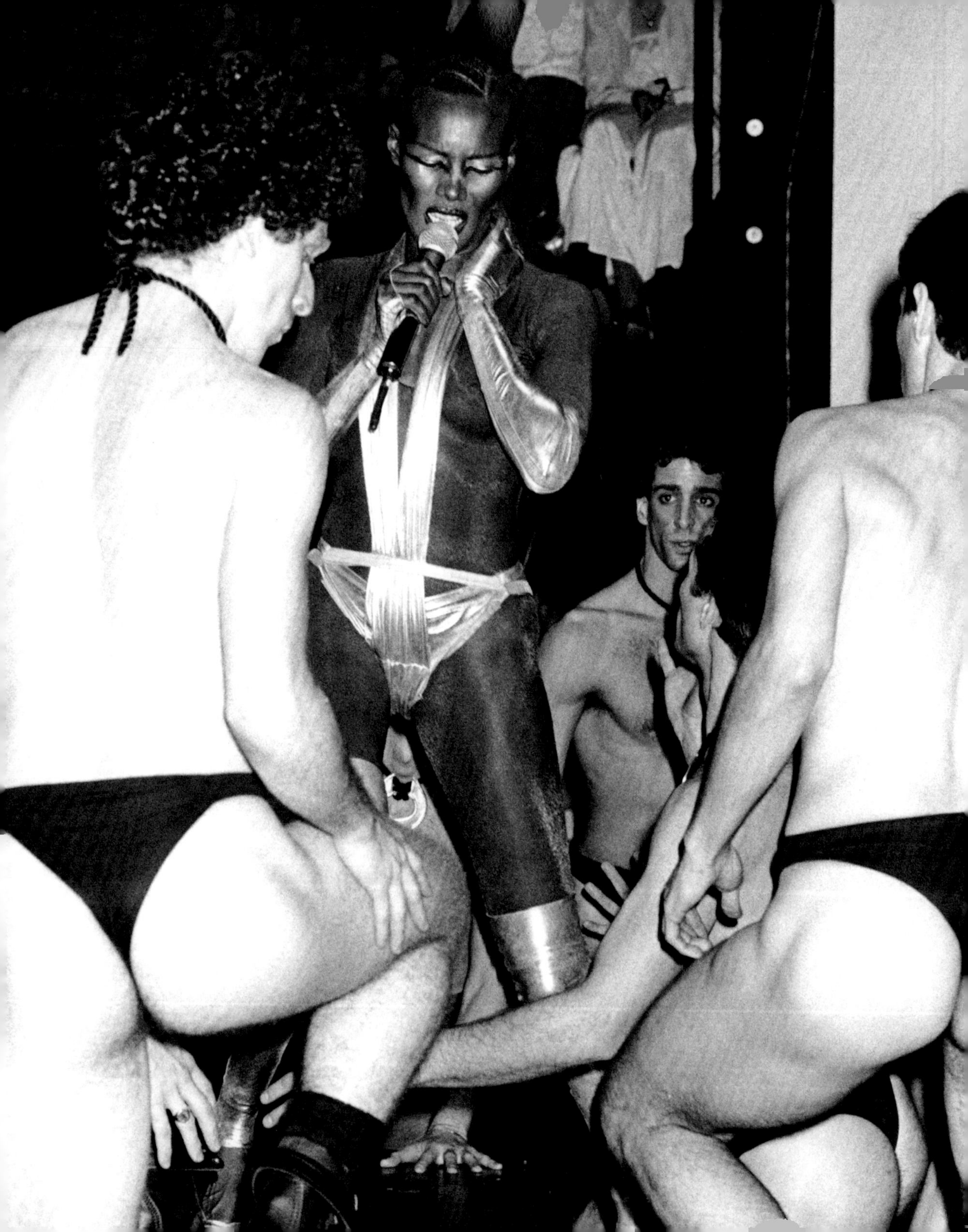

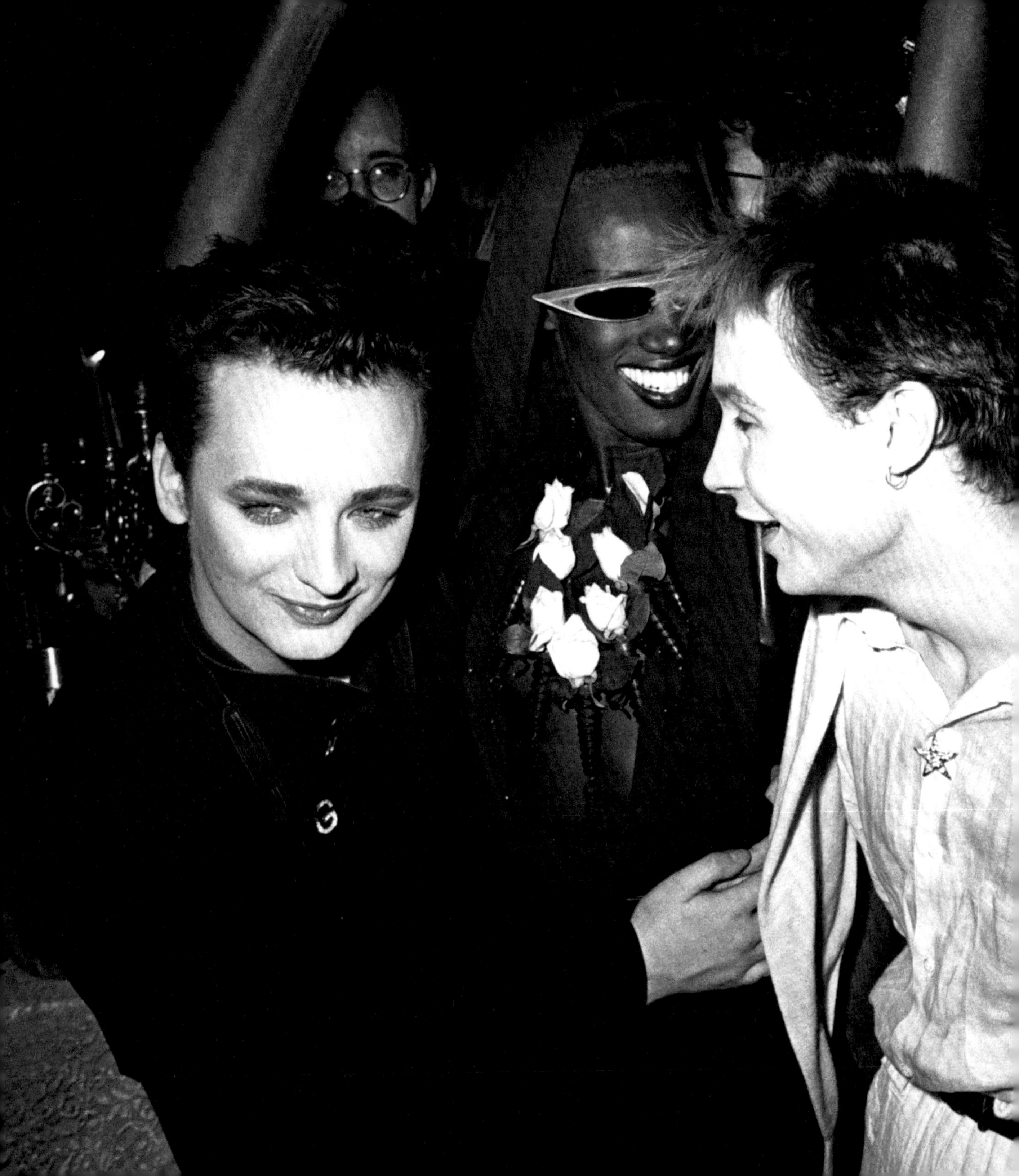

BOY & GRACE
15. Mai 1985: New York – Boy George und
Grace Jones bei der Eröffnung des Palladium.
May 15, 1985: New York—Boy George and
Grace Jones attend the opening of Palladium.

GRACE

31. Dezember 1987: New York – Grace Jones gibt
ein Silvesterkonzert im Roseland Ballroom.
December 31, 1987: New York—Grace Jones performs
during her New Year's Eve concert at Roseland Ballroom.

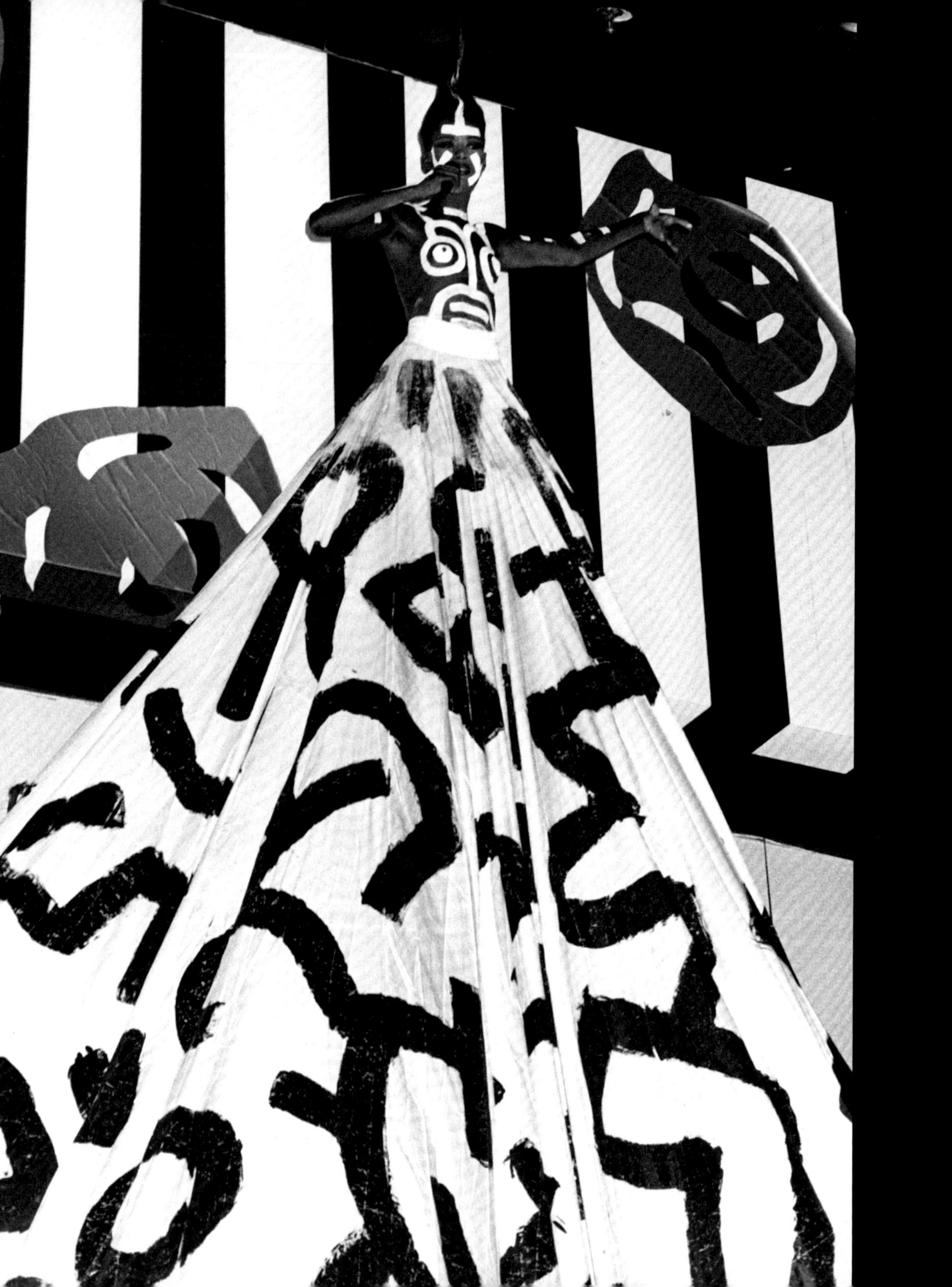

MUSICIANS

Ron Galella

FRANK

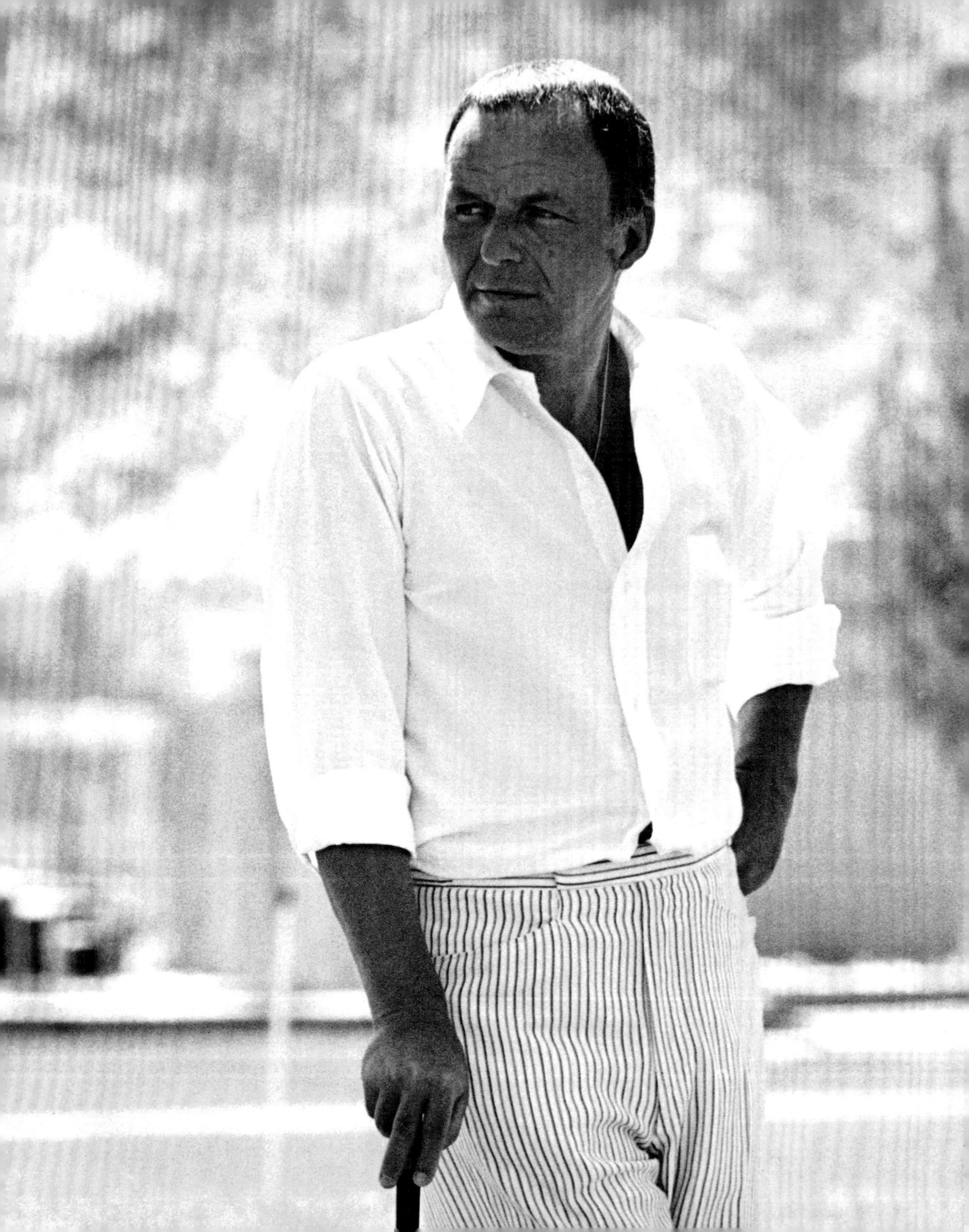

FRANK

18. Oktober 1967: New York – Frank Sinatra am Set von *The Detective* im Polizeirevier des 67. Bezirkes von New York.

October 18, 1967: New York—Frank Sinatra on the set of *The Detective* at New York Police Department's 67th Precinct.

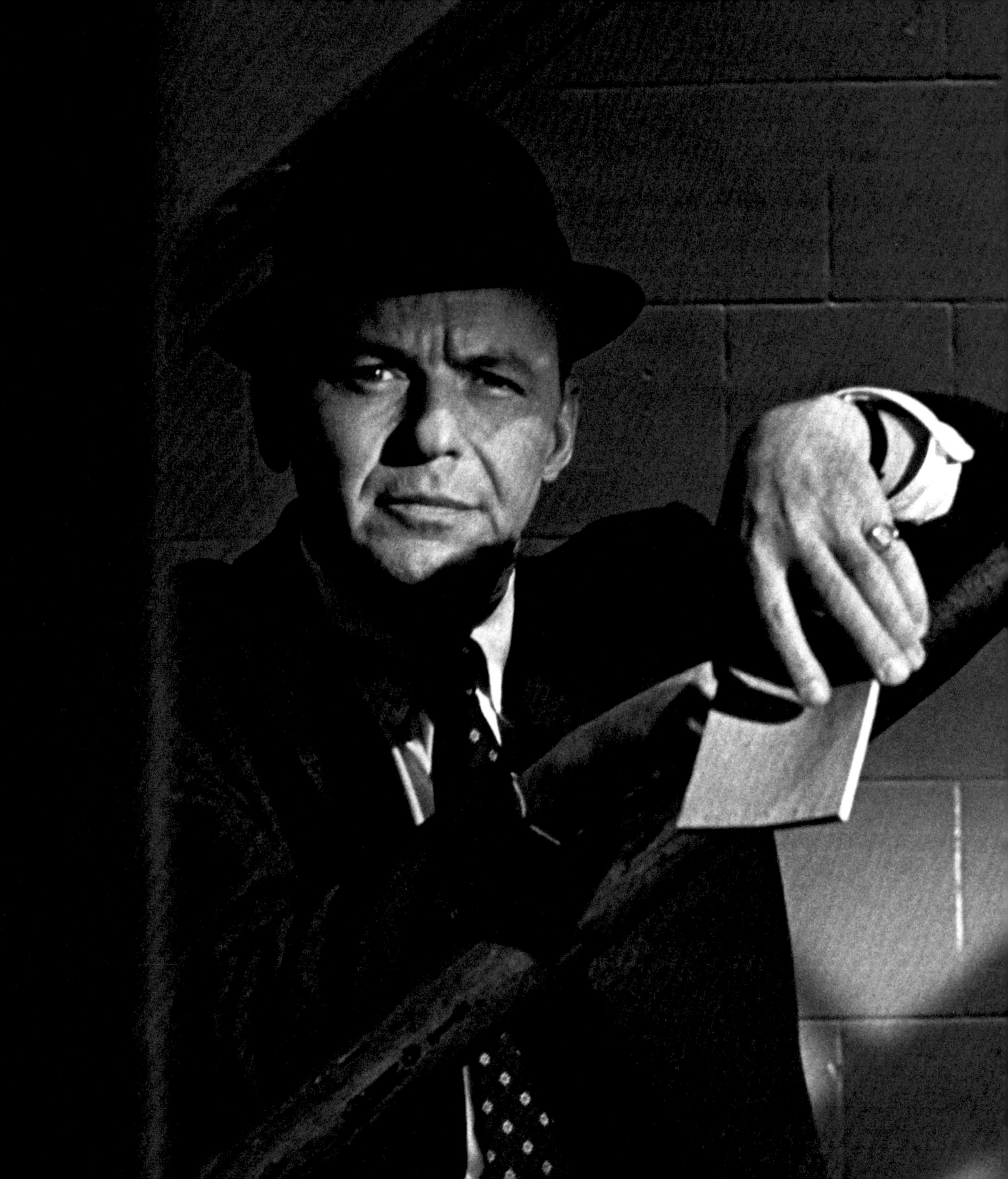

Sept. 20, 1983: Frank Sinatra and Dean Martin teamed up for their buddy Steve Wynn, who is a victim of the dreaded eye disease, Retinitis Pigmentosa at the Waldorf in New York City, benefiting the eye disorder. The old Rat Pack buddies raised more than $750,00 from the packed house. Their duet was sensational! Martin and Sinatra had a ball, after Frankie brought the house down with "New York, New York." They toasted each other and then did a duet, joking all the way. Martin got the biggest laugh, kidding himself. "You know my father made a lot of money fast when he first came to this country, and he only knew three words in English," Martin quipped, "Stick 'em up!". Dino, nowhere near the boozer he used to ne, kidded himself about his old drinking habits and about Sinatra's voice. "You still got it man, you really belt it out," said Dean. "Your eyes are popping out but you're still singing." Dino's 66 to Sinatra's 67. "Together," said Sinatra in noting the new reunion with his old buddy, "we're older than the United States!" There were, however, no godfather jokes. In the benefit booklet Sinatra's page stated, "I am honored to be part of this special evening for Retinitis Pigmentosa as we support the Foundation's continued efforts to increase public awareness and understanding of degenerative retinal diseases. This hardworking organization sustains nine research centers internationally, including centers at Columbia University and New York University Medical Center. And the Foundation needs our continued attention." Martin's stated, "I drink to the more than 22,000 dedicated and untiring volunteers throughout the nation who spearhead the important work of the Retinitis Pigmentosa Foundation and everyone here this evening for their support. Retinitis Pigmentosa is a hereditary disease that strikes people of all ages and may lead to total blindness. Let's help find a cure!"

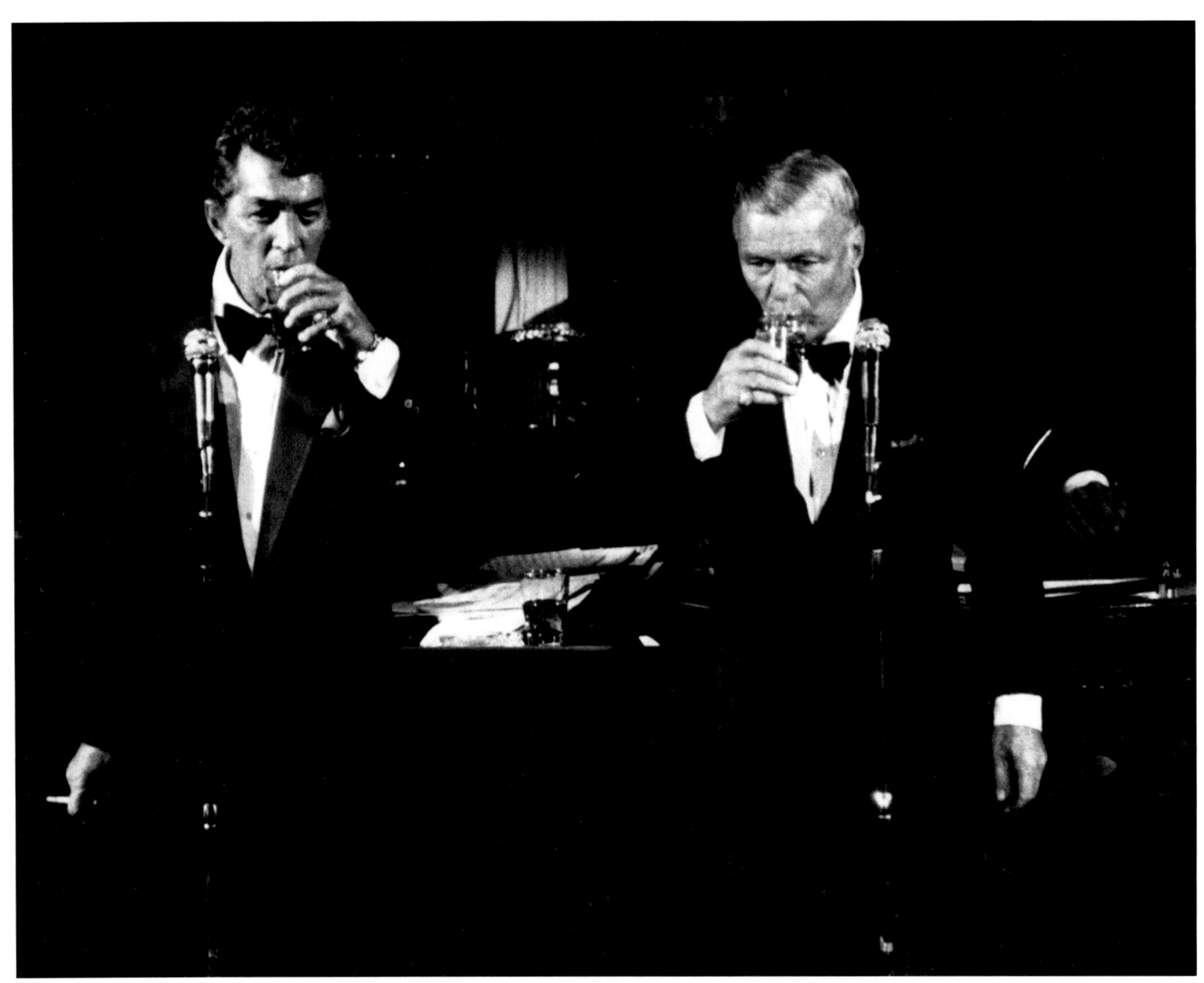

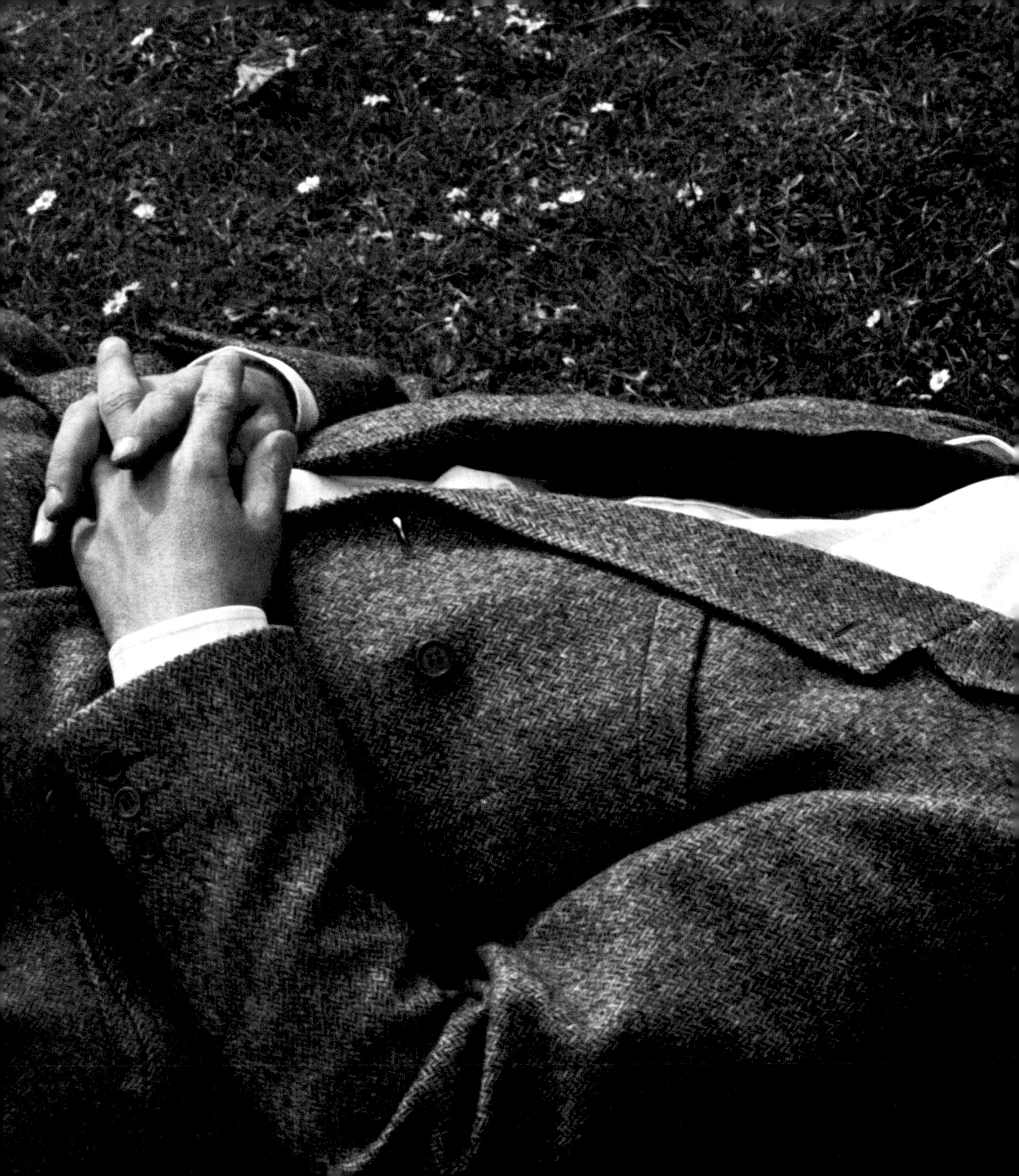

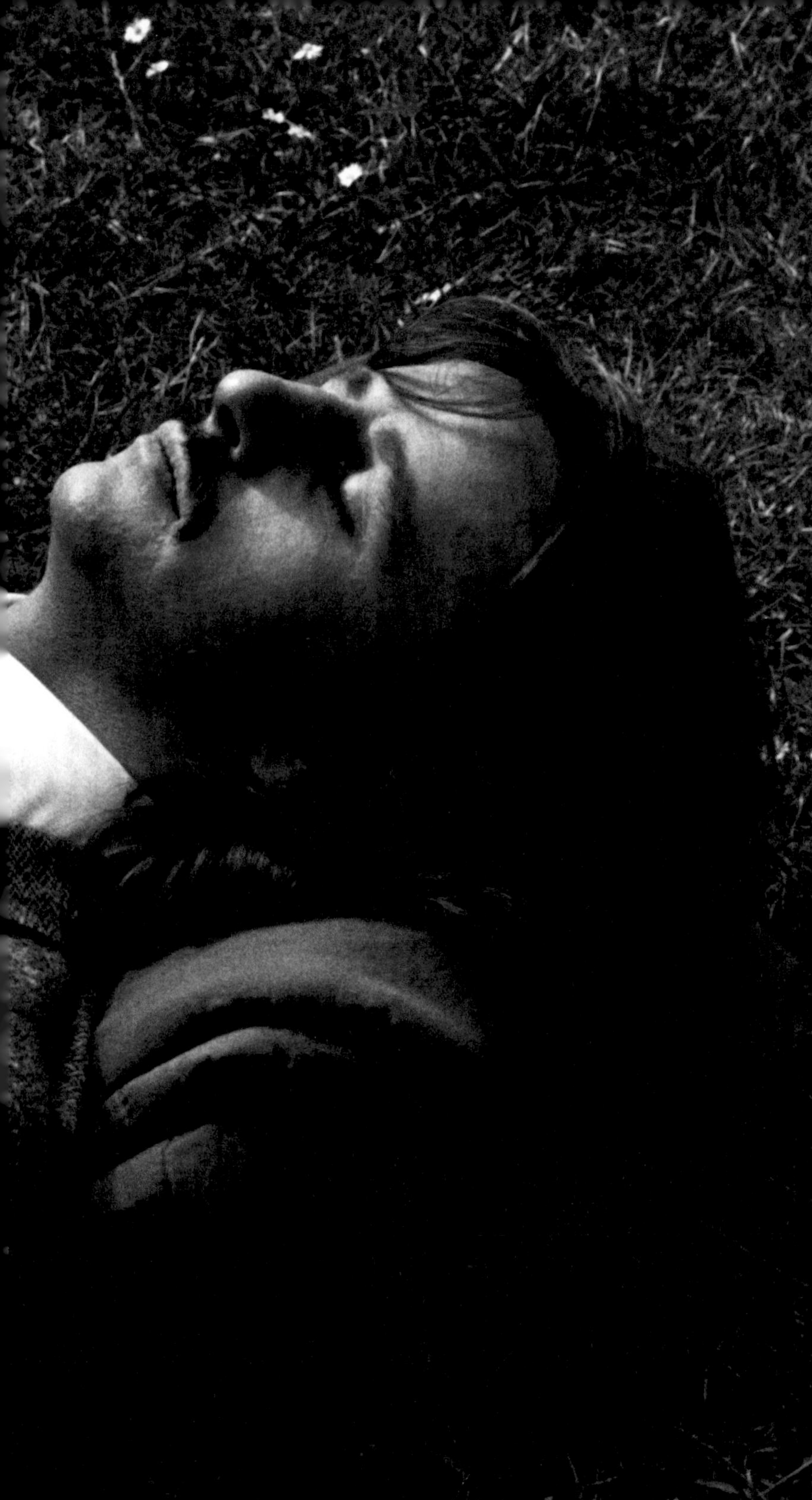

RINGO

September 1969: London – Ringo Starr am Set von *The Magic Christian* im St. James's Park.
September, 1969: London—Ringo Starr on the set of *The Magic Christian* in St. James's Park.

RINGO & PETER

September 1969: London, England – Ringo Starr und
Peter Sellers drehen *The Magic Christian* im St. James's Park.
September, 1969: London, England—Ringo Starr and
Peter Sellers filming *The Magic Christian* in St. James's Park.

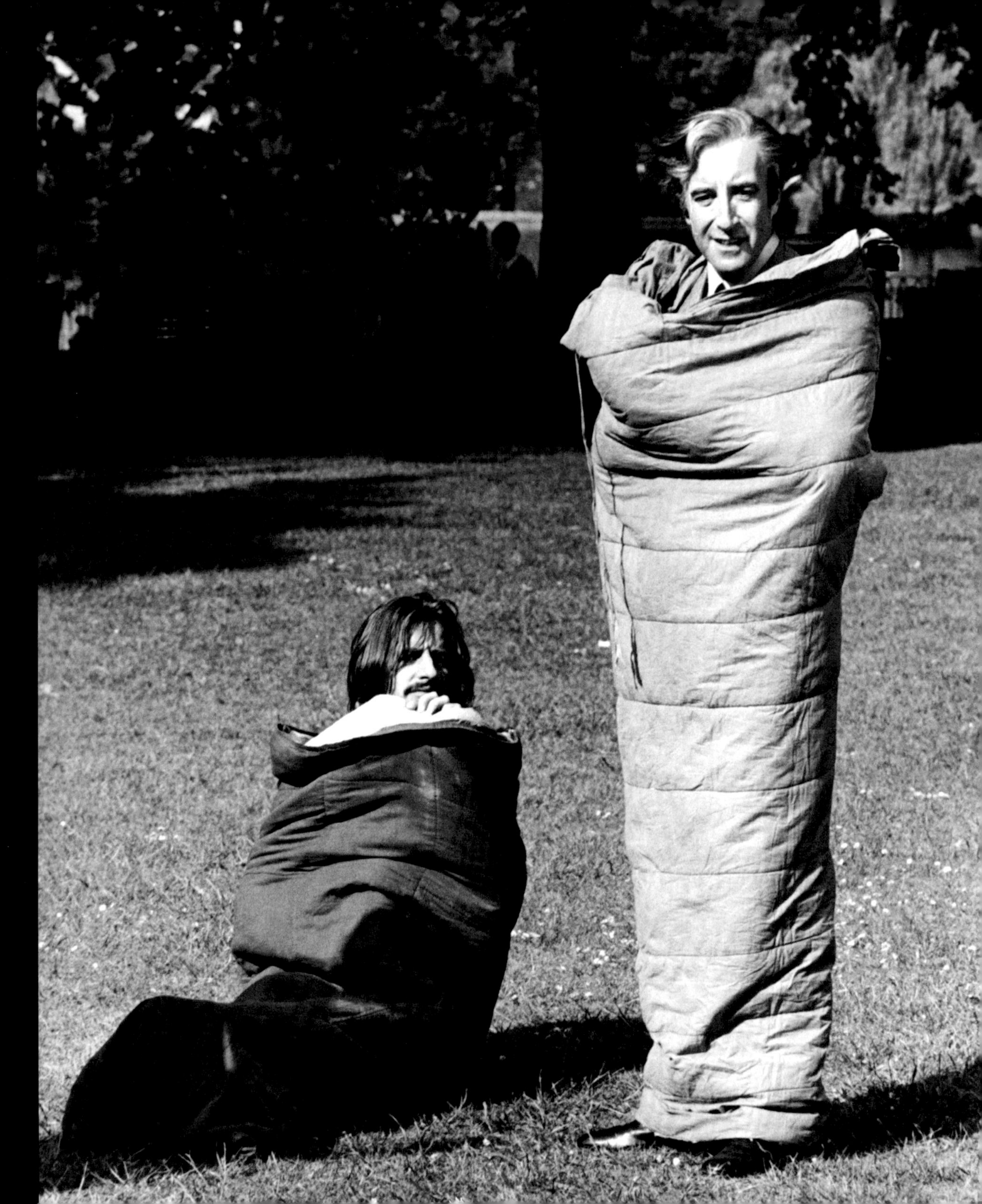

JOHN & MAY

17. November 1974: New York – John Lennon und May Pang
bei der Premiere von *Seargent Pepper's Lonely Hearts Club
Band On the Road* im Beacon Theater.

November 17, 1974: New York—John Lennon and May Pang
attend the opening of *Seargent Pepper's Lonely Hearts Club
Band On the Road* at Beacon Theater.

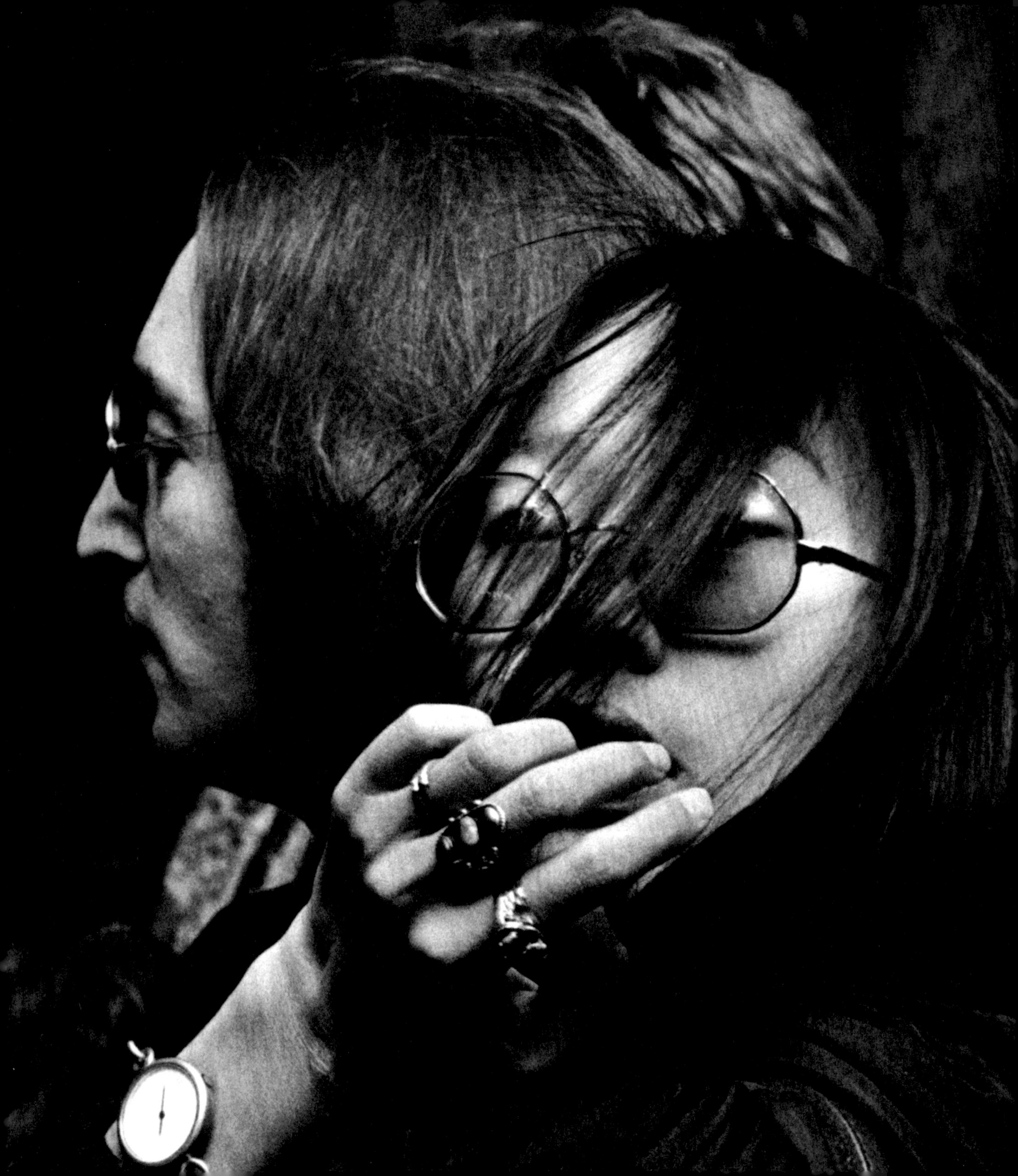

JOHN & MICK

13. März 1974: Los Angeles, Kalifornien – Mick Jagger und
John Lennon bei der Verleihung des zweiten »Annual American
Film Institute Life Achievement Award« an James Cagney
im Hotel Century Plaza. Nach Lennons Tod gab Mick Jagger
Ron Barret ein Interview, in dem er über seine Freundschaft
mit dem gerade verstorbenen John Lennon sprach. Mick sagte,
»Wenn ein guter Freund stirbt, bleibt dir nur noch, dich an die
guten Zeiten zu erinnern.«
March 13, 1974: Los Angeles, California—Mick Jagger and
John Lennon at the Second Annual American Film Institute Life
Achievement Award Salute to James Cagney at the Century
Plaza Hotel. After Lennon's death, Mick Jagger held an interview
with Ron Barret and spoke of his friendship with the late
John Lennon. Mick said, "when a good friend dies all you can
do is remember the good times."

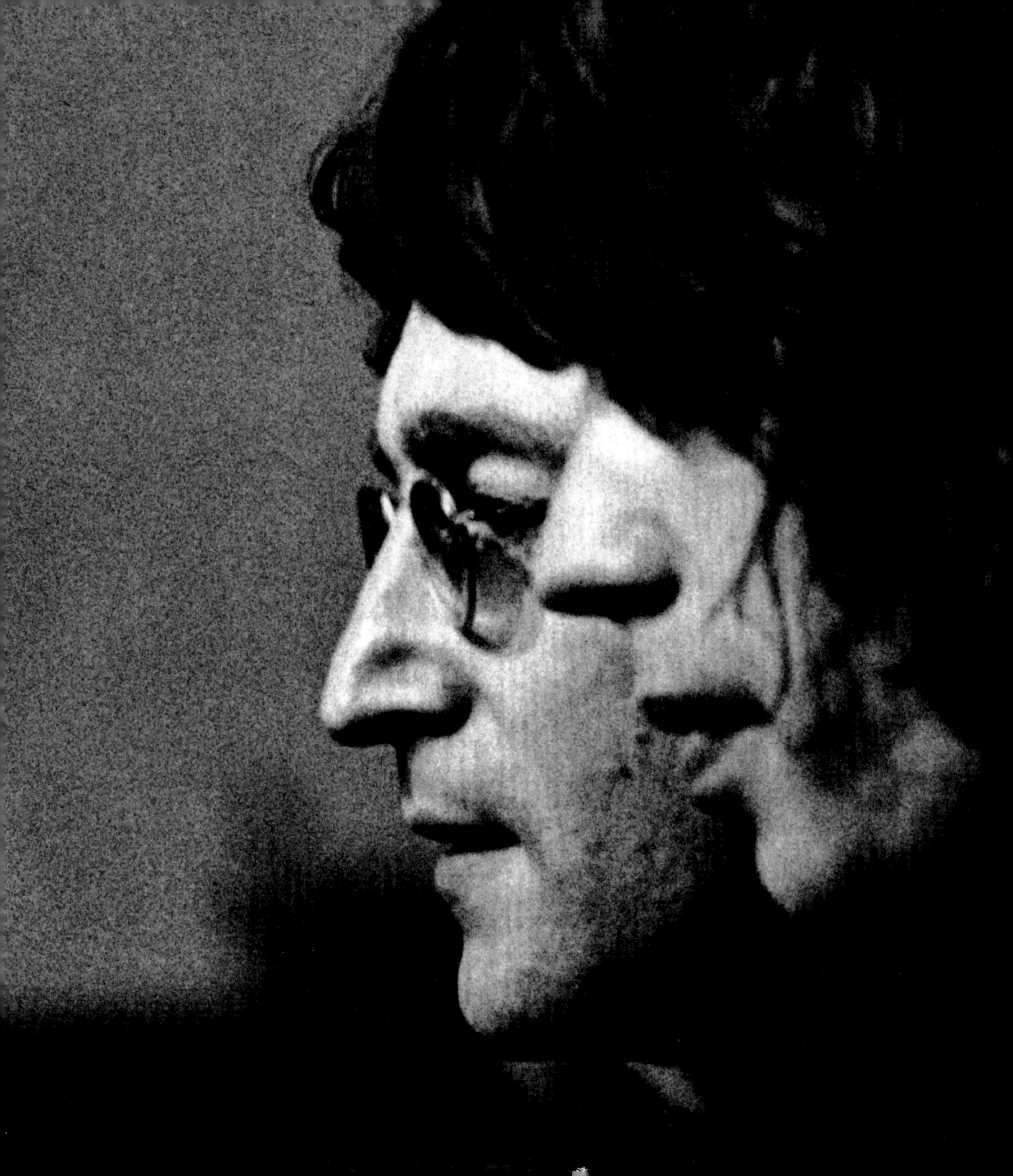

March 13, 1974: Two of rock's all
time greats, the late John Lennon
and "Rolling Stone's" Mick Jagger
at the AFI Salute to James Cagney
at the Century Plaza Hotel in California. John's former secretary
and lover, has just completed a
book on her life with John titled
"Loving John", which is being
published by Warner Books and ex-
cerpts of the book can be read in
the July issues of US MAGAZINE.
The most revealing fact from the
book is that May was urged to
date John, by John's wife, Yoko
Ono.

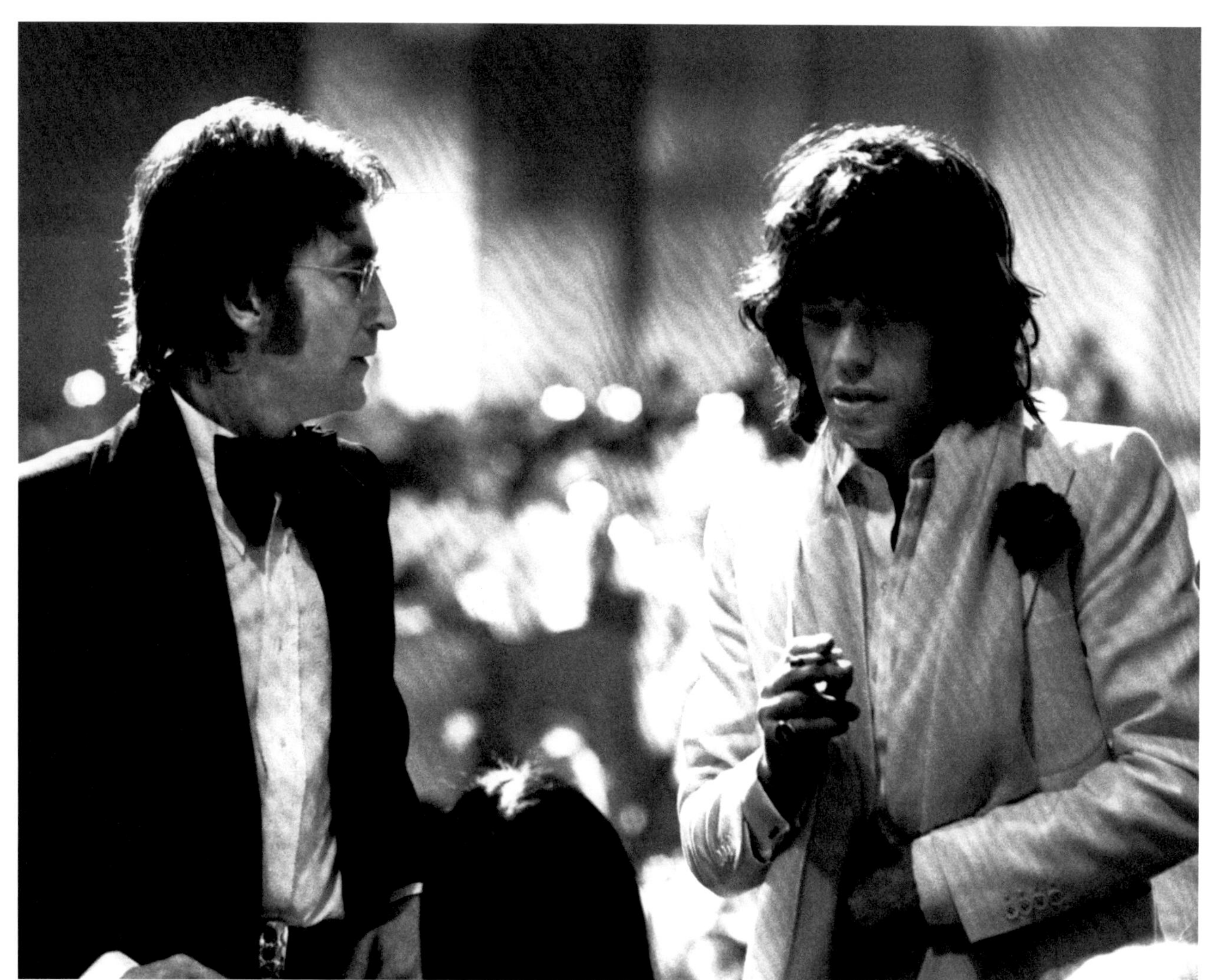

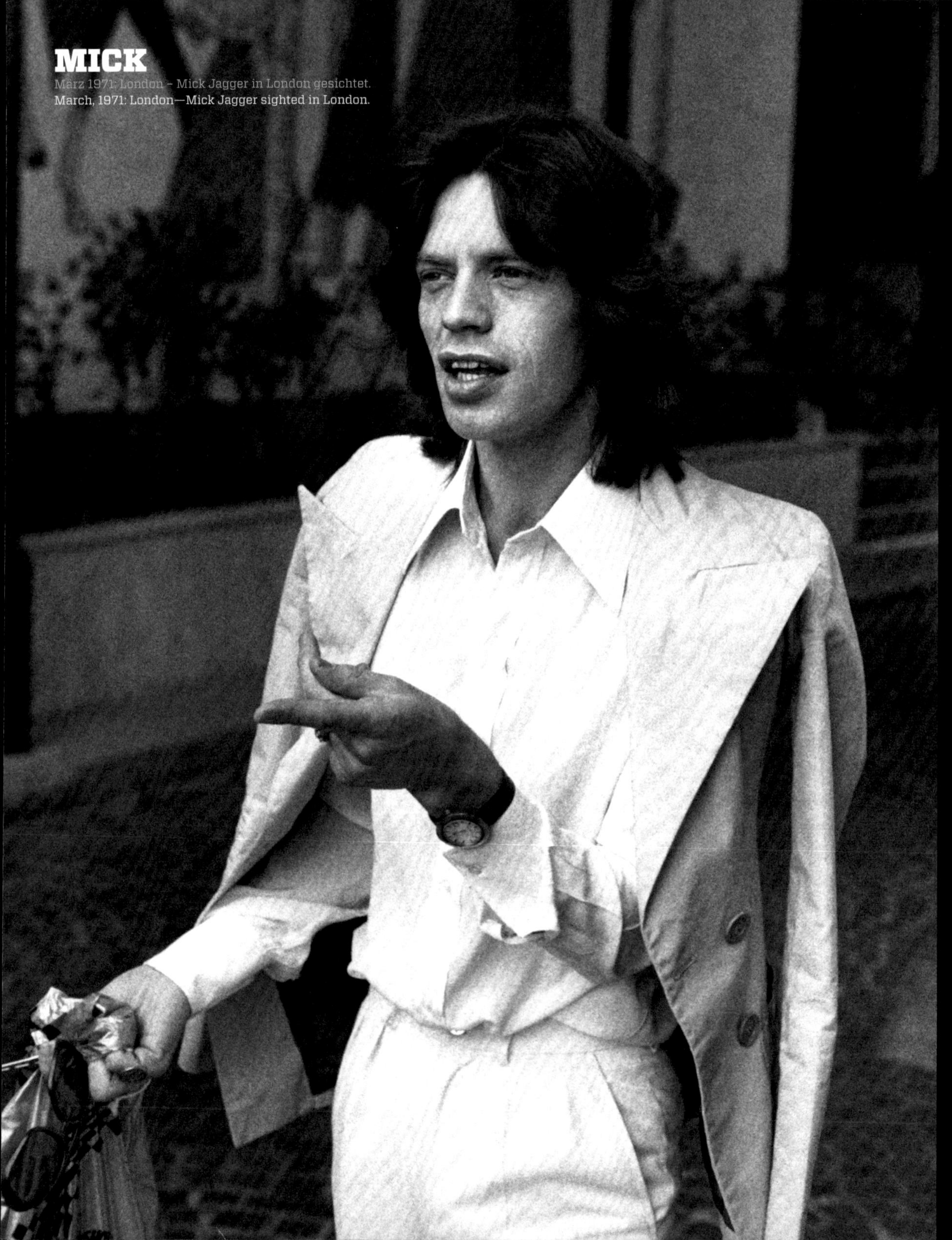

MICK
März 1971: London – Mick Jagger in London gesichtet.
March, 1971: London—Mick Jagger sighted in London.

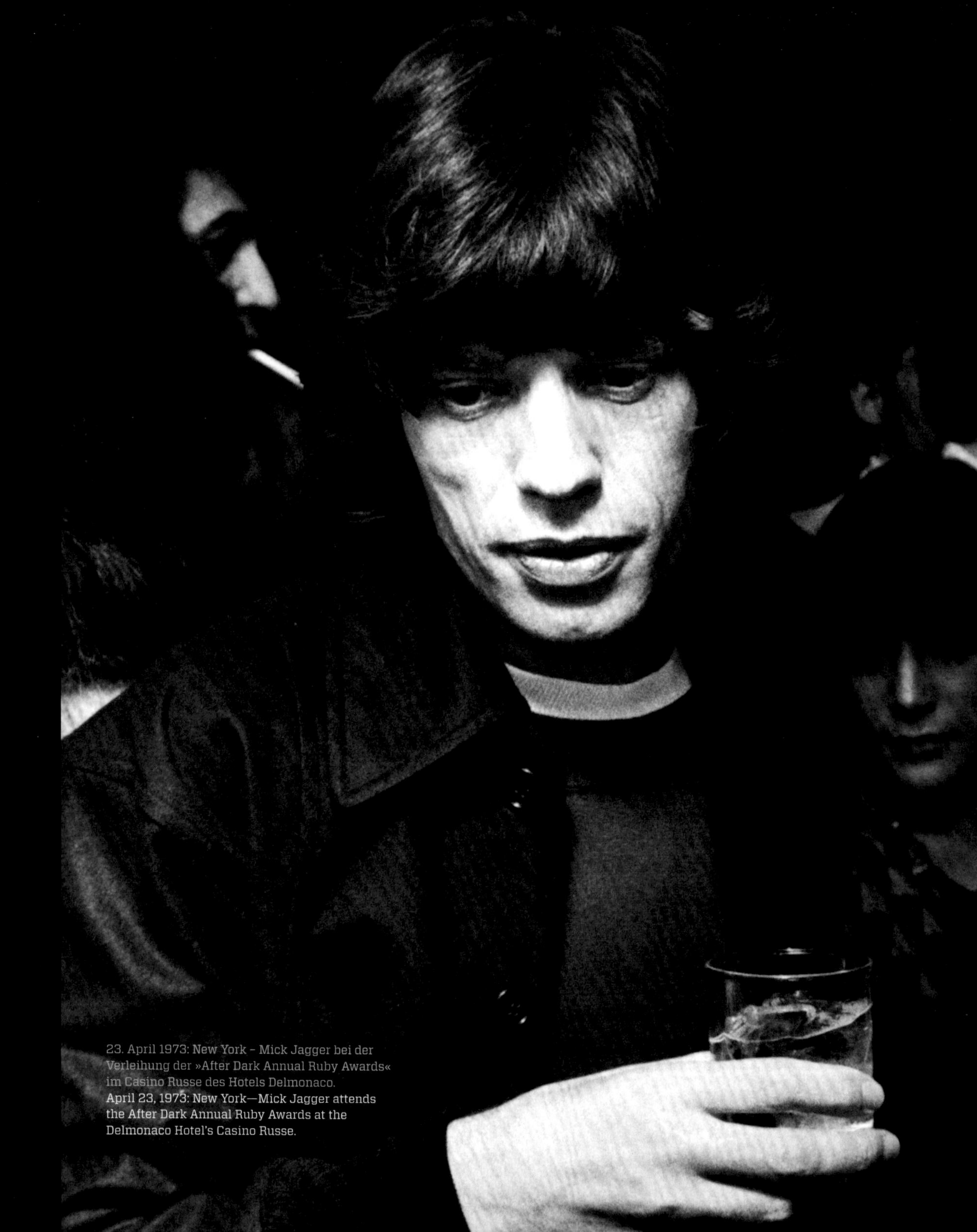

23. April 1973: New York – Mick Jagger bei der
Verleihung der »After Dark Annual Ruby Awards«
im Casino Russe des Hotels Delmonaco.
April 23, 1973: New York—Mick Jagger attends
the After Dark Annual Ruby Awards at the
Delmonaco Hotel's Casino Russe.

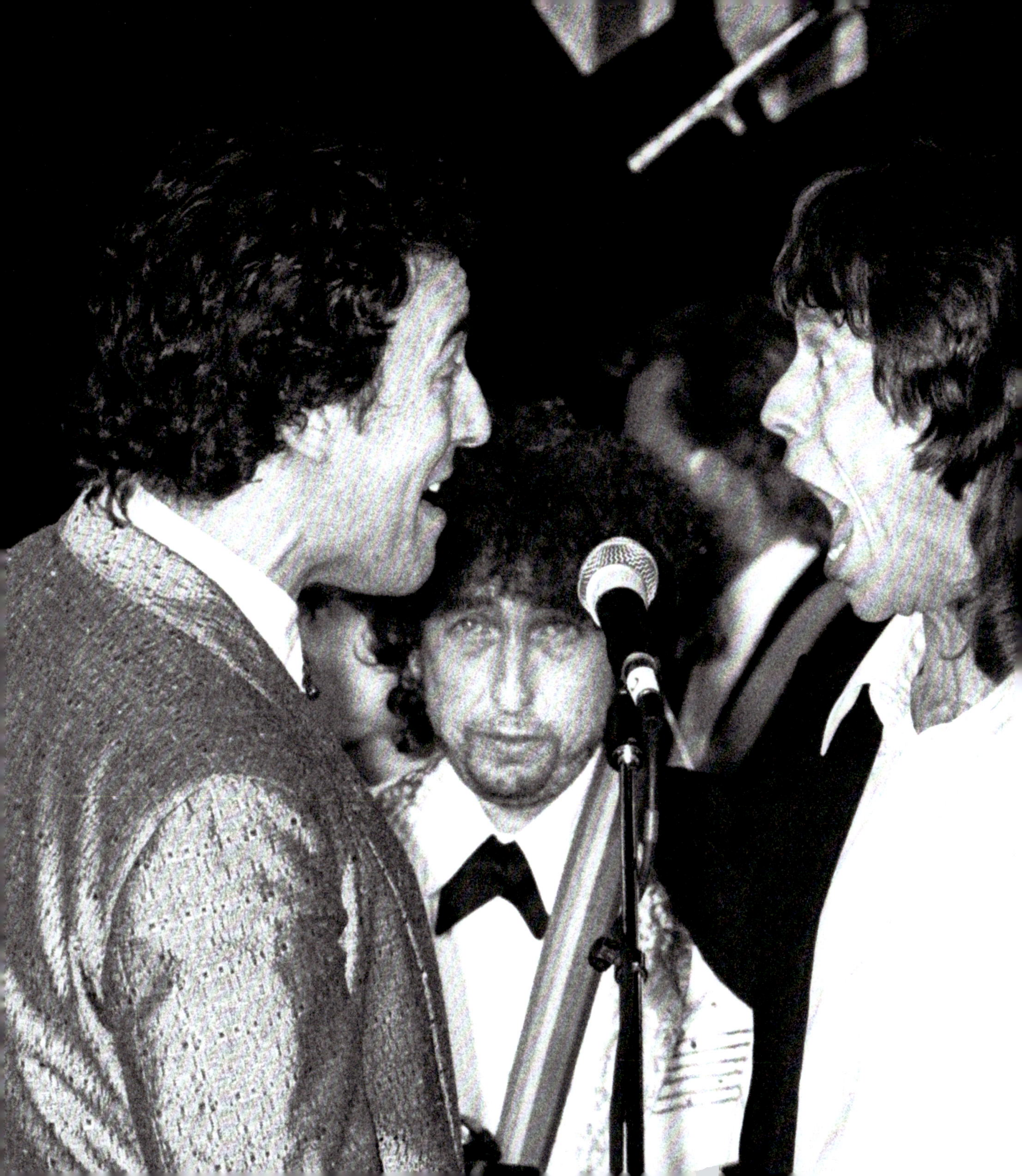

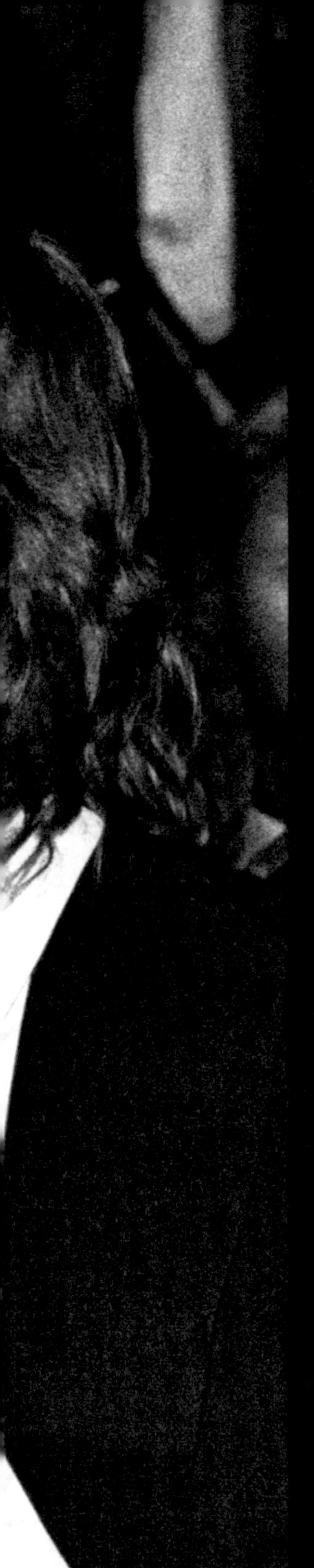

KEITH & PATTI
13. Juni 1988: New York – Keith Richards und
Patti Hansen bei der Benefizveranstaltung
»You Can Do Something About AIDS« im Club MK.
June 13, 1988: New York—Keith Richards and
Patti Hansen at Club MK for the You Can Do
Something About AIDS benefit.

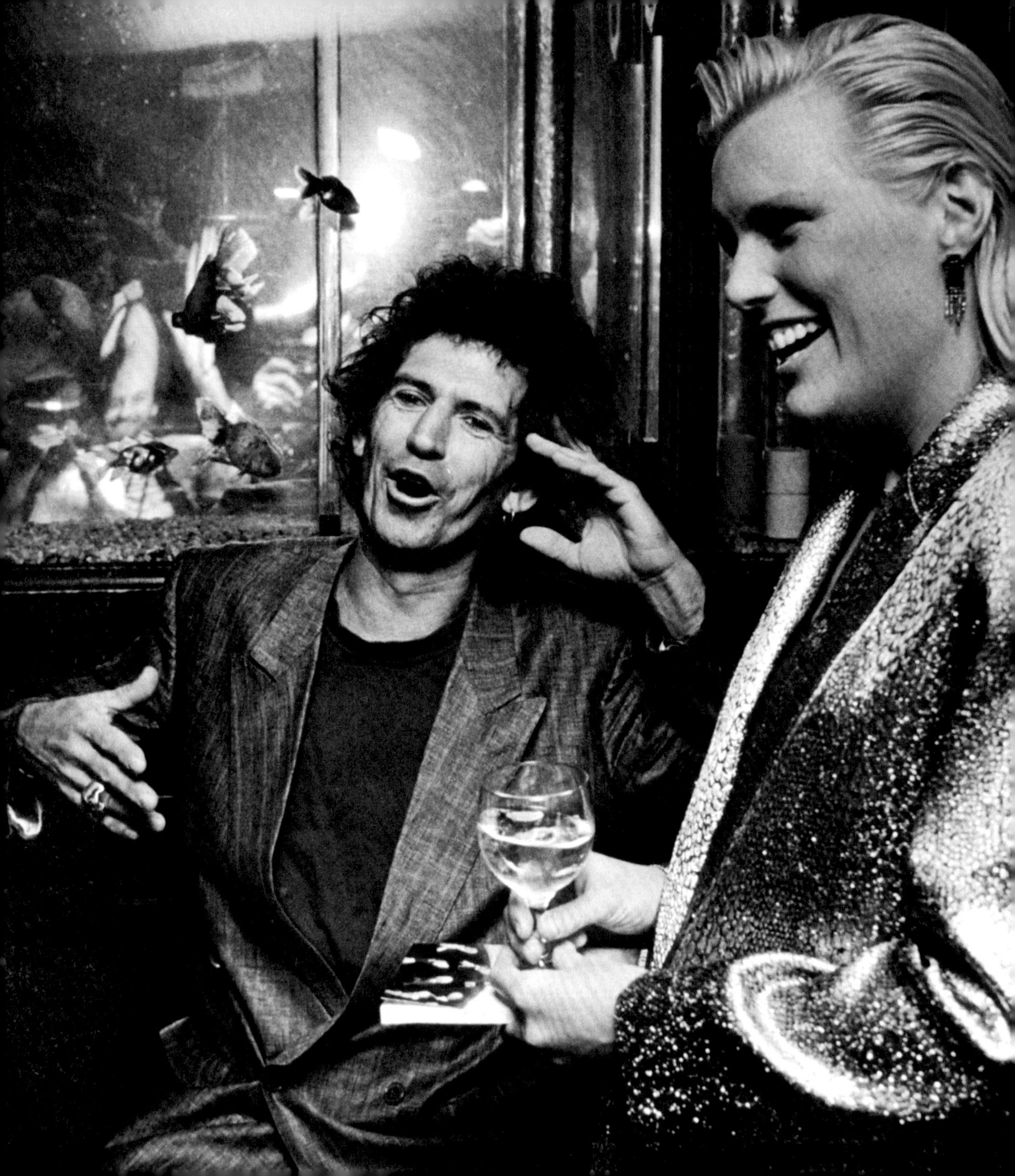

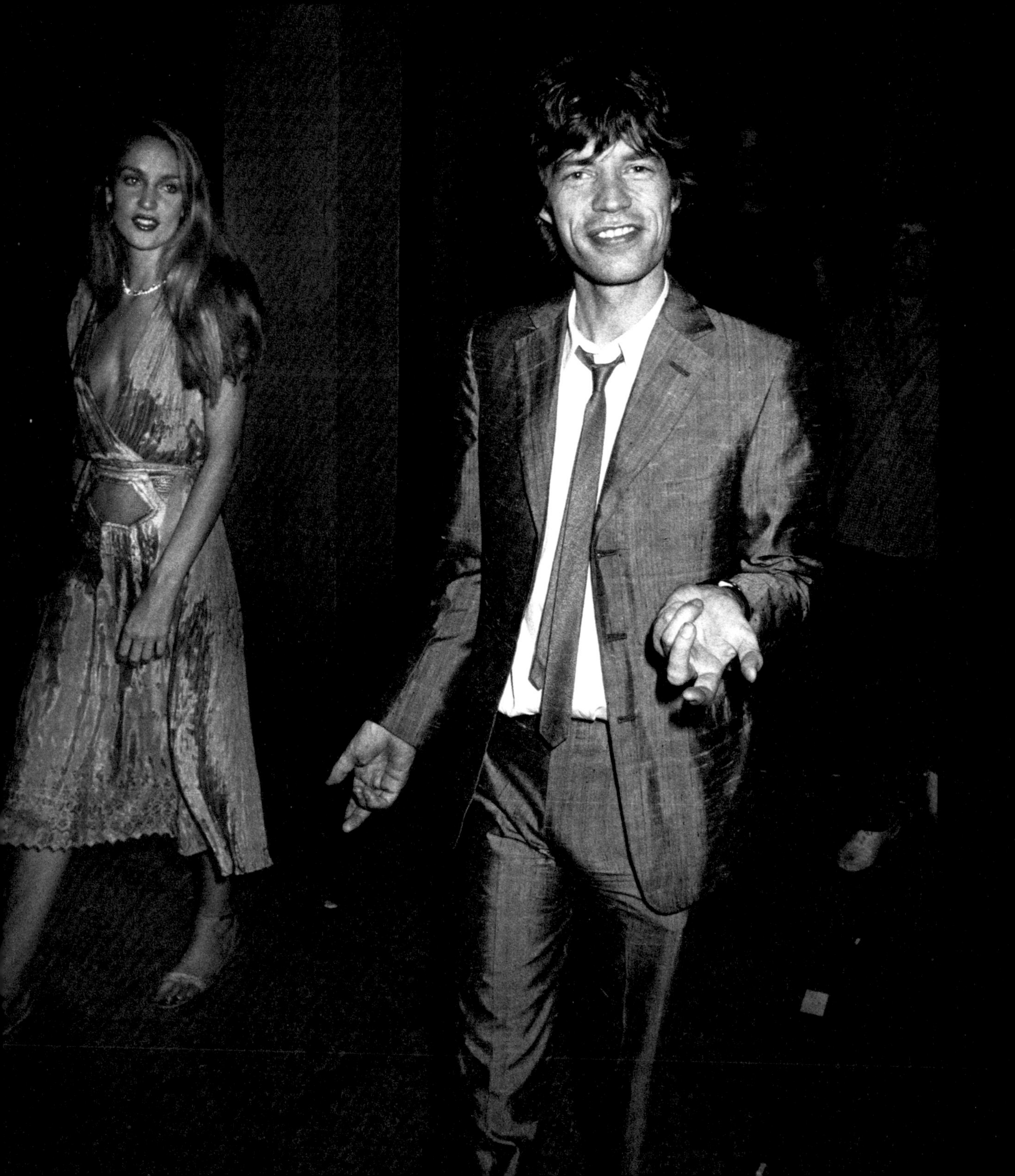

BIANCA & HALSTON

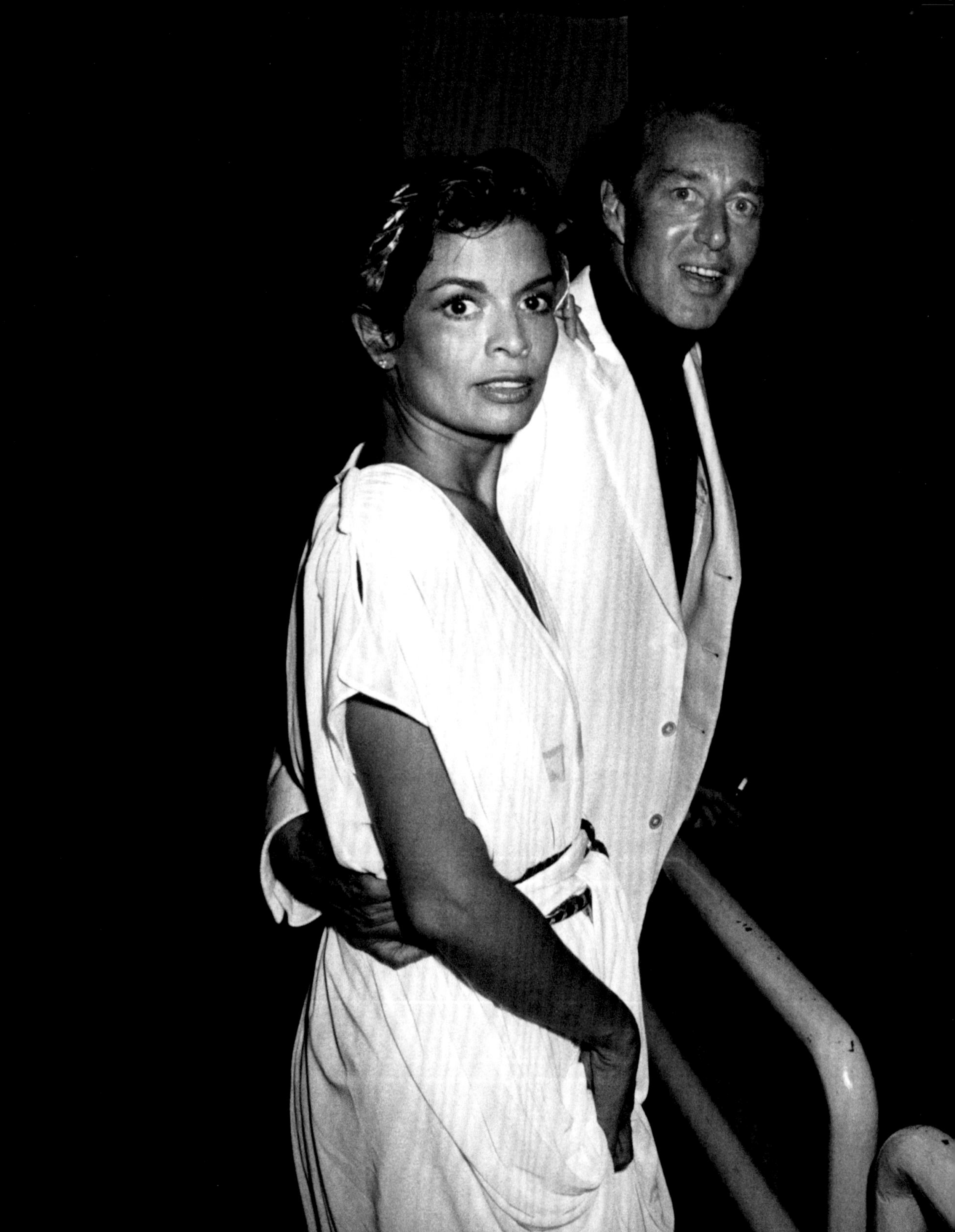

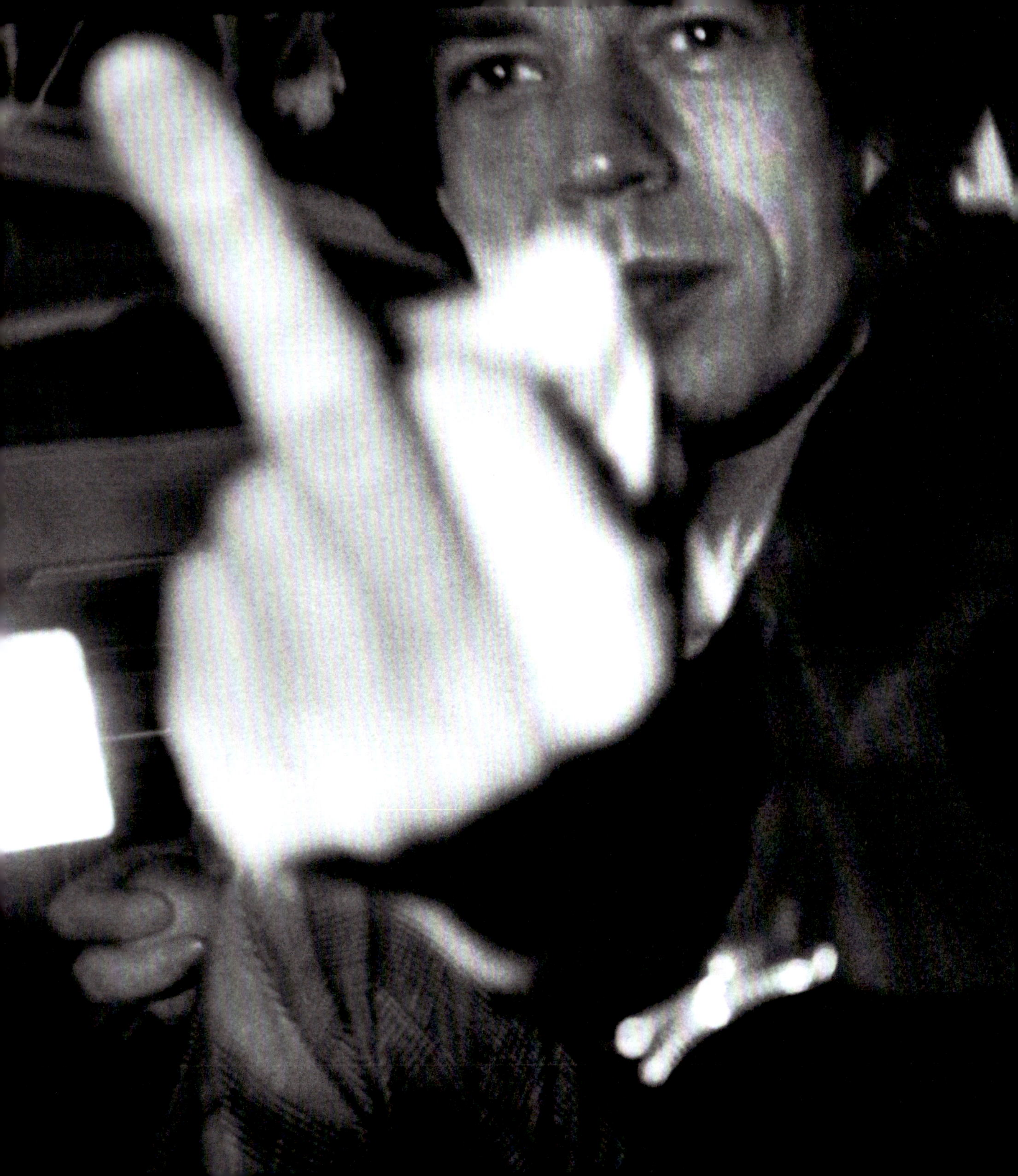

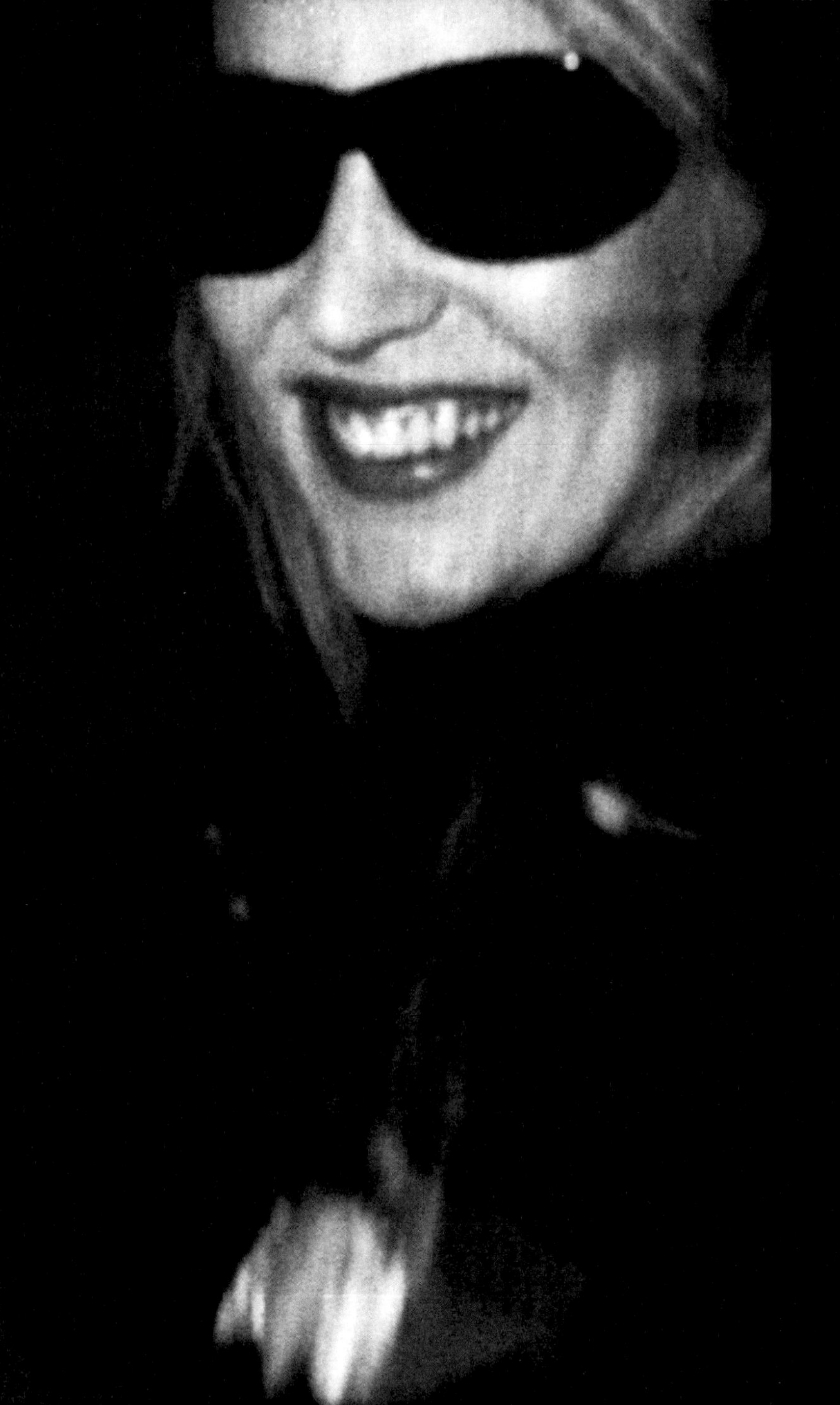

MICK & JERRY

16. Januar 1983: Los Angeles, Kalifornien –
Mick Jagger und Jerry Hall bei einem Essen
anlässlich einer Ausstellungseröffnung
in der Mizuno Gallery.
January 16, 1983: Los Angeles, California—
Mick Jagger and Jerry Hall attending an
opening luncheon at Mizuno Gallery.

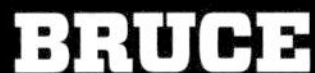

BRUCE

24. August 1988: New York – Bruce Springsteen im Hotel Westbury.
Bruce »Der Boss« Springsteen sprang bei Stings Konzert im Madison
Square Garden auf die Bühne und ging dann zu einer Party zu seinen
Ehren in die Canal Bar, wo ich dieses Foto im Regen machte. Bruce
brachte seine angeblich schwangere Freundin und Background-
sängerin Patti Scialfa mit, die er später heiratete. Wir knipsten die
beiden, als sie in eine Limousine einstiegen, und folgten ihnen bis
zum Hotel Westbury. »Was machen Sie hier, Ron?« scherzte der Boss.
»Sie sind schwer zu kriegen!« sagte Ron zu seinem sich schnell
bewegenden Ziel.

August 24, 1988: New York—Bruce Springsteen at the Westbury Hotel.
Bruce "The Boss" Springsteen jumped onstage at Sting's Madison
Square Garden concert and went on to a party in his honor at the
Canal Bar, where I captured this photo in the rain. Bruce brought
along his reportedly preggers gal pal and backup singer Patti Scialfa,
whom he later married. We snapped the duo as they departed in a
limo, trailing them to the Westbury Hotel. "What are you doing here
Ron?" quipped The Boss. "You're hard to get!" said Ron to his fast-
moving target.

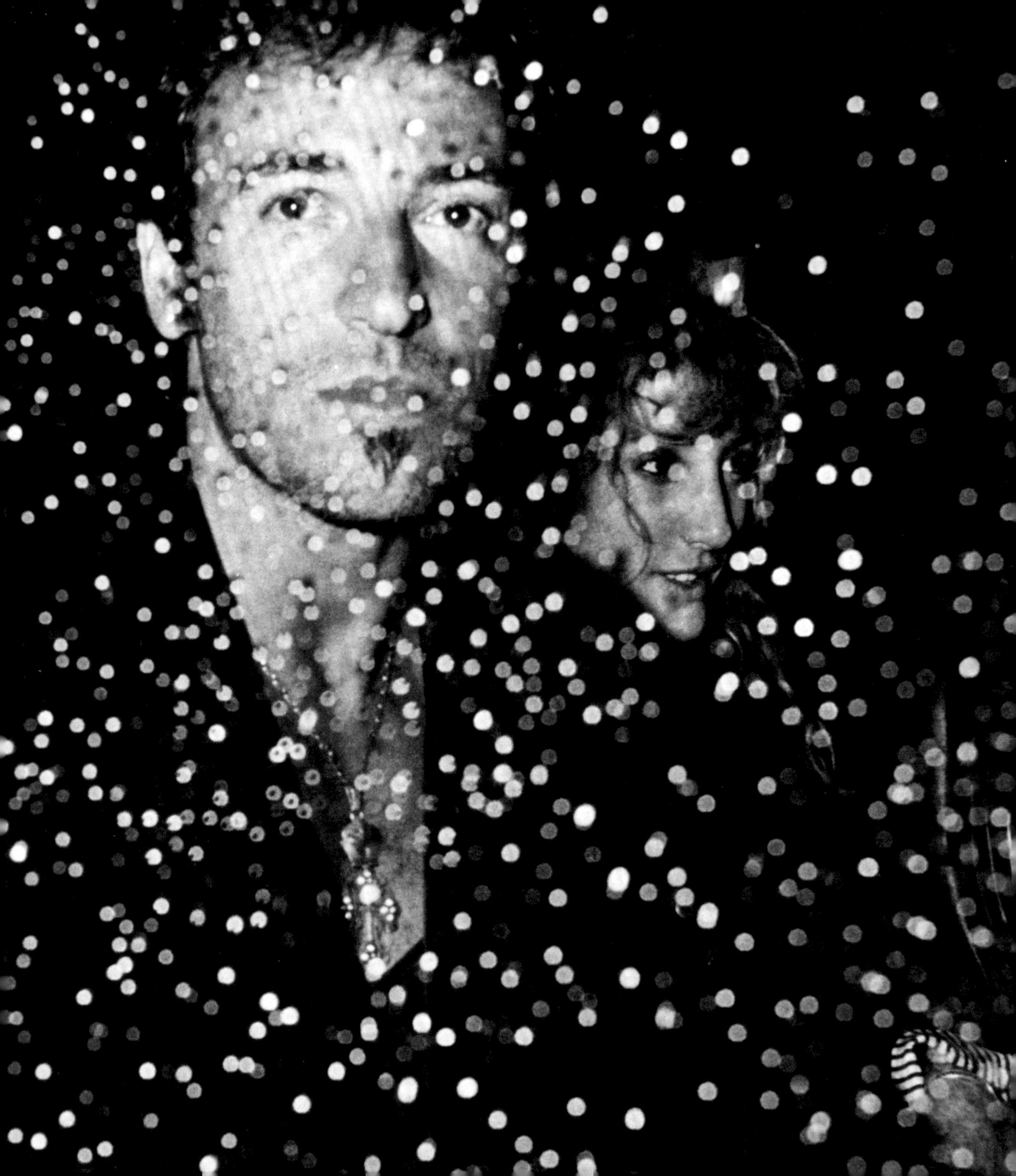

TOM

18. April 1984: Beverly Hills – Tom Jones beim
Galadinner der British Olympic Association USA
im Hotel Beverly Wilshire.
April 18, 1984: Beverly Hills—Tom Jones attends
the British Olympic Association USA Gala Dinner
at the Beverly Wilshire Hotel.

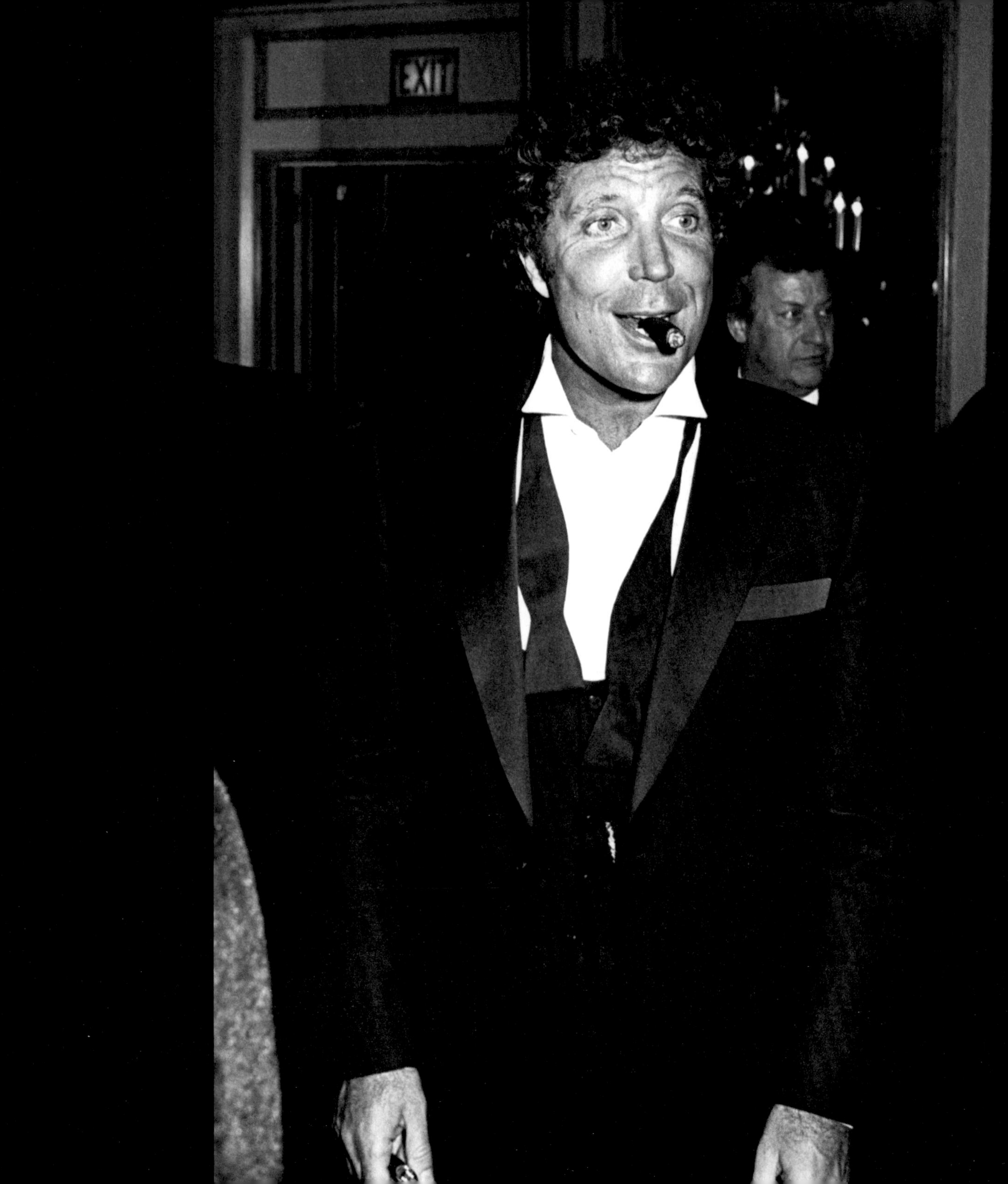

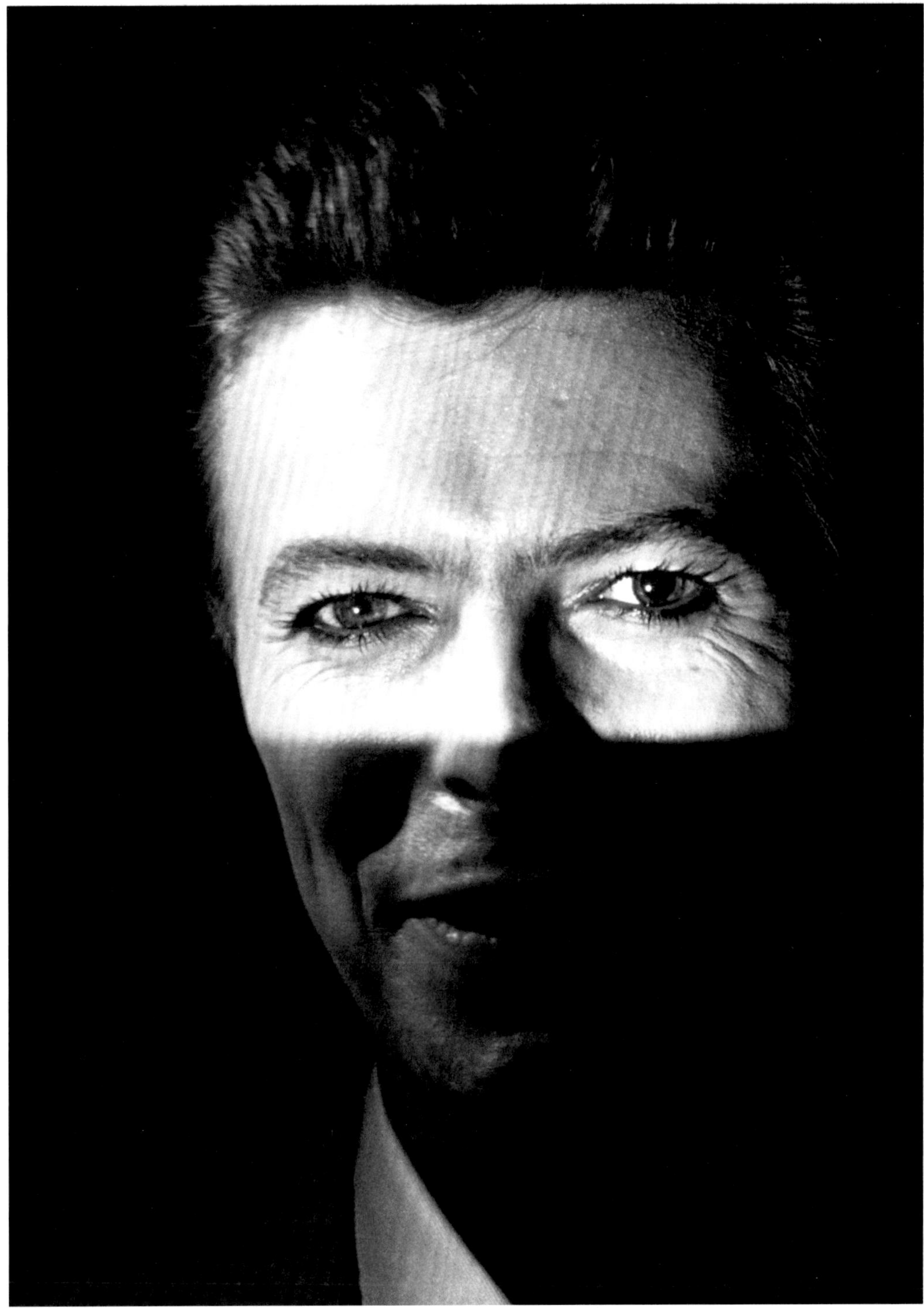

Sept. 28, 1980: David Bowie opens in the "ElephantMan" on Broadway at the Booth Theatre. Here's a 1983 update on Bowie. He is a star of many faces, an artist of many styles, the supreme pop chameleon. For more than a decade, in a spectacular array of different guises, he has played the part of the outsider, becoming a rock legend in the process-David Bowie, who now, he says, is a man intent on being himself. This is the man who crashed into public wearing mascara and dresses, who declared Adolf Hitler, "one of the first rock stars"; and who officially retired after his farewell-to-Ziggy Stardust concert in 1973. Yet now he appears almost convincingly as a normal kind of man, intent on making an "uplifting" kind of pop music. In the last three years, Bowie has made a concerted effort to escape from what he calls the "blinkered" life style of most rock stars. He lives off the beaten path in Switzerland and paints for his own pleasure. His film career began in earnest with "The Man Who Fell to Earth" in 1976. Since then he has played a Prussian stuffed tuxedo in "Just A Gigolo" (1978), a rapidly aging vampire in "The Hunger" (1983) and a tough willed prisoner of war in "MerryChristmas Mr. Lawrence." On broadway he won praise for his performance as John Merrick in "The Elephant Man" (1980). Bowie is currently on a world tour to promote his latest album "Let's Dance" and has a new lady to escort him. Her name is Jee-Ling and she is featured with Bowie on his new video disc, "China Girl".

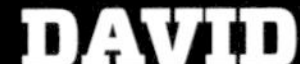

1. März 1975: New York – David Bowie bei der After-Party
der 17. »Annual Grammy Awards« im Essex House.
March 1, 1975: New York—David Bowie at the 17th
Annual Grammy Awards After Party at Essex House.

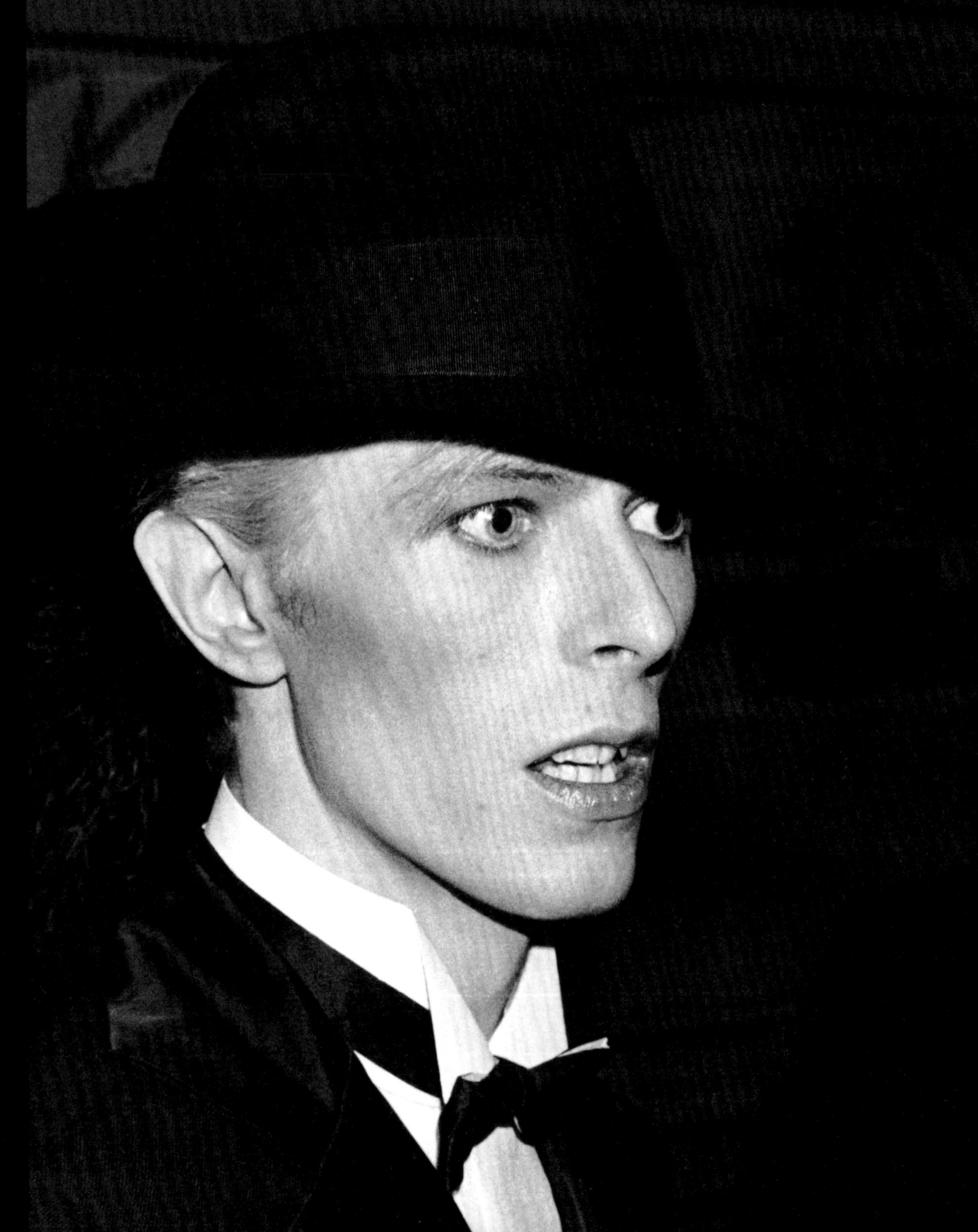

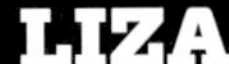

LIZA

2. April 1974: Beverly Hills, Kalifornien – Liza Minnelli bei der
Pre-Party der 46. »Annual Academy Awards« im Pips Club.
April 2, 1974: Beverly Hills, California—Liza Minnelli at
Pips Club for a 46th Annual Academy Awards Pre-Party.

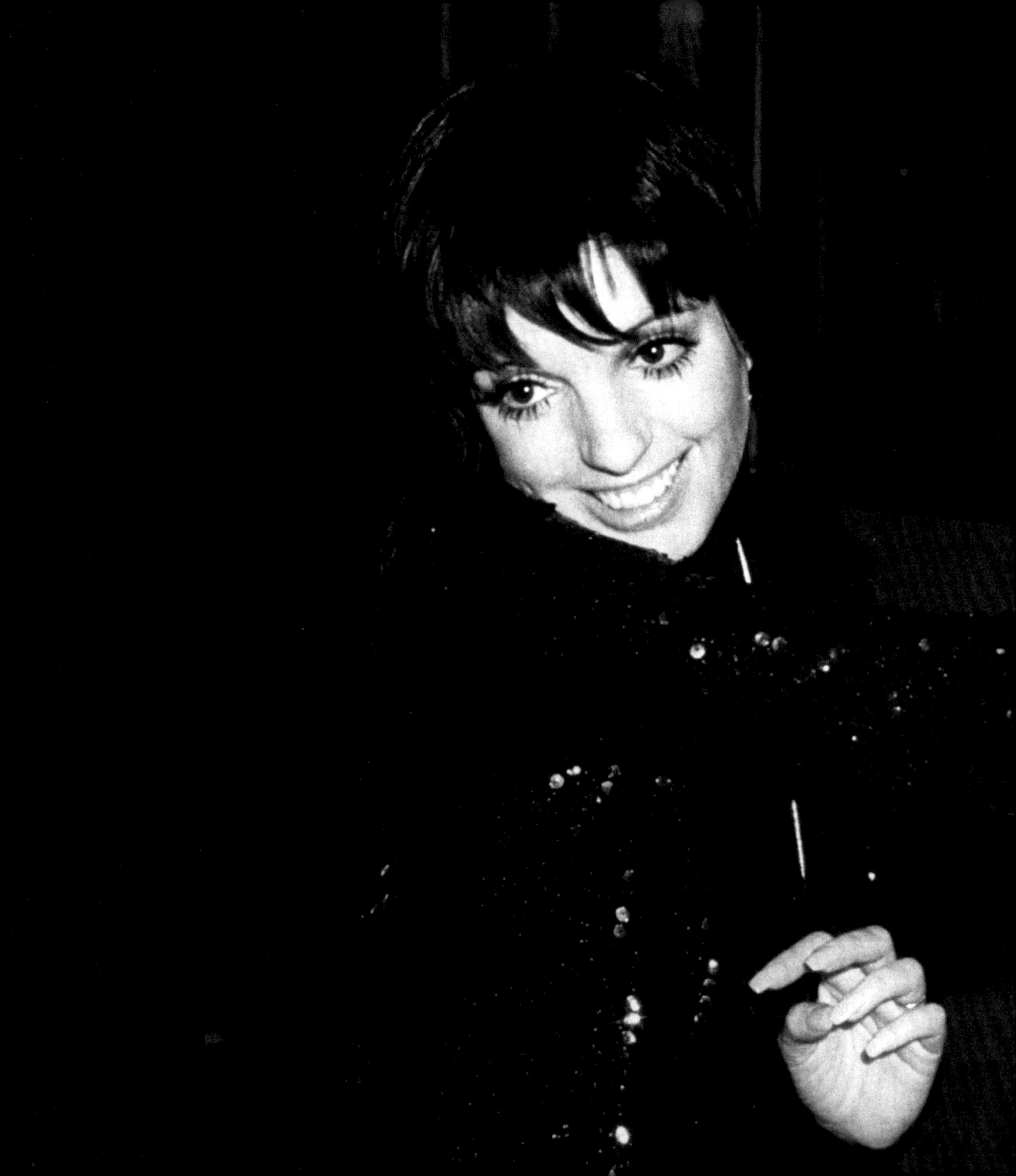

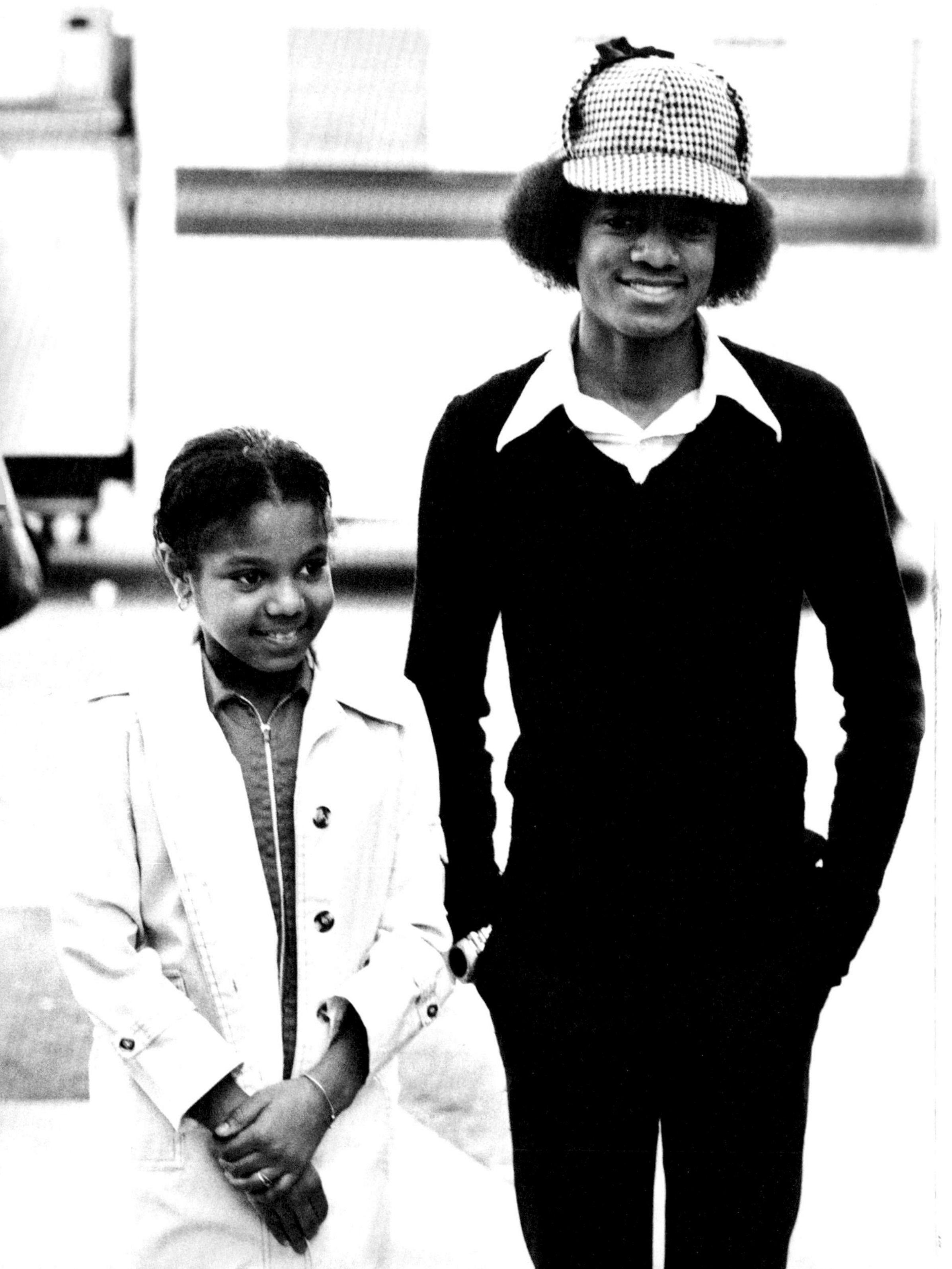

MICHAEL & JANET

30. Januar 1977: Santa Monica, Kalifornien – Janet Jackson (10)
und Michael Jackson (18) bei den Proben der Verleihung der
4. »Annual American Music Awards« in der Stadthalle von
Santa Monica.
January 30, 1977: Santa Monica, California—Janet Jackson (10)
and Michael Jackson (18) at the 4th Annual American Music
Awards Rehearsals at Santa Monica Civic Auditorium.

MICHAEL

10. März 1978: Irvine, Kalifornien – Michael Jackson
beim ersten »Annual Rock and Roll Sports Classic«
an der University of California.
March 10, 1978: Irvine, California—Michael Jackson
at University of California for the 1st Annual Rock
and Roll Sports Classic.

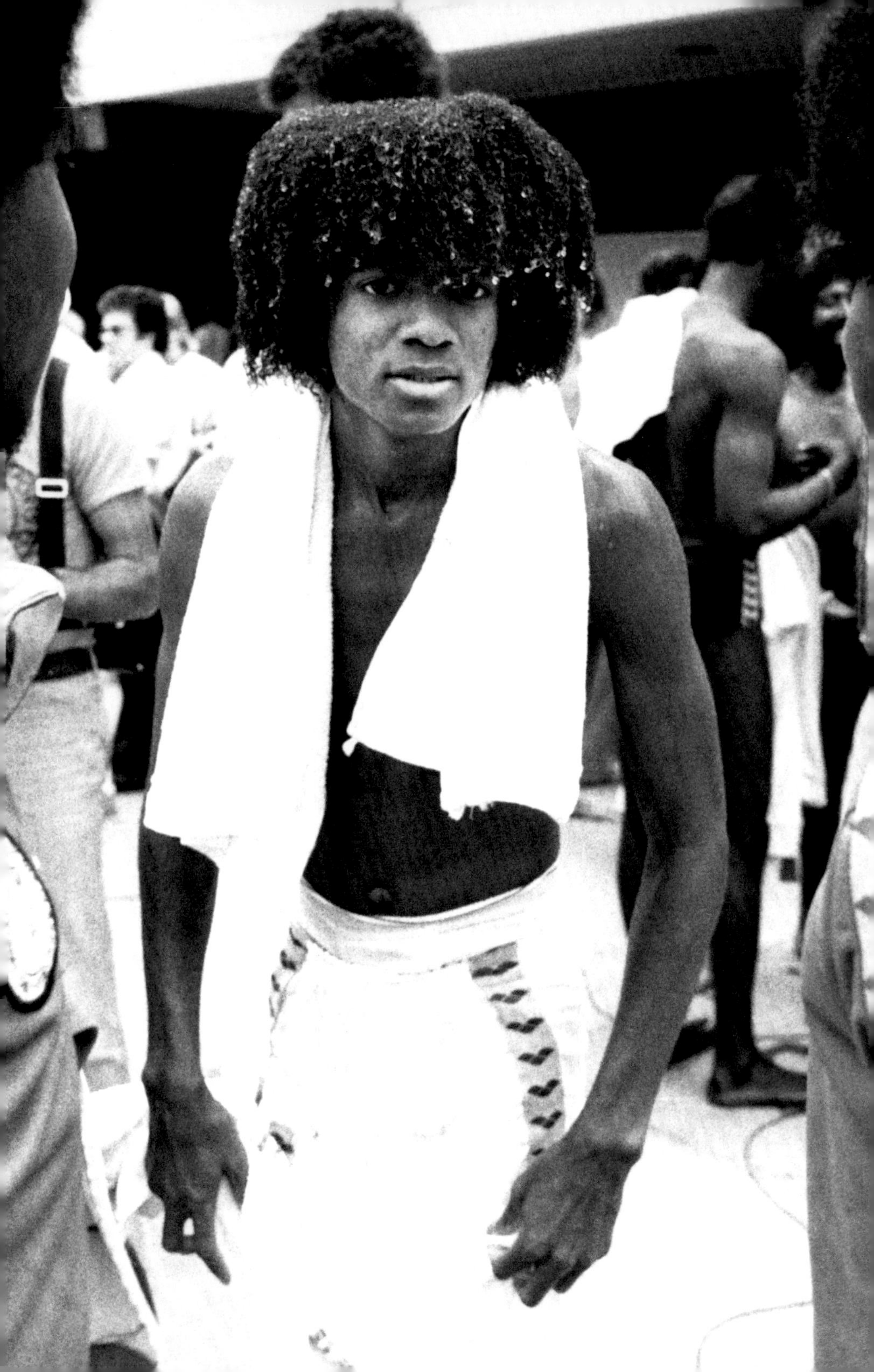

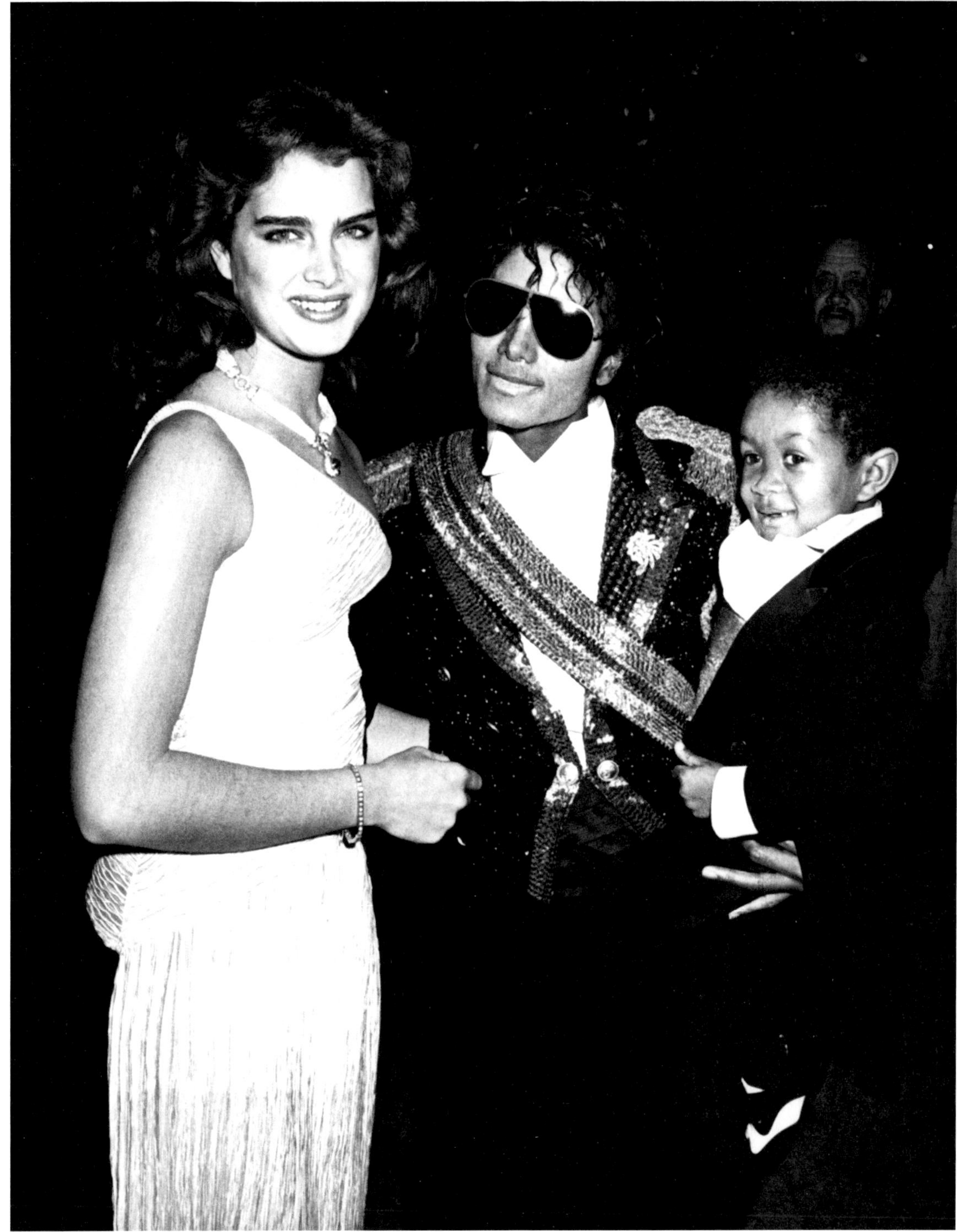

February 28, 1984: It was a trium-
phant evening when Michael Jackson
hit the jackpot with an unprecedented
8 Grammy Awards! The 25-year-old
superstar shared the evening with
date Brooke Shields and his little
friend Emmanuel Lewis of "Webster."
..The trio were snapped as Michael
and Emmanuell escorted Brooke to
the L'Ermitage Hotel in Beverly Hills
California.

THIS IS AN ORIGINAL PHOTOGRAPH BY RON GALELLA:

RON GALELLA

PHOTO CREDIT: RON GALELLA, Ltd.

Photography with the ▮▮▮▮▮▮▮▮ *approach*

17 GLOVER ▮▮▮▮▮▮▮▮ RON GALELLA (914) 237-2988

MICHAEL

19. November 1986: New York – Michael Jackson
versucht bei der U-Bahn-Station Botanical Garden
in der Bronx sein Gesicht abzuschirmen.
November 19, 1986: New York—Michael Jackson
tries to shield his face at the Botanical Garden
Subway Line in the Bronx.

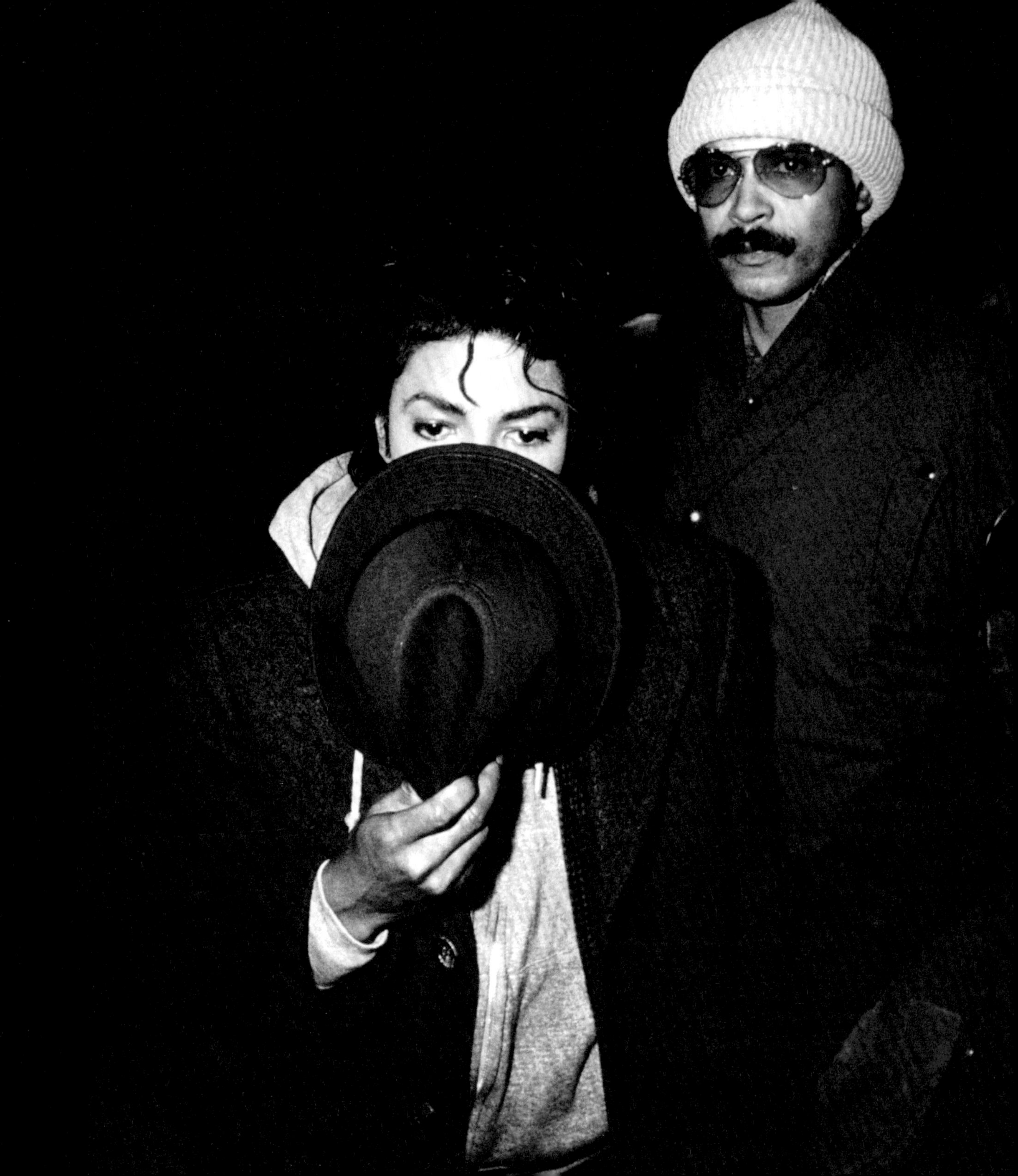

NOBLES

Ron Galella

DAVID & WALLIS

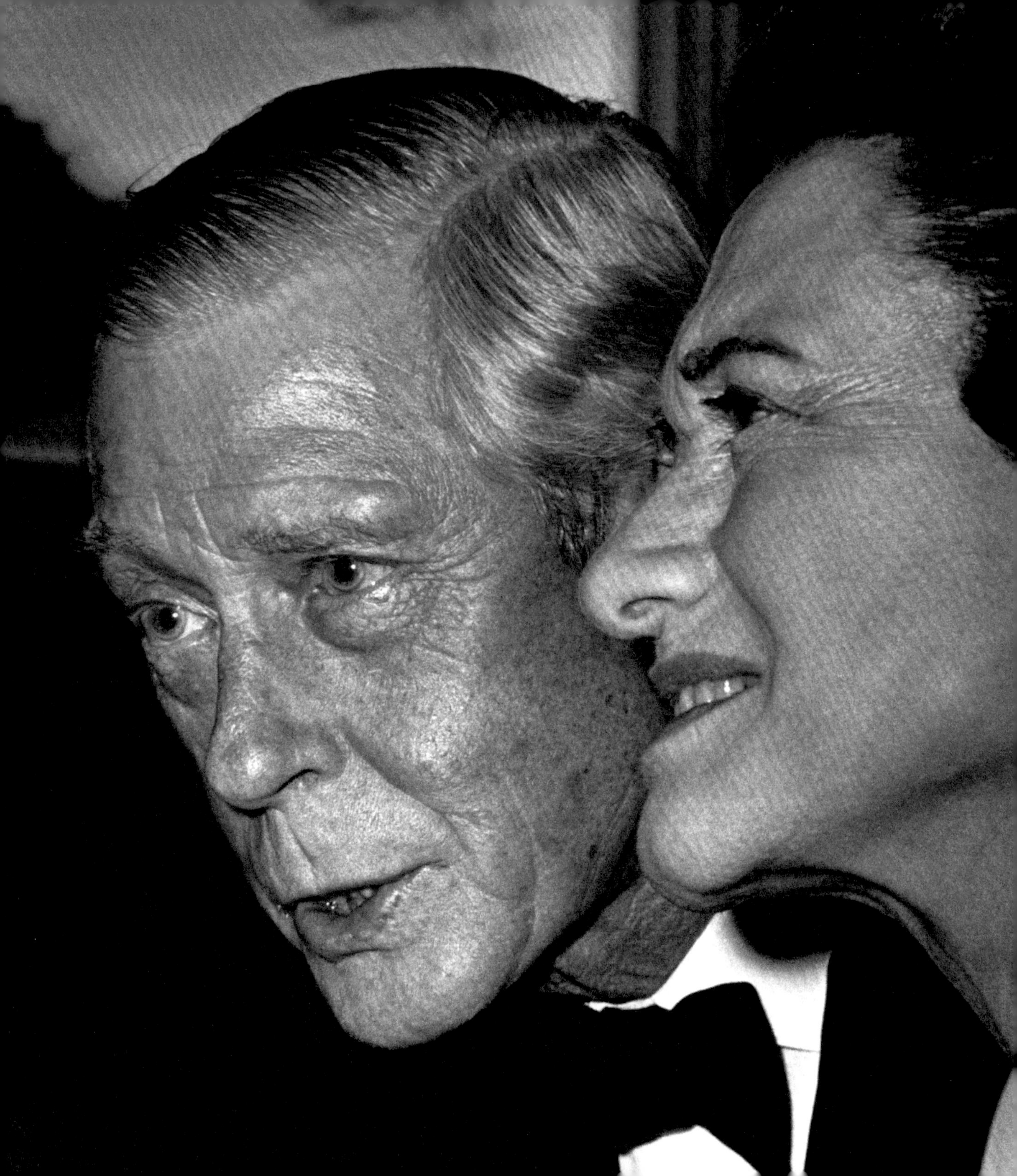

ANNE

26. September 1976: London, England –
Prinzessin Anne bei den »Wyle Horse Trials«.
September 26, 1976: London, England—
Princess Anne at the Wyle Horse Trials.

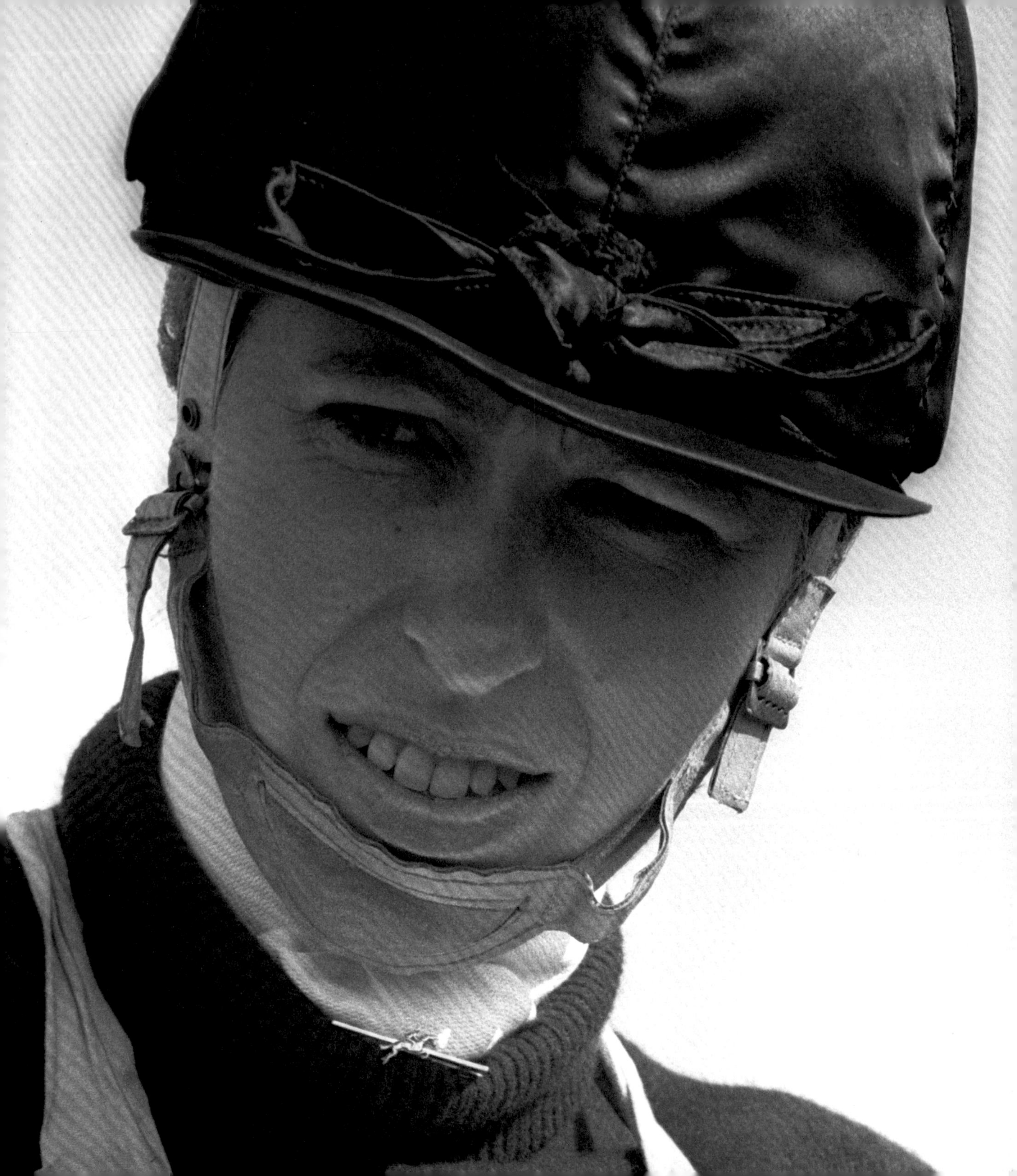

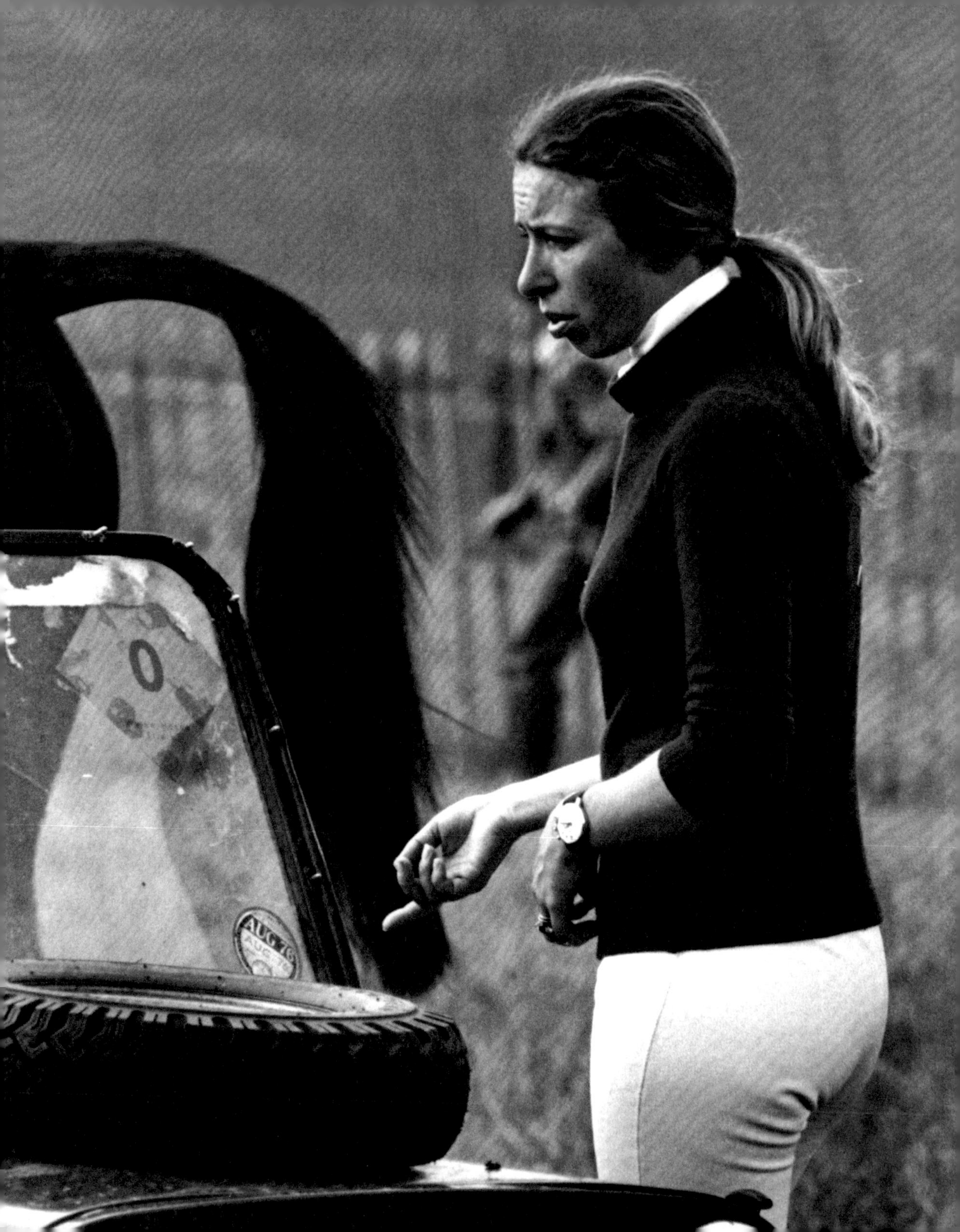

ANNE

26. September 1976: London, England –
Prinzessin Anne bei den »Wyle Horse Trials«.
September 26, 1976: London, England—
Princess Anne at the Wyle Horse Trials.

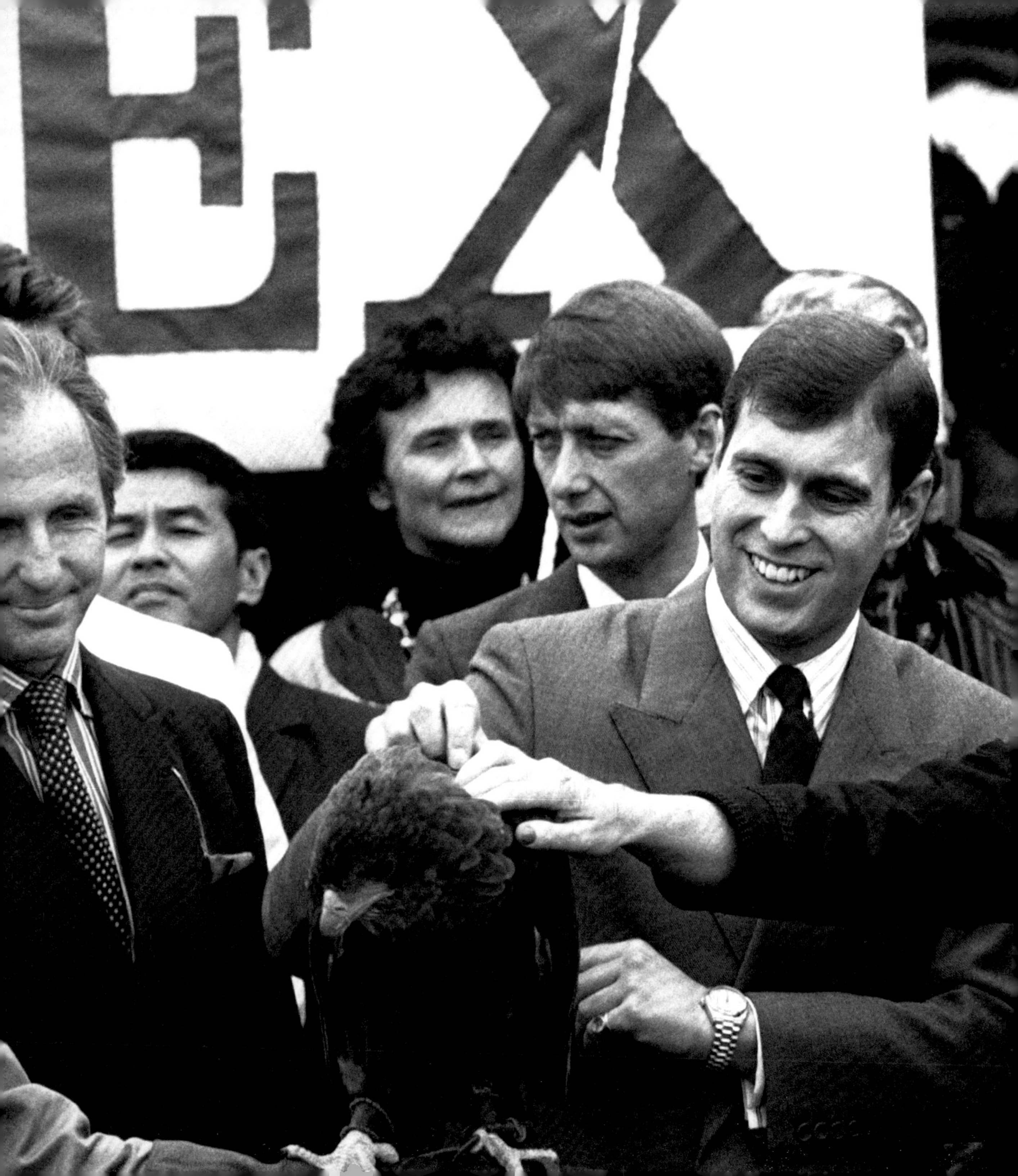

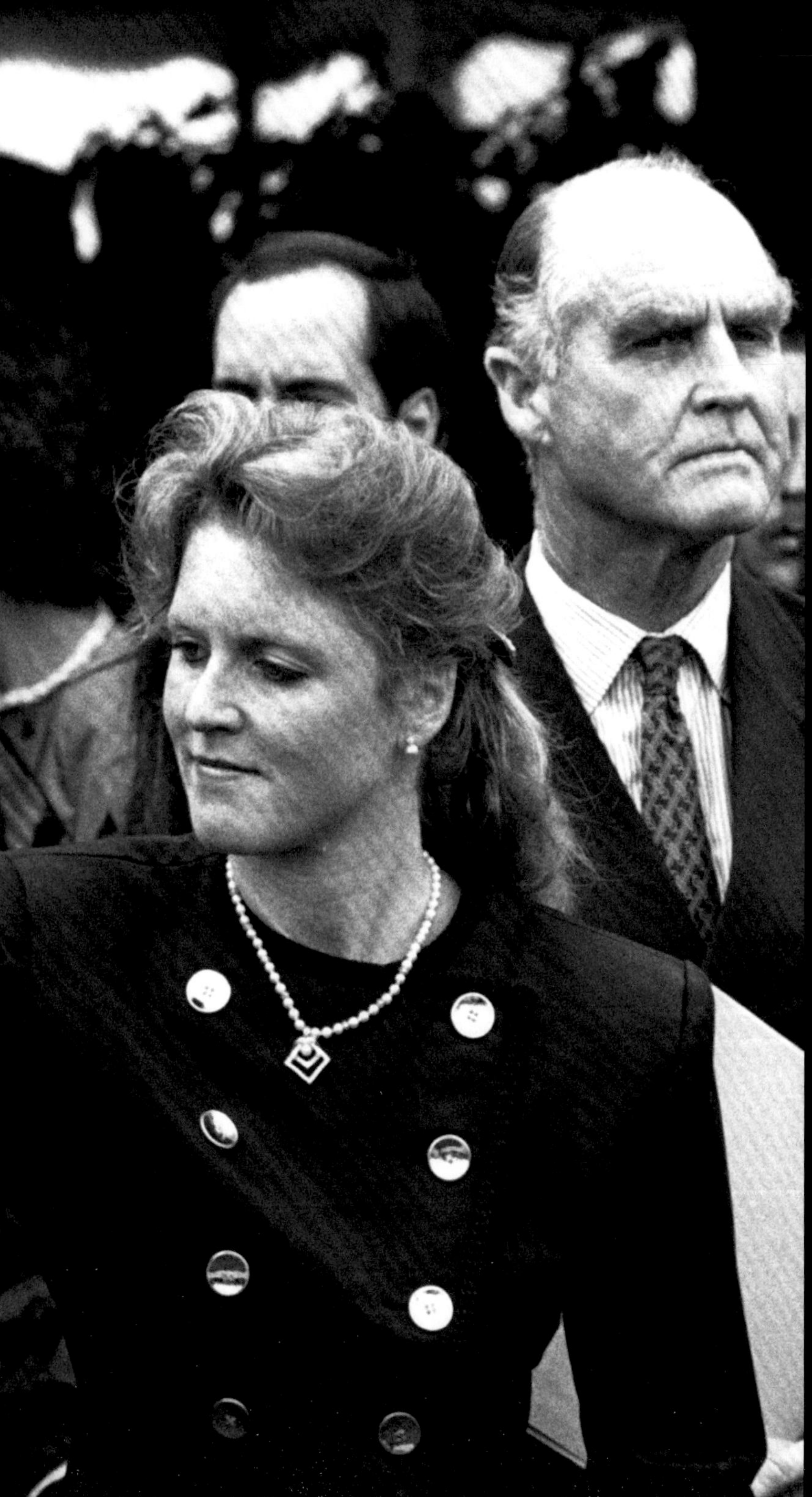

ANDREW & SARAH

19. September 1987: Greenwich, Conneticut – Prinz Andrew
und Sarah Ferguson bei einer Benefizveranstaltung des
World Wildlife Fund im Greenwich Polo Club. Der Herzog
und die Herzogin von York, auch bekannt als Prinz Andrew
und Sarah Ferguson, auf der Conyers Farm, Heimat des
Greenwich Polo Club in Conneticut. Die Polowettkämpfe
wurden wegen Regens abgesagt, aber die königlichen
Hoheiten nahmen an einer von Jim Fowler moderierten
Wildtier-Vorführung zu Gunsten des World Wildlife Fund
teil. Fergie sprang vor Entsetzen zurück, als eine Python-
schlange gezeigt wurde, erwärmte sich aber für die Vögel
und Elefanten. Ihr Vater Major Ferguson und ihre Mutter
Susan Barrantes waren zur Stelle.

September 19, 1987: Greenwich, Conneticut—Prince Andrew
and Sarah Ferguson attend a World Wildlife Fund benefit
at Greenwich Polo Club. The Duke & Duchess of York, aka
Prince Andrew and Sarah Ferguson at Conyers Farm, home
of the Greenwich Polo Club in Conneticut. Polo matches
were cancelled due to rain but the Royals took in a wildlife
demo hosted by Jim Fowler for the benefit of the World
Wildlife Fund. Fergie recoiled in horror when a python
was shown, but took kindly to the birds and elephants.
Her father Major Ferguson and mother, Susan Barrantes
were on hand.

GLORIA & JOHANNES

23. Oktober 1987: New York – Prinzessin Gloria und Prinz Johannes
von Thurn und Taxis beim 36. »Annual April in Paris Ball« im Hotel
Waldorf-Astoria.

October 23rd, 1987: New York City—Princess Gloria and Prince
Johannes von Thurn und Taxis at the 36th Annual April in Paris
Ball at the Waldorf-Astoria Hotel.

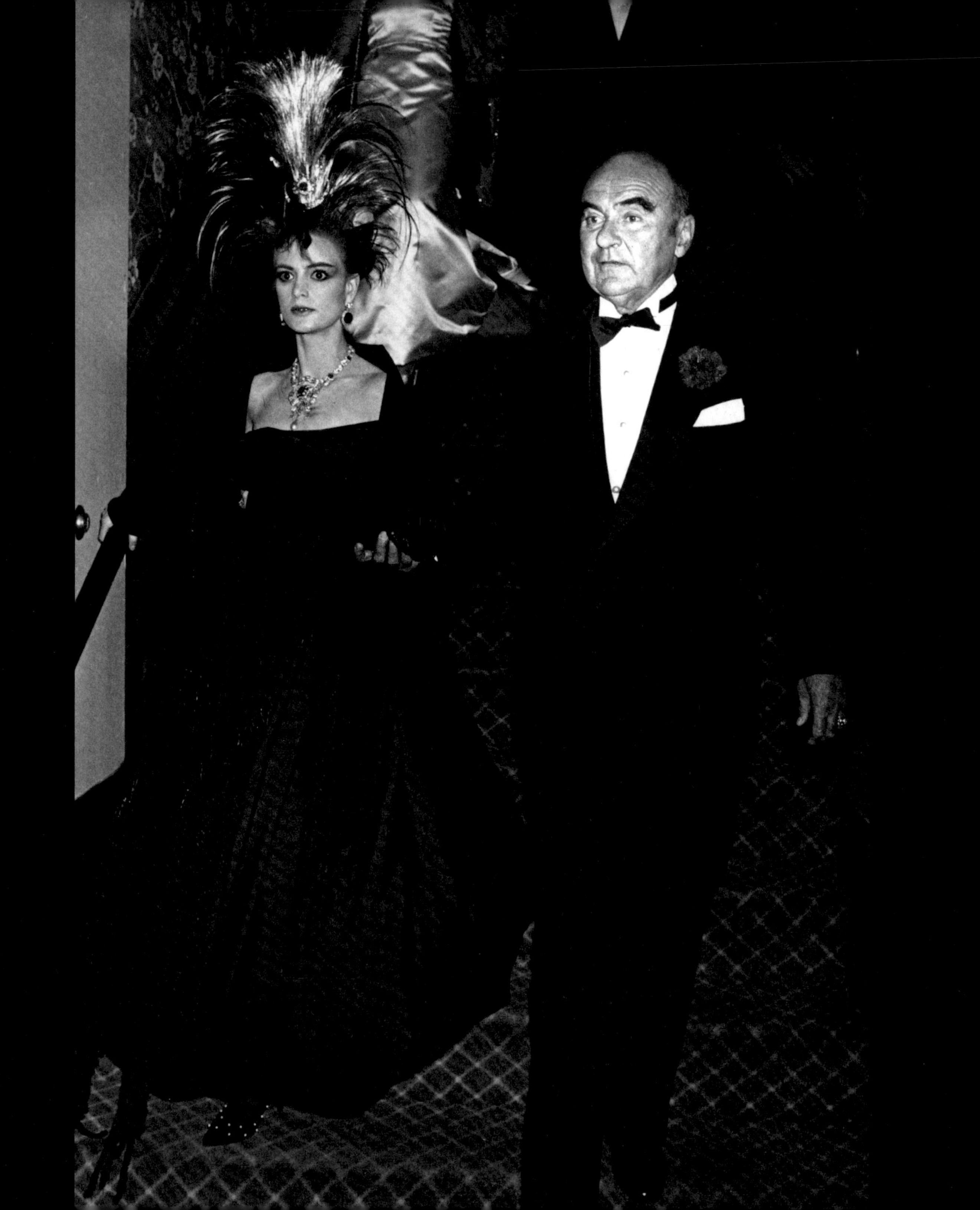

GLORIA

23. Oktober 1987: New York – Prinzessin Gloria von
Thurn und Taxis beim 36. »Annual April in Paris Ball«
im Hotel Waldorf-Astoria.
October 23rd, 1987: New York City—Princess Gloria von
Thurn und Taxis at the 36th Annual April in Paris Ball
at the Waldorf-Astoria Hotel.

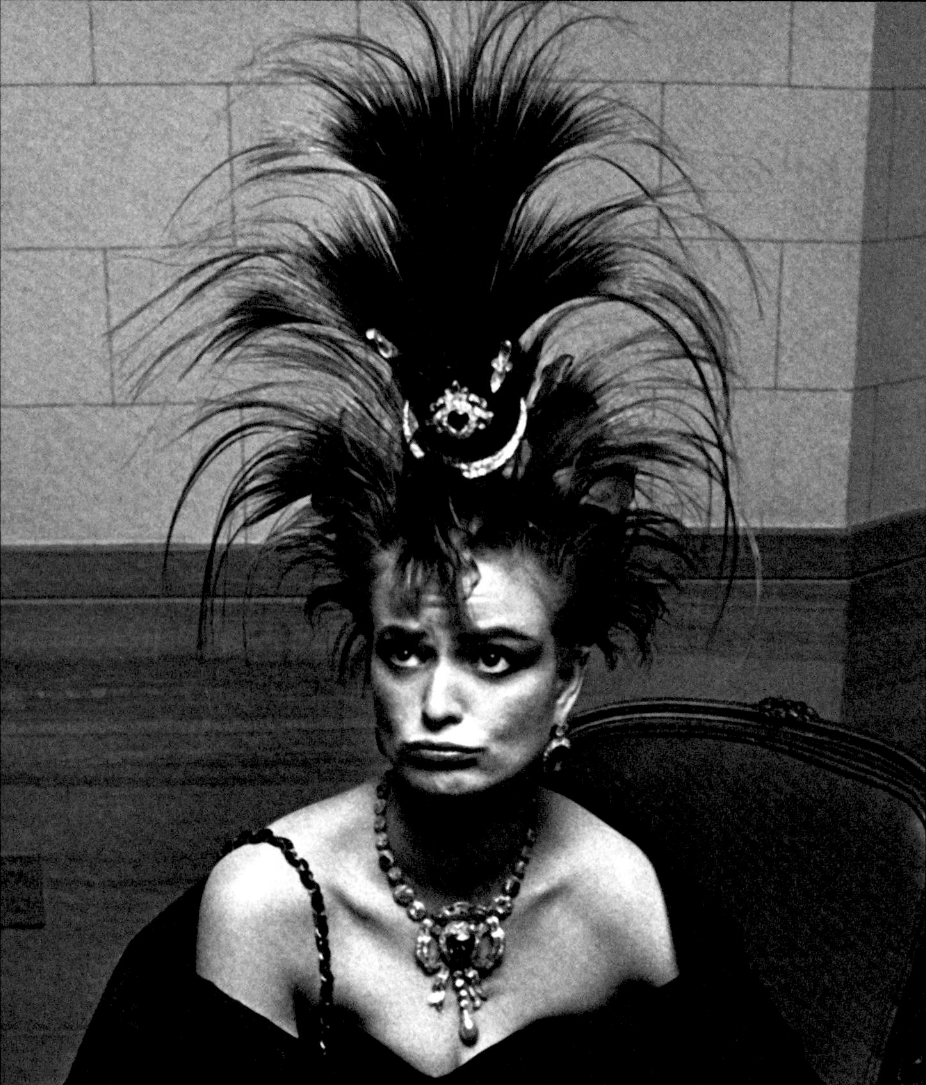

Magazin *Life*, Titel und Doppelseiten, 31. März 1972.
Life magazine, title and double pages, March 31, 1972.

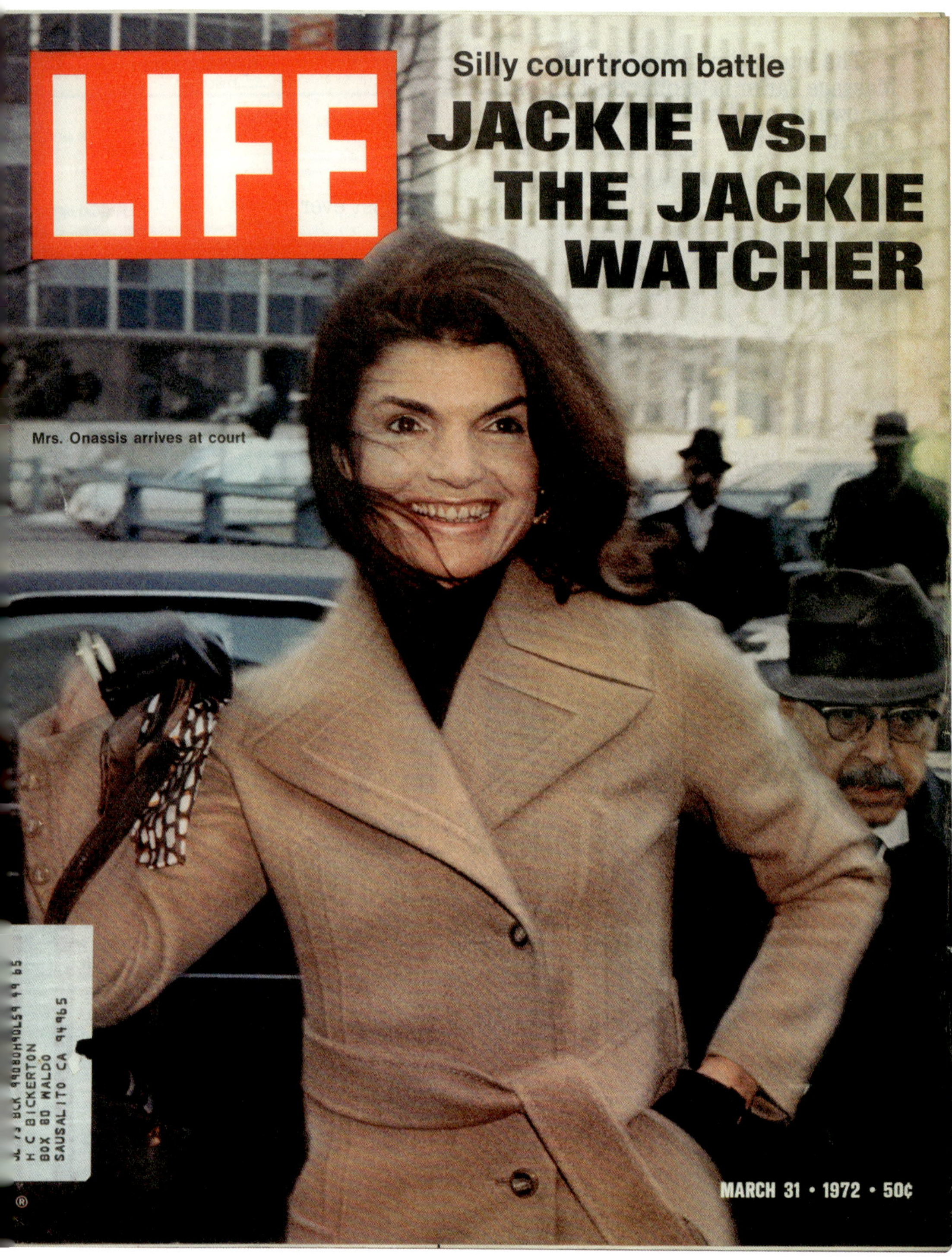
Silly courtroom battle
LIFE
JACKIE vs. THE JACKIE WATCHER
Mrs. Onassis arrives at court
MARCH 31 • 1972 • 50¢

One man's running battle with

Seldom has a court of law been put to such a glamorous but trivial test. At issue is whether the woman below, whom most of the world instantly recognizes as Jacqueline Kennedy Onassis, is a private person, as she insists. Or is she a global celebrity whose every footstep is a legitimate news event, which is the contention of the man with the cameras scuttling along behind her on a New York street? Is he a pest, or worse, a menace? Has he frightened her? Has she interfered with his livelihood? Did she have him flung into a snowbank? Does anybody care?

The questions are under endless consideration in Courtroom No. 1506 of Manhattan's Federal Courthouse. The case is *Ronald Galella, Plaintiff, vs. Jacqueline Onassis, Defendant,* and after six weeks of testimony, about the only unchallenged fact to emerge is that *Defendant* looks terrific, even under the most rigorous cross-examination. By comparison, all else seems irrelevant and immaterial.

Still, for the record, Galella is the freelance who for several years has made a modest but agreeable living taking pictures of celebrities (mostly Jackie) and selling them to magazines here and abroad (including LIFE). It is a career not wholly unfamiliar to Jackie, who in the days before she married John Kennedy was an Inquiring Photographer for a Washington paper. In getting people to pose, she relied on an unobtrusive charm. Galella, by his own admission, puts more faith in aggressive pursuit. He is, the testimony suggests, about as obtrusive as a building falling down.

Nevertheless, Galella claims that Mrs. Onassis has repeatedly thwarted his picture-taking by siccing the Secret Service and other police on him. They have shoved him, he says, tried to smash a camera, and once, in Central Park, threw him into a snowbank. Galella is asking $1.3 million in damages, about 50 times what he earns annually taking pictures.

Mrs. Onassis countersued, charging Galella with invasion of privacy and harassment, and the two cases are being heard together. The testimony thus far revolves around certain incidents of Galella's aggressive pursuit. As described by Jackie, they suggest that Galella stalks her everywhere, popping out from doorways and shrubs, bobbing and weaving, taking dozens of photographs, while emitting a curious "grunting" sound. Galella,

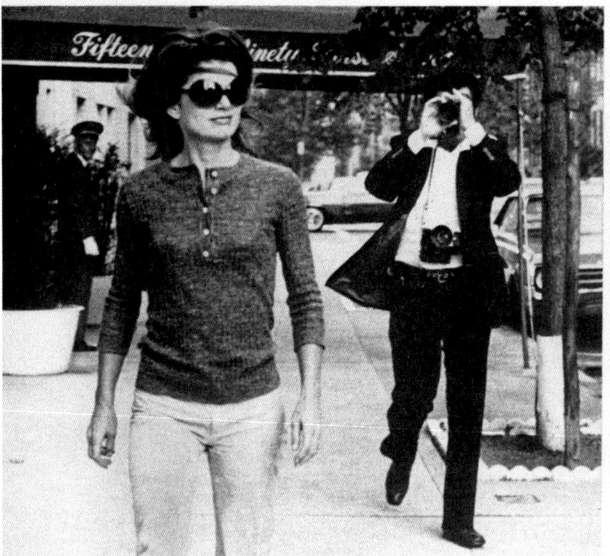

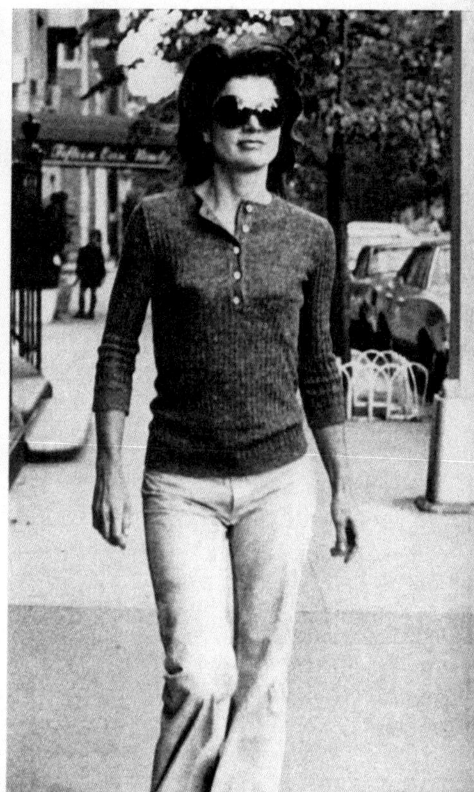

Peering through the camera, coattails flying, photographer Ron Galella snaps a picture of Mrs. Jacqueline Kennedy Onassis (above), then hurries to catch up (right) for a different angle. These two scenes of Galella in action were made by a friend who accompanied him on one of his routine "spot checks" of Mrs. Onassis's neighborhood. Out of this encounter, Galella says, came his favorite picture of Jackie (far right).

64

Jackie

she says, "terrifies" her. She wants the court to order the photographer to stay at least 50 yards away from her and 100 yards away from her home at all times. In Galella's version of the same incidents, he implies that Mrs. Onassis is unnaturally camera-shy and uncooperative.

Behind the staggering pettiness of the details of their dispute, of course, lies a serious issue: the unfettered pursuit of a bona fide story vs. an individual's privacy. Jackie's case is based in large part on the notion that, her supercelebrity status aside, she has the right to be left alone in public. But it seems doubtful that Mrs. Onassis can ever hope to enjoy real anonymity. During her days on the witness stand the courtroom was jammed. As soon as she had finished testifying, most of the spectators left.

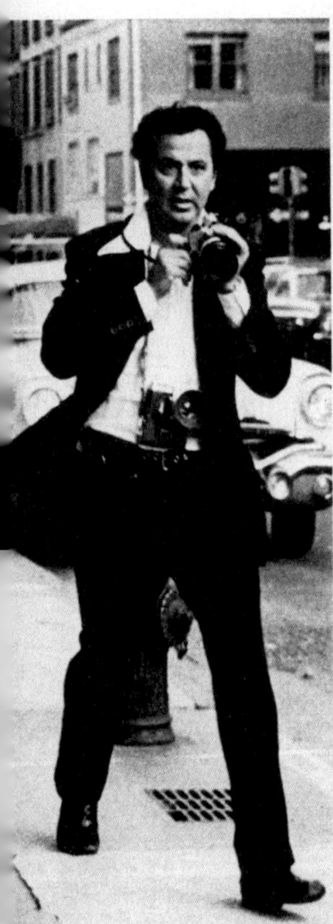

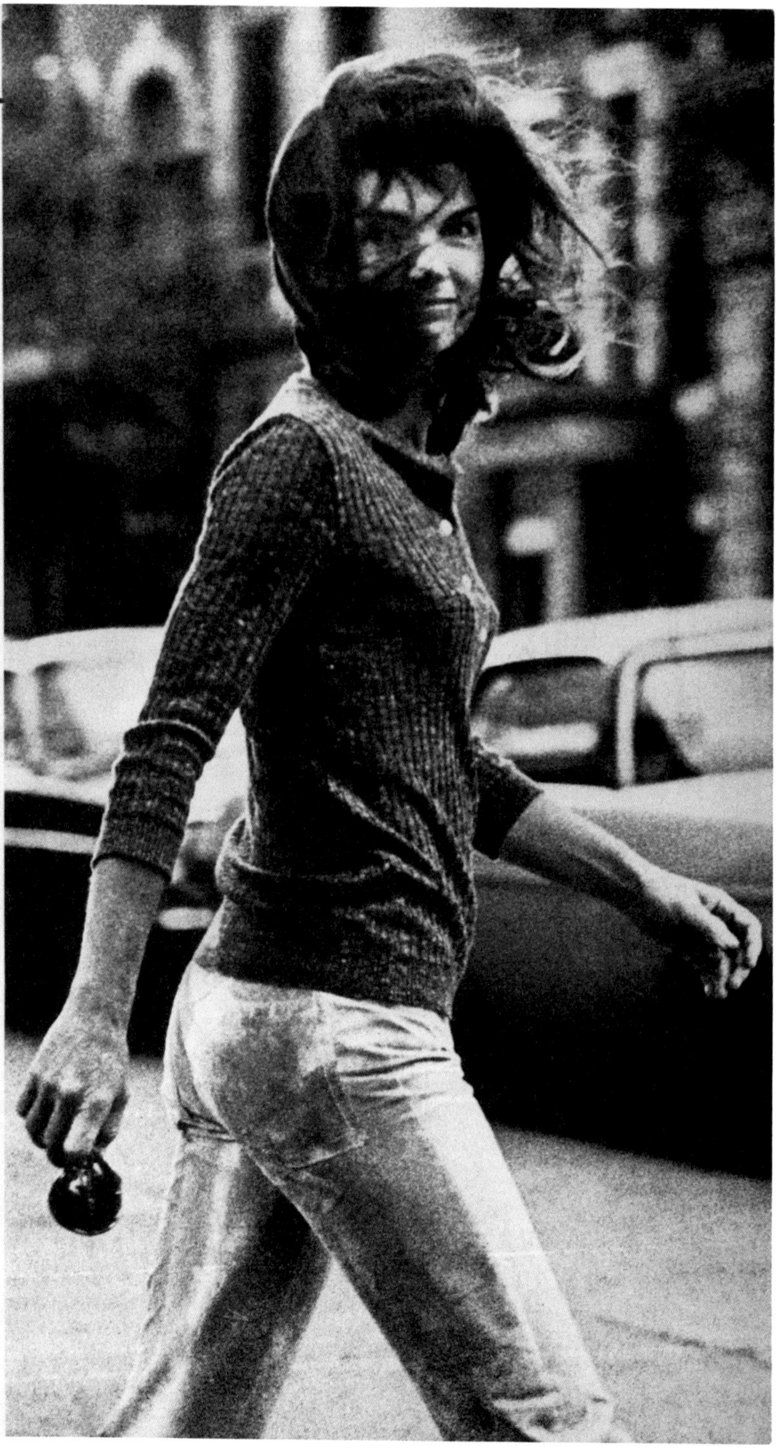

A series of head-on encounters

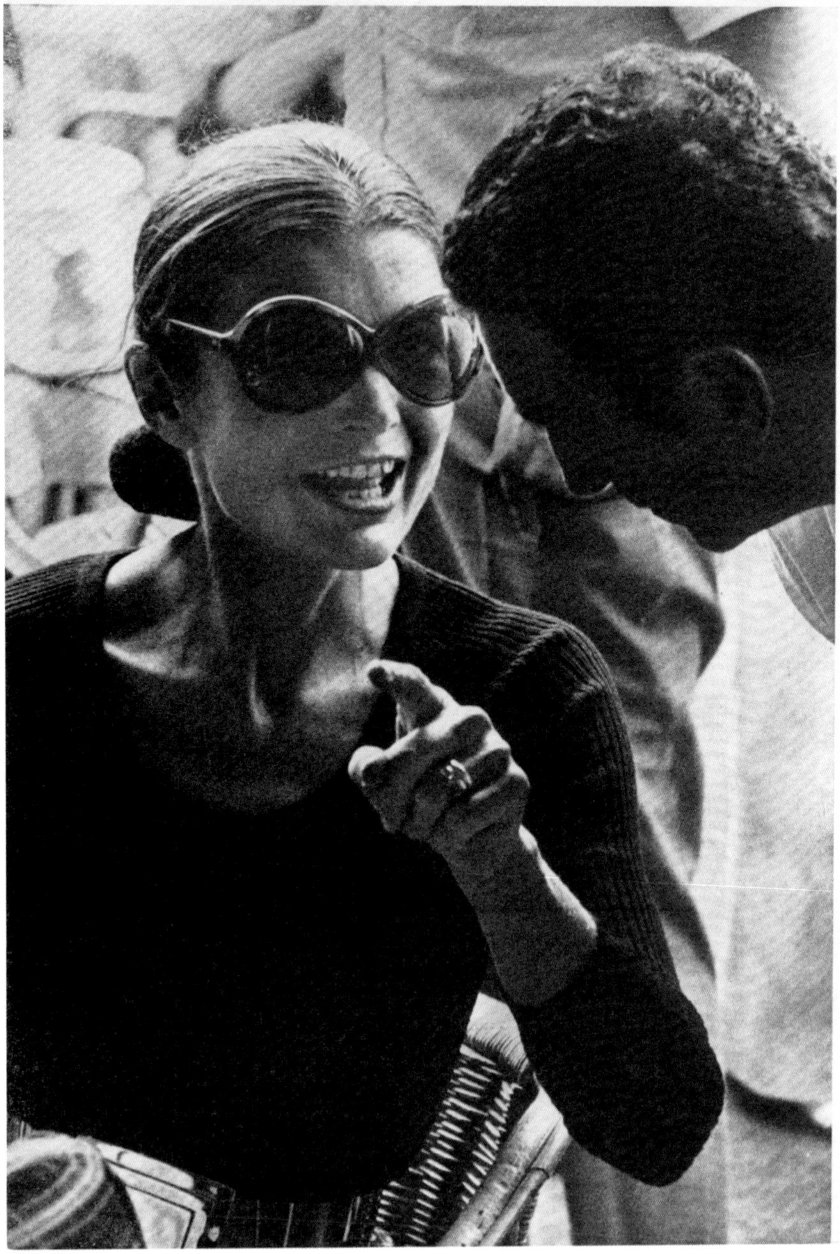

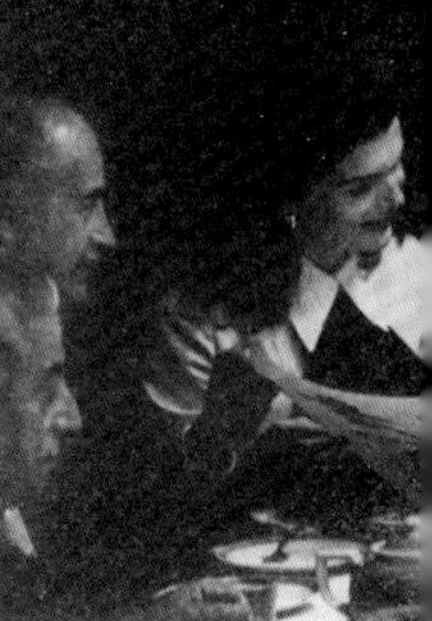

The Chinese restaurant coatrack incident

Jackie testified that during a dinner hosted by architect I. M. Pei (right, above) at a Chinese restaurant in 1969, Galella suddenly materialized and began taking pictures, causing the party to break up. Galella claims the restaurant manager invited him, fed him, and helped him hide behind a coatrack.

The 21 Club ruse an fast getaway inciden

Riding in a limousine one eve ning last year, Jackie notice that Galella was following her She ordered her driver to stop at the 21 Club (right). "I opene the car door as if I was goin to get out," she testified. "Tha caused Galella to get out of hi car. . . . [Then] I leapt back in slammed the car door and tol my driver to go as fast as h could to get away." The rus was effective, Galella agreed

The Isle of Capri sidewalk café incident

In August of 1970 Jackie spent an afternoon on Capri and encountered Galella, who was dressed up, she testified, in "a white sailor suit with a little white sailor hat on. . . . He came running along. He yelled at me . . . 'Hiya, Jackie. Are you surprised to see me here? How do you like me? I've joined the navy.'" Later at a sidewalk café (left), Galella claims, Jackie pointed at him and told one of the waiters to chase him away. Jackie denies having said anything of the sort.

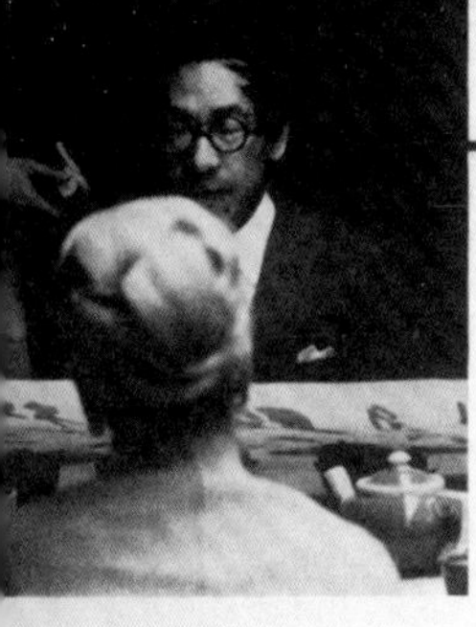

The Third Avenue stroll and record shop incident

After a luncheon at P. J. Clarke's restaurant last year, Mrs. Onassis and her husband decided to stroll up Third Avenue, only to be spotted by Galella. "He was leaping around, taking pictures, running ahead of us, taking them, running back," Jackie testified. When Ari's withering glare (right) failed to dissuade Galella, the couple ducked into a record shop. Galella followed them, but was ordered to leave by a clerk. Jackie stayed around and bought a couple of records.

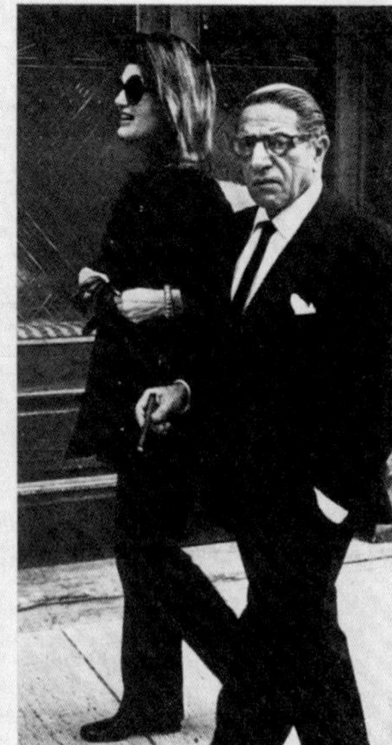

The Mother's Day bouquet camouflage incident

Galella, hiding behind a corner of Jackie's apartment building on Mother's Day in 1969, saw his favorite subject pull up in an automobile and get out. But just as he was about to snap her picture, he says, she raised a bouquet and hid her face (right). Galella claims (although not in his formal complaint) that Jackie frequently tries to ruin his pictures by concealing herself behind large, dark sunglasses. She also wears black quite often—to foil his use of color film, Galella suspects.

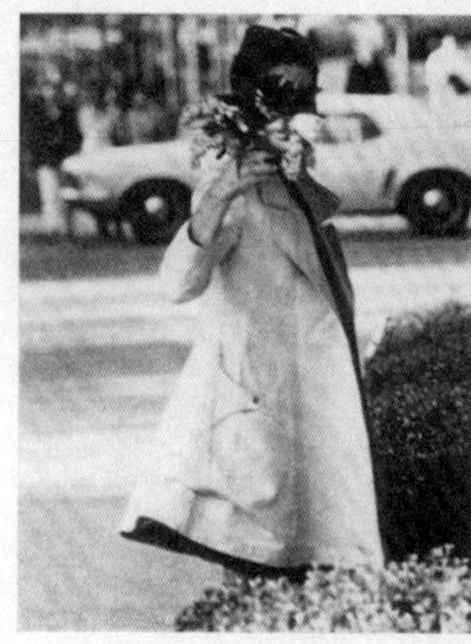

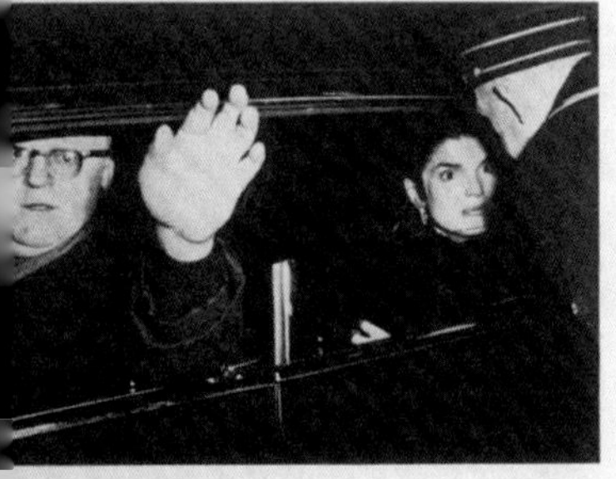

The Secret Service agent on a bike in the park incident

In 1969 Jackie and son John were bicycling through Central Park (below) when Galella leaped out of the shrubbery, she testified, causing John to swerve "violently." Jackie contends this was the end of the incident. Galella claims she ordered a Secret Service agent who was following on a bicycle to "smash his camera." No blows were struck, but Galella was arrested for harassment. The charge was dismissed. The arrest, Galella says, prompted his suit against Mrs. Onassis.

The persistent man in the Santa suit incident

Coming out of her apartment one December evening in 1970, Jackie was greeted by a man dressed as Santa Claus. He was "pushing, trying to get next to me, pushing Mr. Meyer [her escort], scuffing . . ." she testified. Galella was there too, she said. "He [was] saying, 'Come on, Jackie, be nice to Santa, won't you? Come on, Jackie, snuggle up to Santa.'" Admitting that Santa was an employee from a concession he operates in New Jersey, Galella explains that he had a holiday assignment from the *National Enquirer* to photograph Jackie and Santa together. The picture was a disappointment, though (left). "She's fast," Galella says, "and Santa was slow."

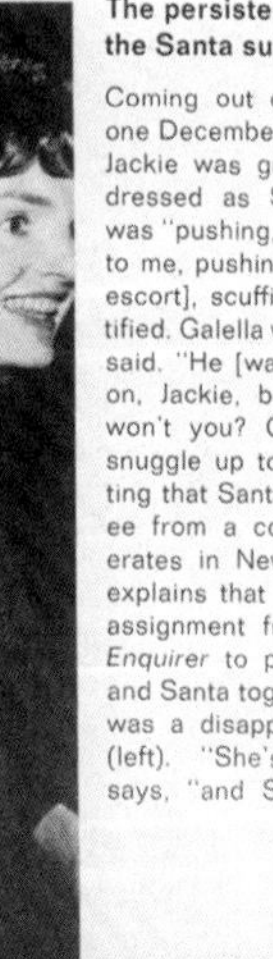

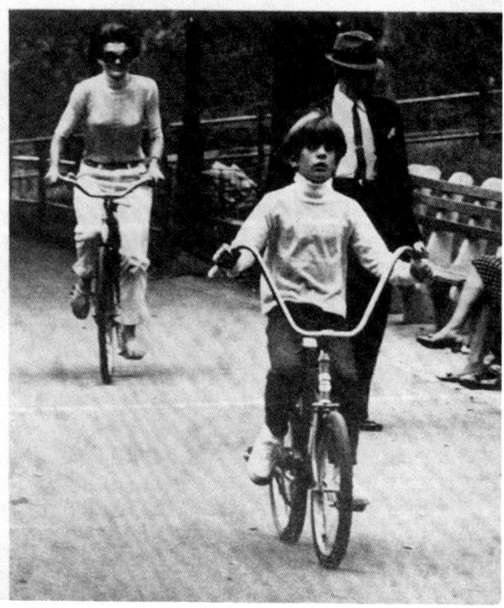

The jogging track incident

Last October in Central Park, Jackie told the court, her daughter Caroline's tennis lesson was interrupted by the appearance of photographer Galella. "He yelled to Caroline," Jackie testified, " 'I'm not making you nervous, am I honey?' And she said, 'Yes, you are.' She turned towards me and there were tears in her eyes." For a moment longer, Jackie stood at the sidelines beside a glowering Secret Service agent (right). Then, as Galella's camera records, she bolted away and ran across the park (far right). With Galella in pursuit, Jackie dashed up a slight hill and past a police cruiser (below), whose occupants apparently did not find the chase out of the ordinary for Central Park. Finally, Jackie wound up on the park's jogging track. Galella, winded by now, was able to squeeze off one last shot before she sprinted around the bend and out of his sight (lower right).

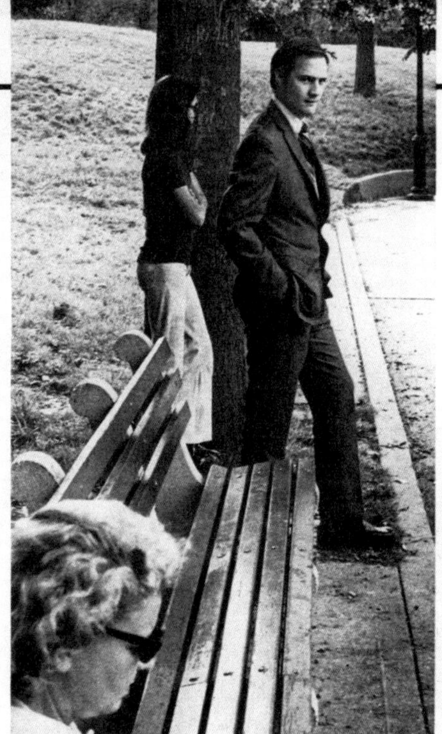

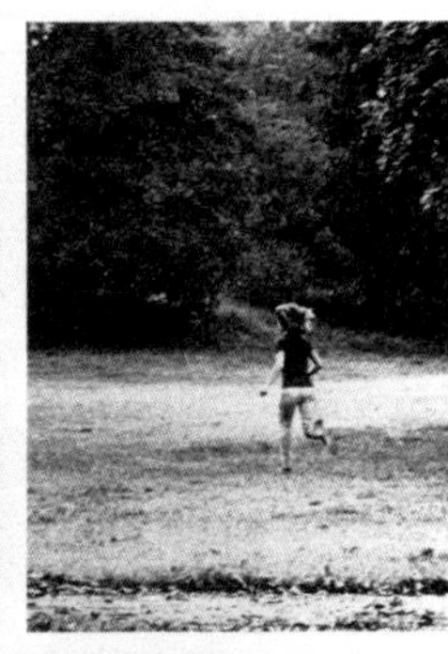

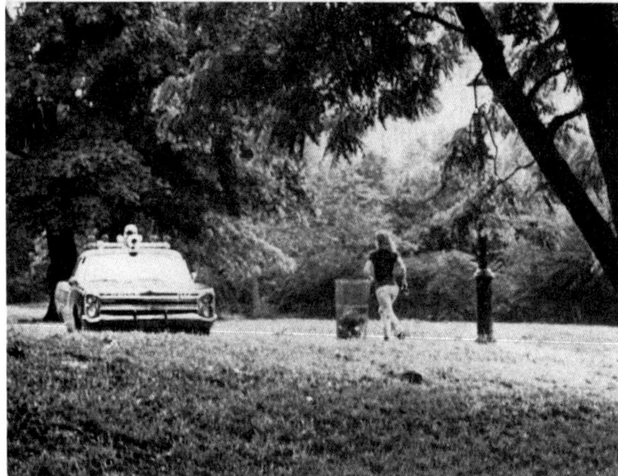

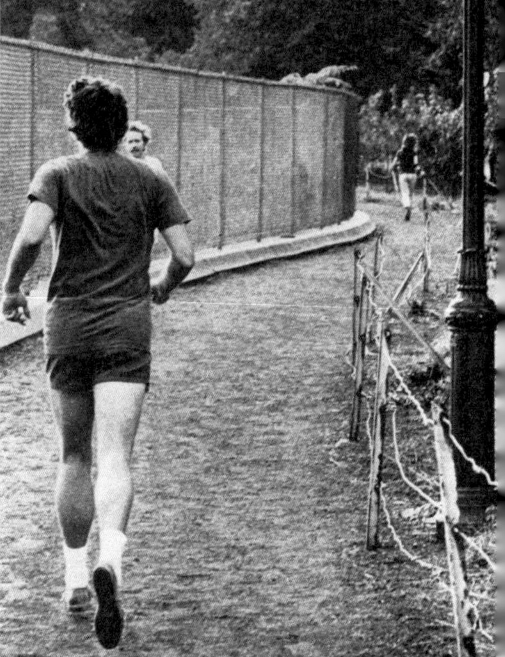

174

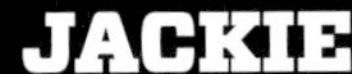

JACKIE

17. Februar 1969: New York – Jackie Onassis im Club 21.
February 17, 1969: New York—Jackie Onassis at 21 Club.

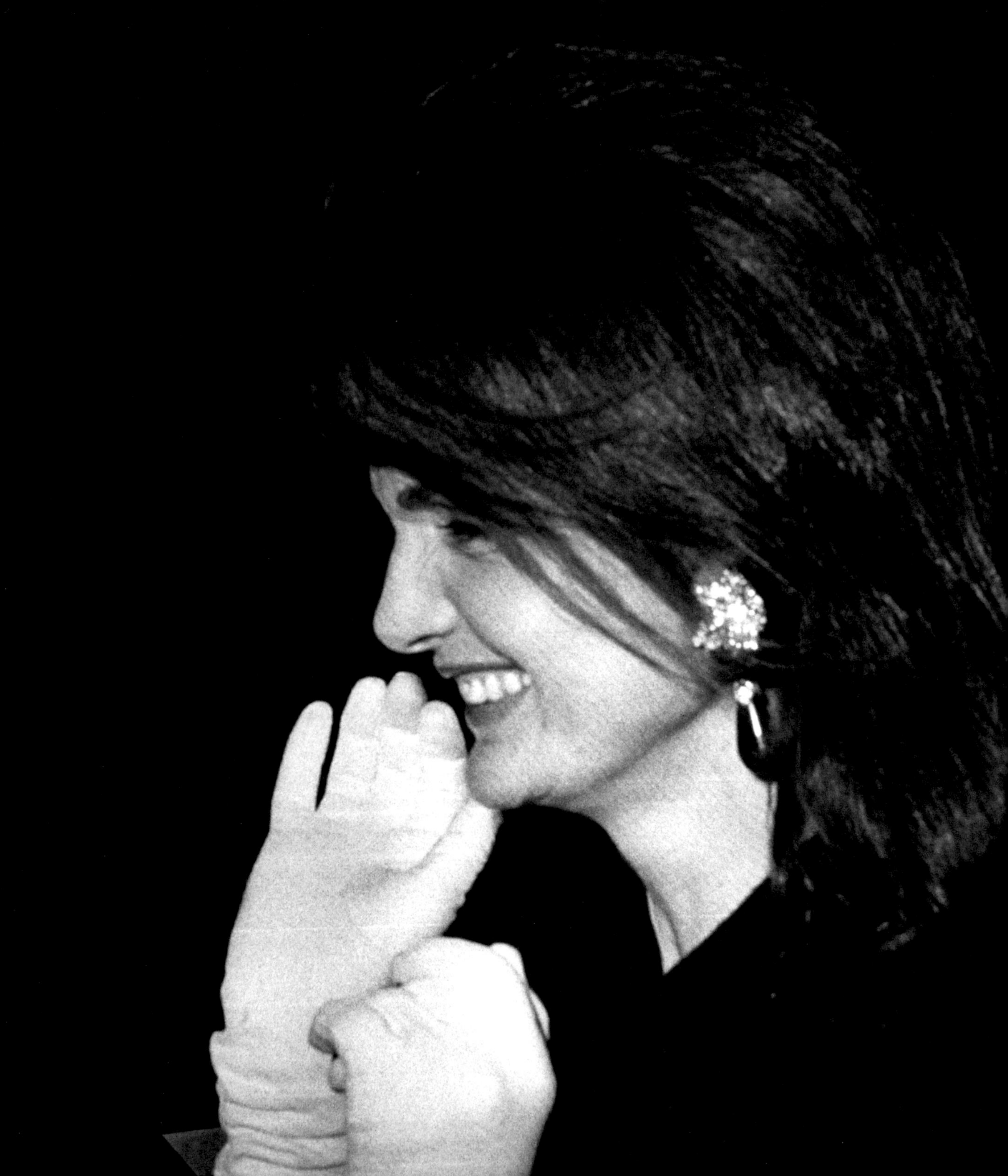

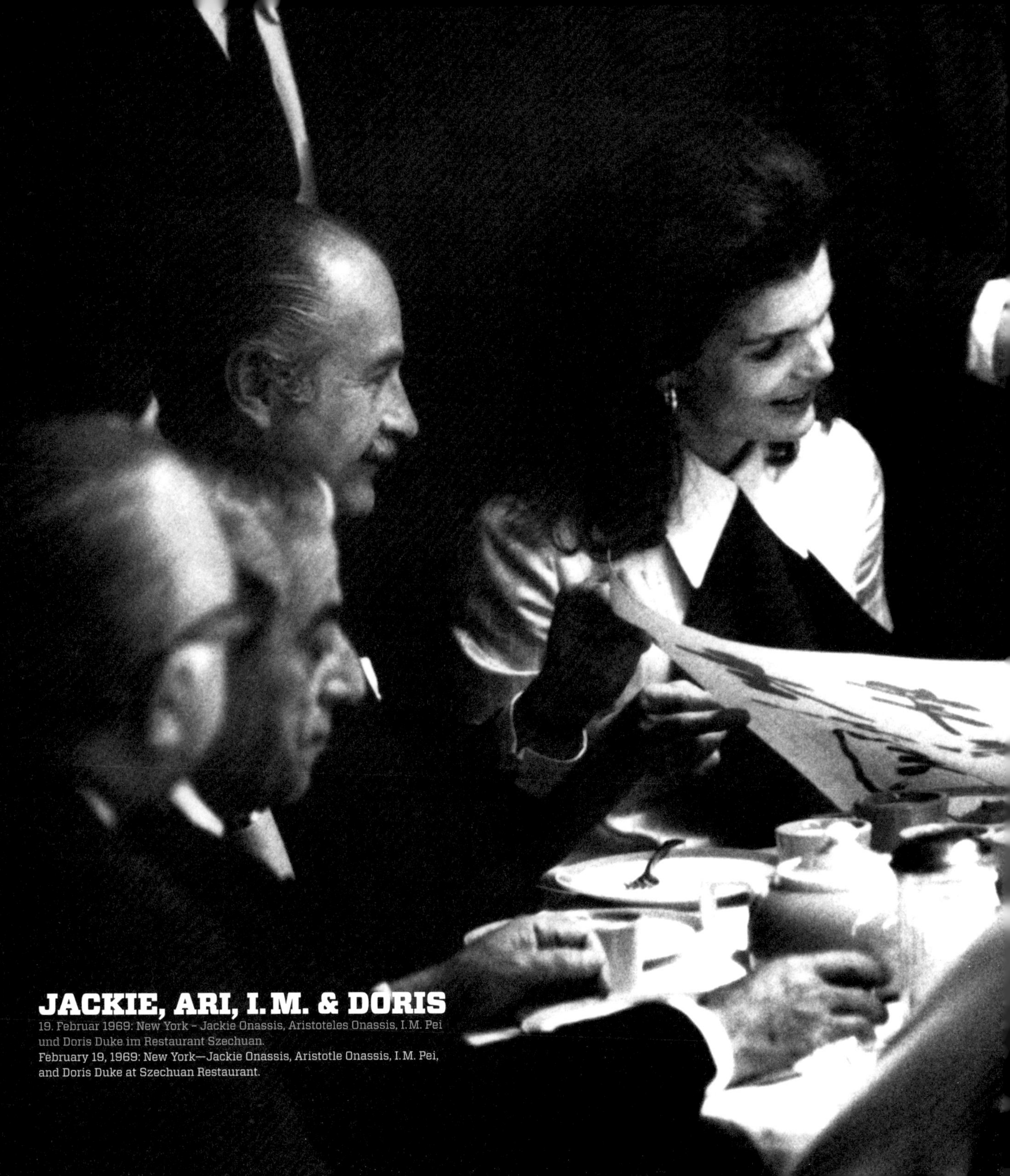

JACKIE, ARI, I.M. & DORIS

19. Februar 1969: New York – Jackie Onassis, Aristoteles Onassis, I.M. Pei
und Doris Duke im Restaurant Szechuan.
February 19, 1969: New York—Jackie Onassis, Aristotle Onassis, I.M. Pei,
and Doris Duke at Szechuan Restaurant.

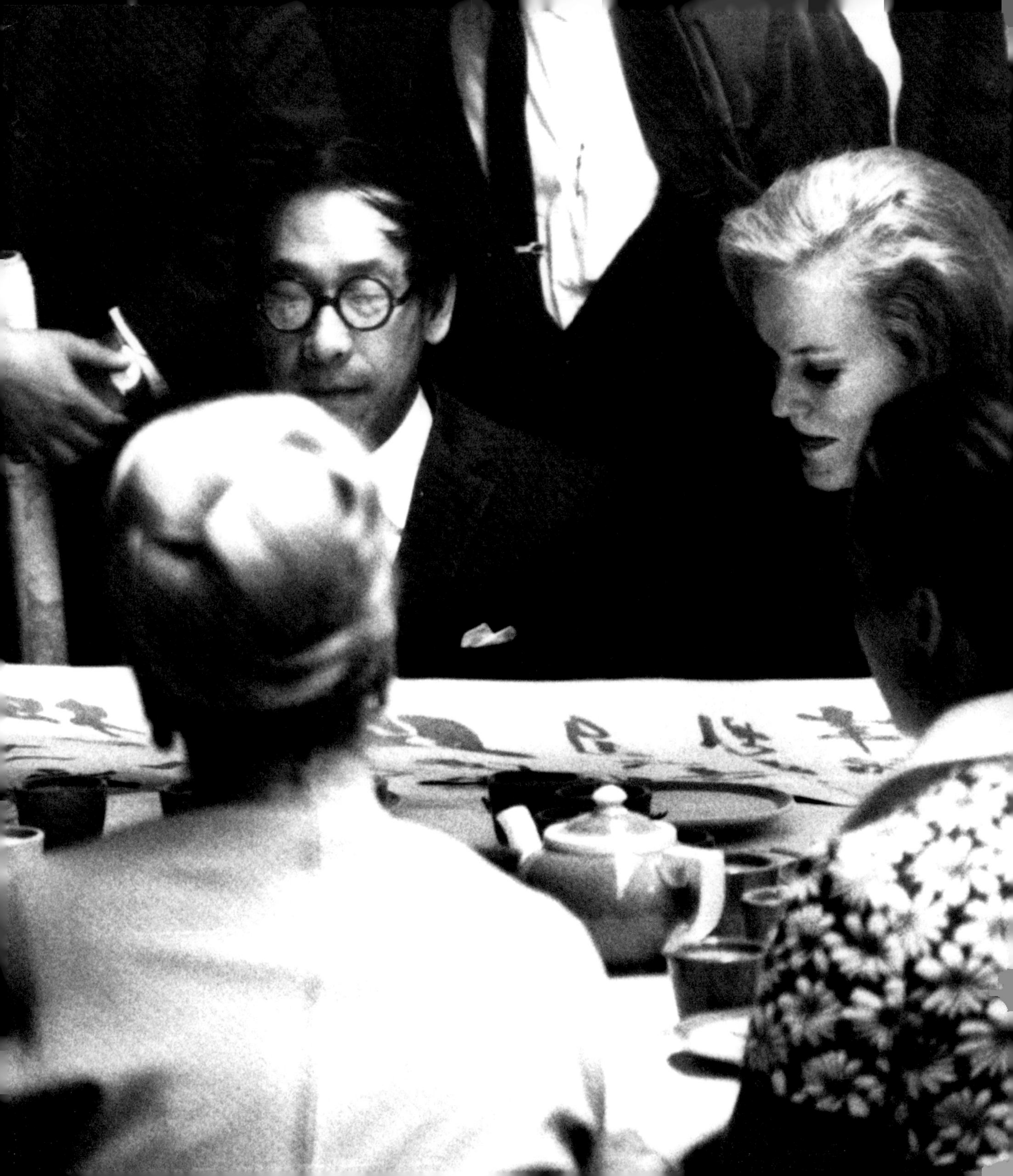

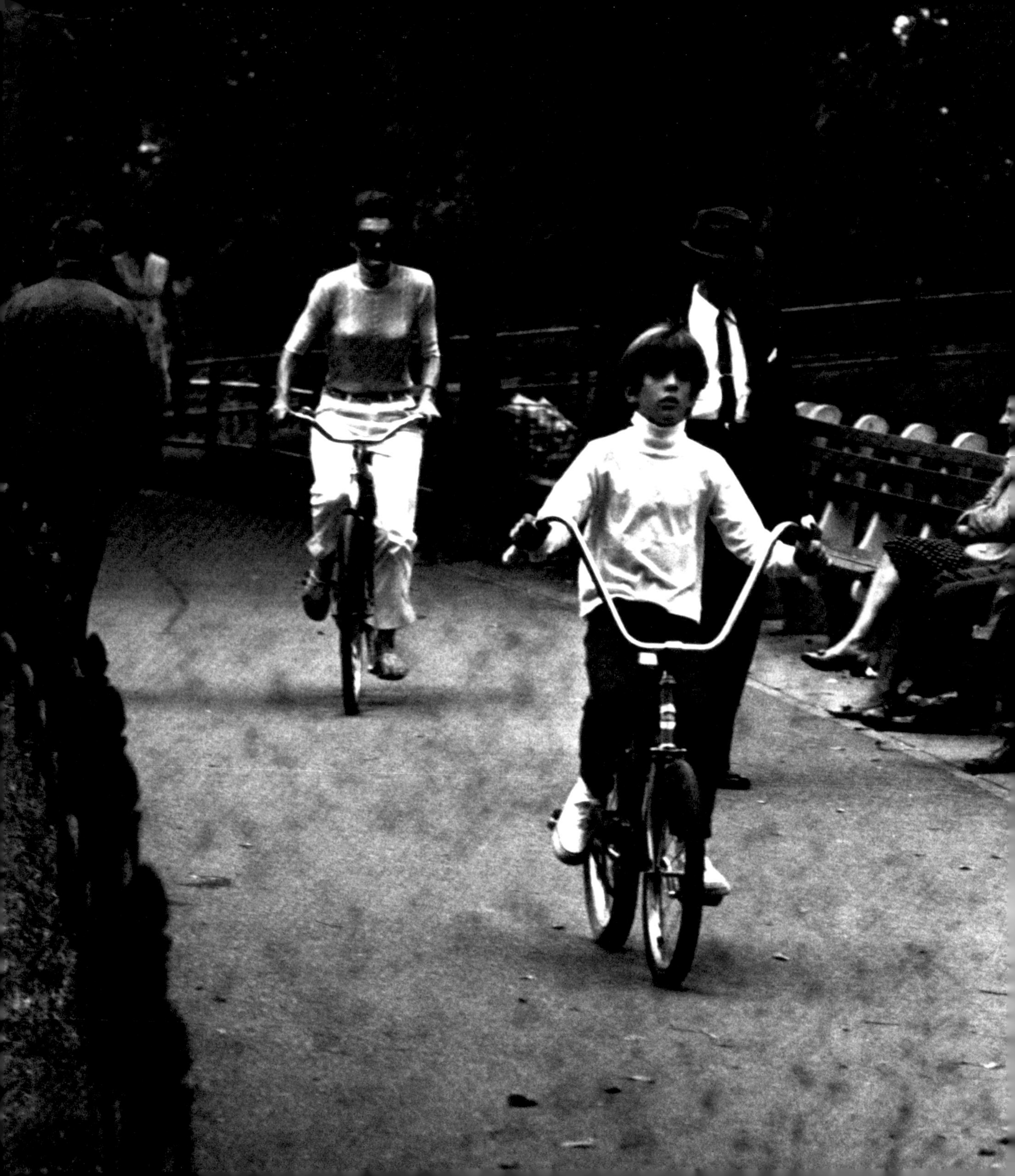

JACKIE & JOHN

24. September 1969: New York – Jackie Onassis und
John F. Kennedy Jr. fahren im Central Park Fahrrad.
September 24, 1969: New York—Jackie Onassis and
John F. Kennedy, Jr. ride bicycles in Central Park.

Sept. 24, 1969: Jackie & John Jr riding bikes in
Central Park. "S mash His Career "
Jackie said to agent mr. Connelly

8 - 9 - 10 - 11

Photography with the **PAPARAZZI** ™ *approach*

17 GLOVER AVE. - • YONKERS, N.Y. 10704 RON GALELLA (914) 237-2988
© 1978 RON GALELLA, ALL RIGHTS RESERVED
THIS PHOTOGRAPH IS LEASED FOR ONE TIME REPRODUCTION ONLY.

John Martin

Feb

THIS IS AN ORIGINAL
PHOTOGRAPH BY
RON GALELLA:

RON GALELLA

Offset
p36 / 84

35

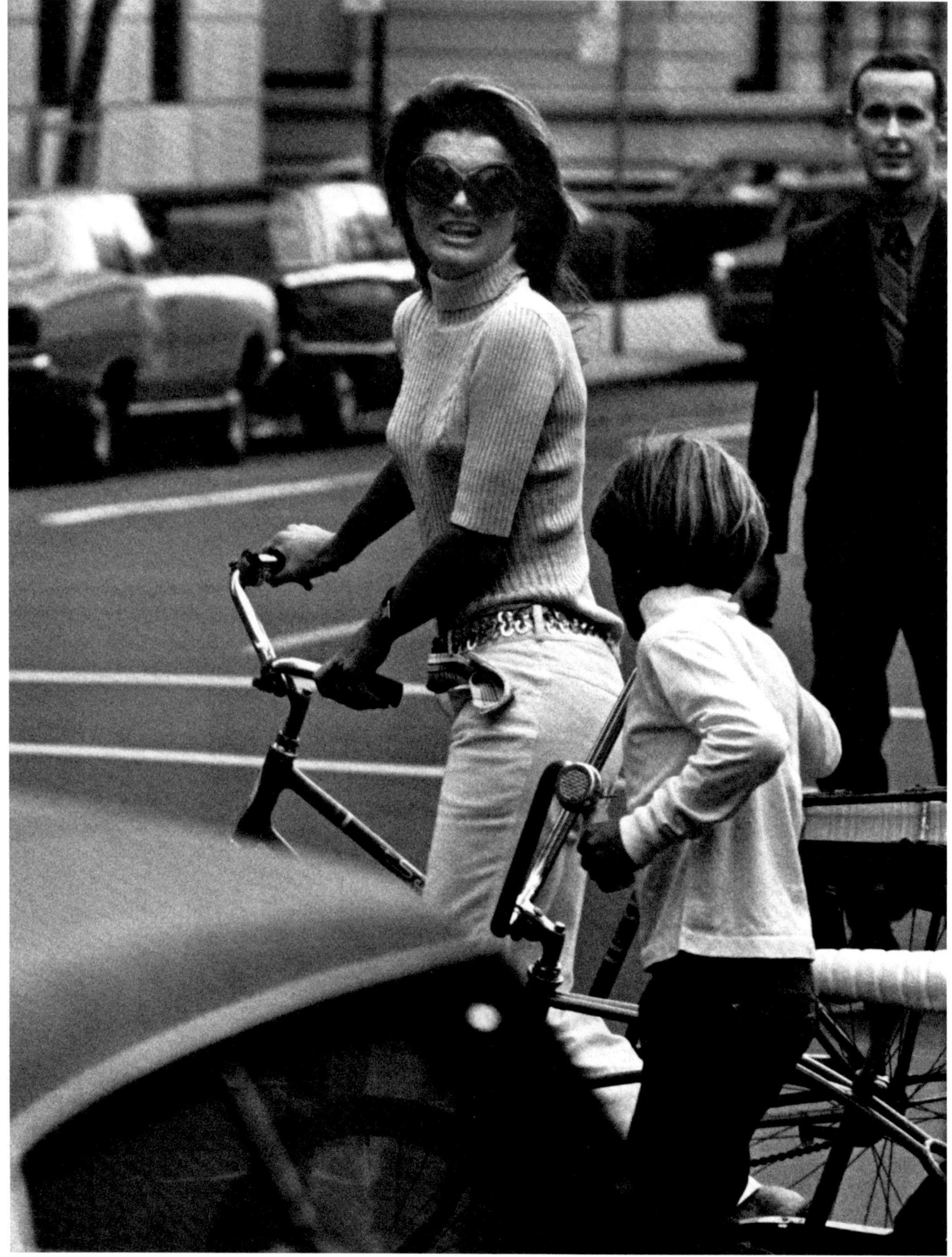

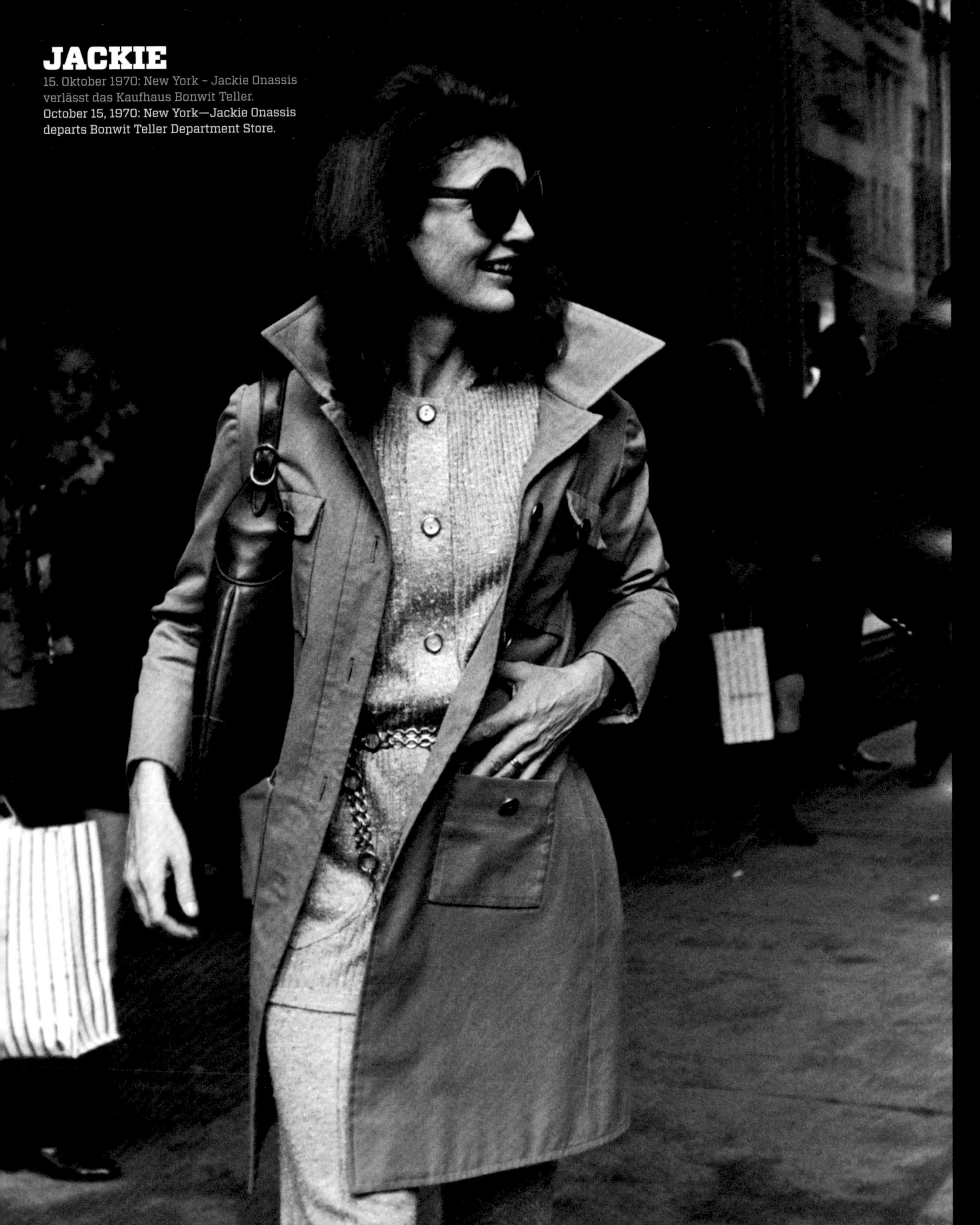

JACKIE

15. Oktober 1970: New York – Jackie Onassis
verlässt das Kaufhaus Bonwit Teller.
October 15, 1970: New York—Jackie Onassis
departs Bonwit Teller Department Store.

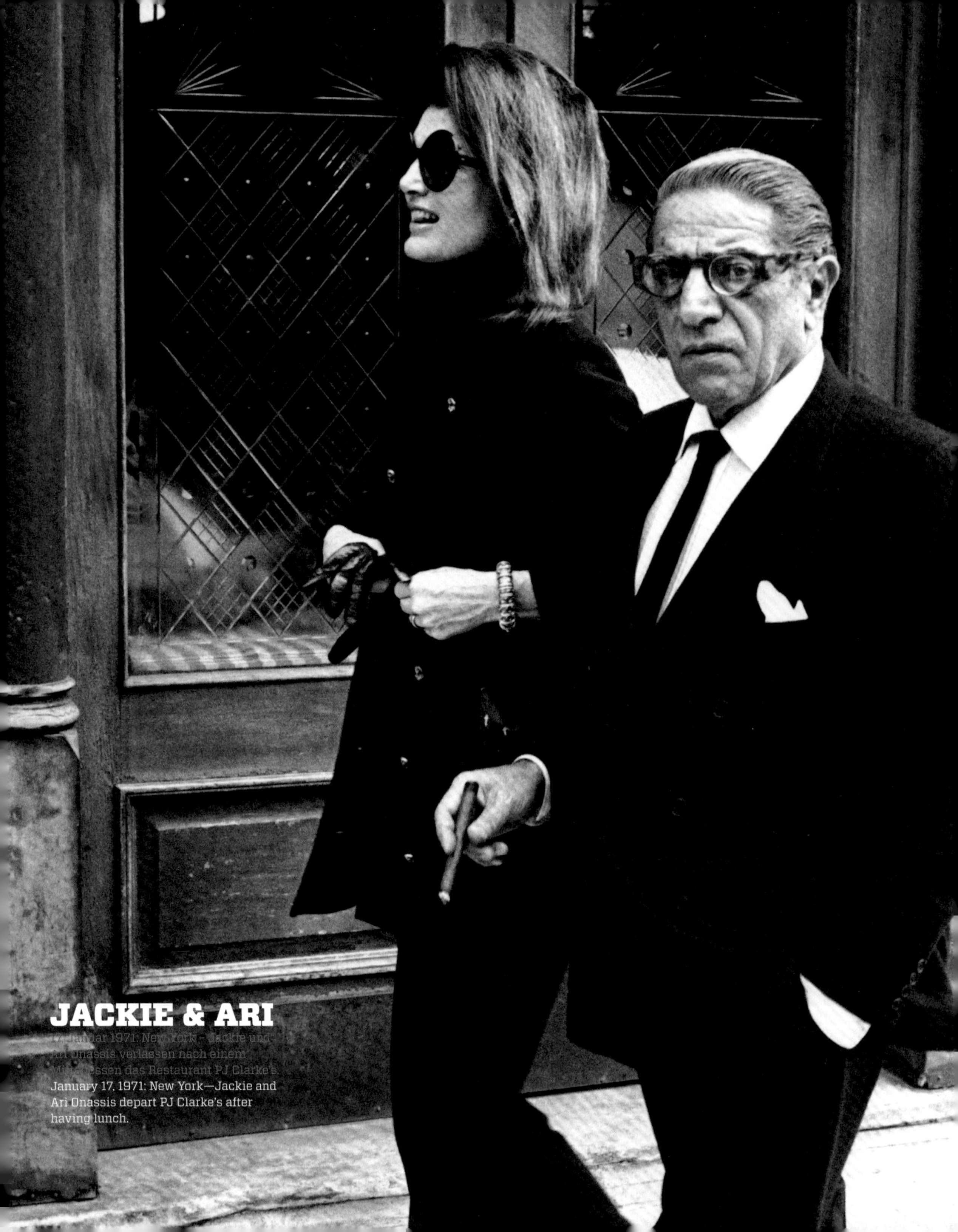

January 17, 1971: New York—Jackie and
Ari Onassis depart PJ Clarke's after
having lunch.

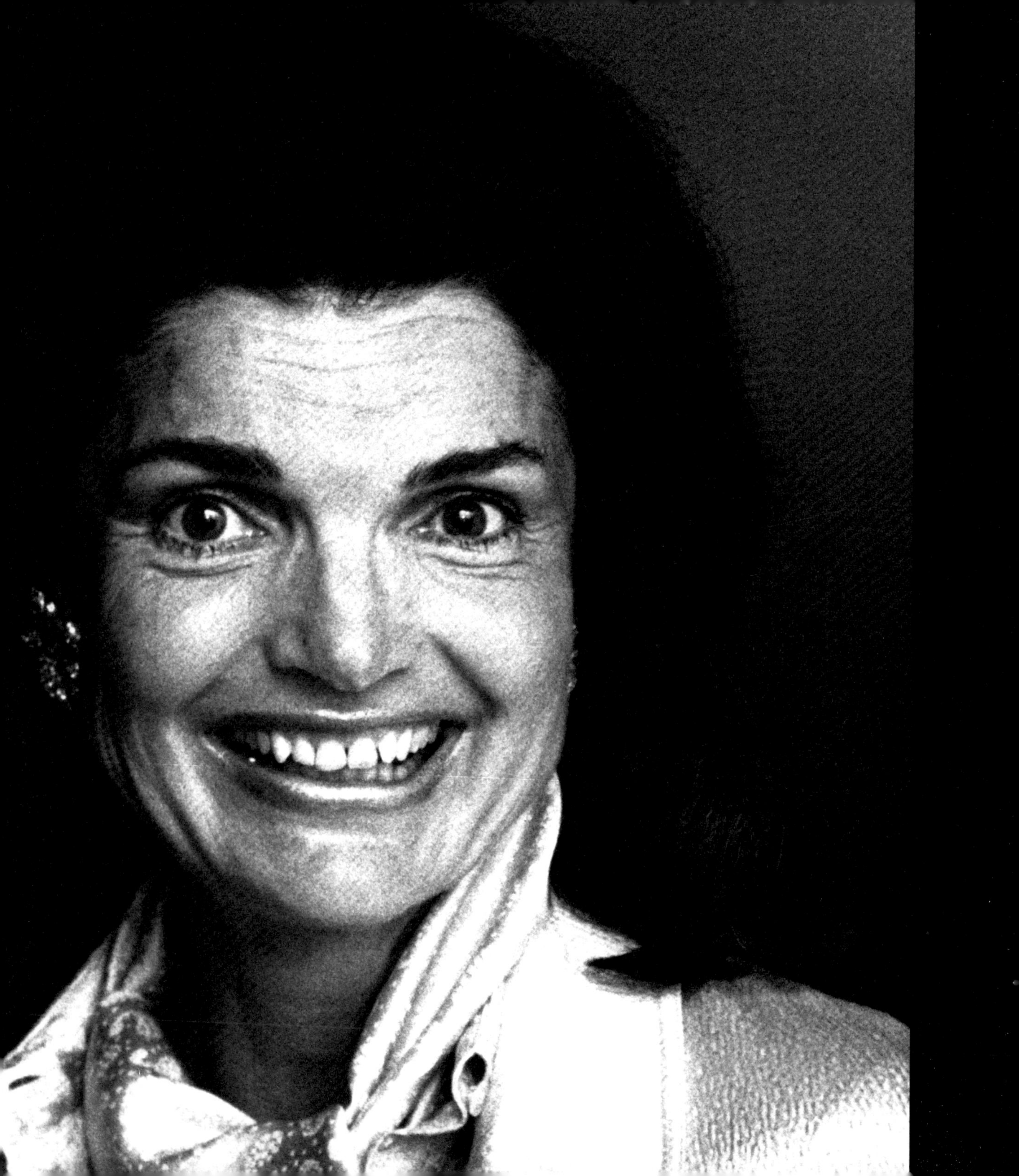

JACKIE

19. April 1976: New York – Jackie Onassis im Palace Theater.
Die Eröffnung von Shirley MacLaines *One-Woman Show* zog viele
Prominente an, inklusive Barbara Walters, Peter und Cheray
Duchin, Liza Minelli und Robert De Niro. Hinter der Bühne strahlte
Jackie Onassis über das ganze Gesicht. Auf ihrem Weg nach
draußen sagte sie zu mir: »Oh … Sie sind's wieder, ich dachte Sie
wären im Gefängnis.«

April 19, 1976: New York—Jackie Onassis at The Palace Theater.
The opening of Shirley MacLaine's *One-Woman Show* drew many
celebrities including Barbara Walters, Peter and Cheray Duchin,
Liza Minnelli and Robert De Niro. Jackie Onassis was all smiles
backstage. On her way out she said to me, "Oh … it's you again,
I thought you were in jail."

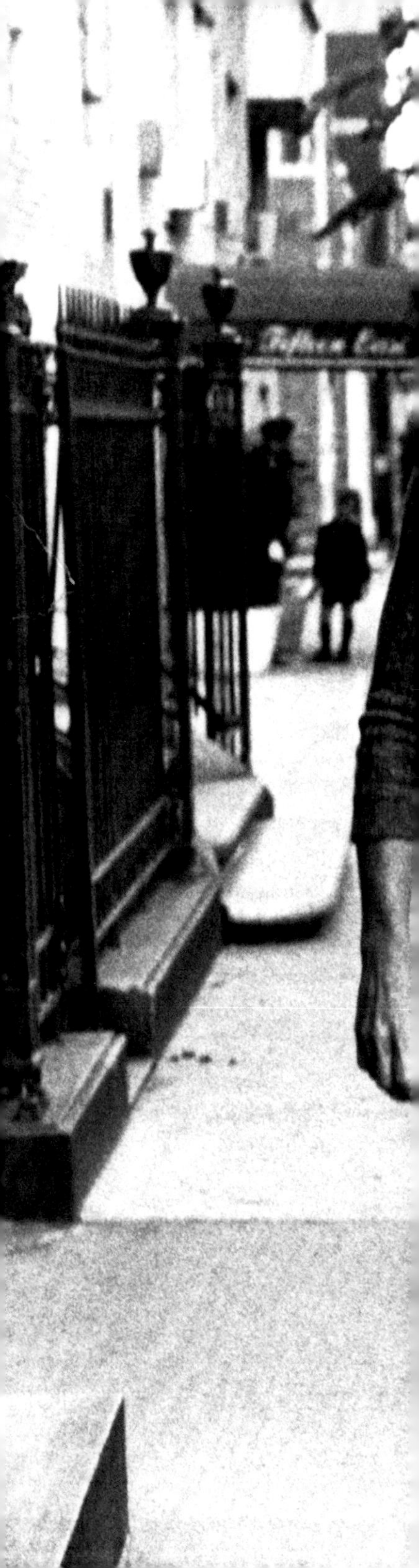

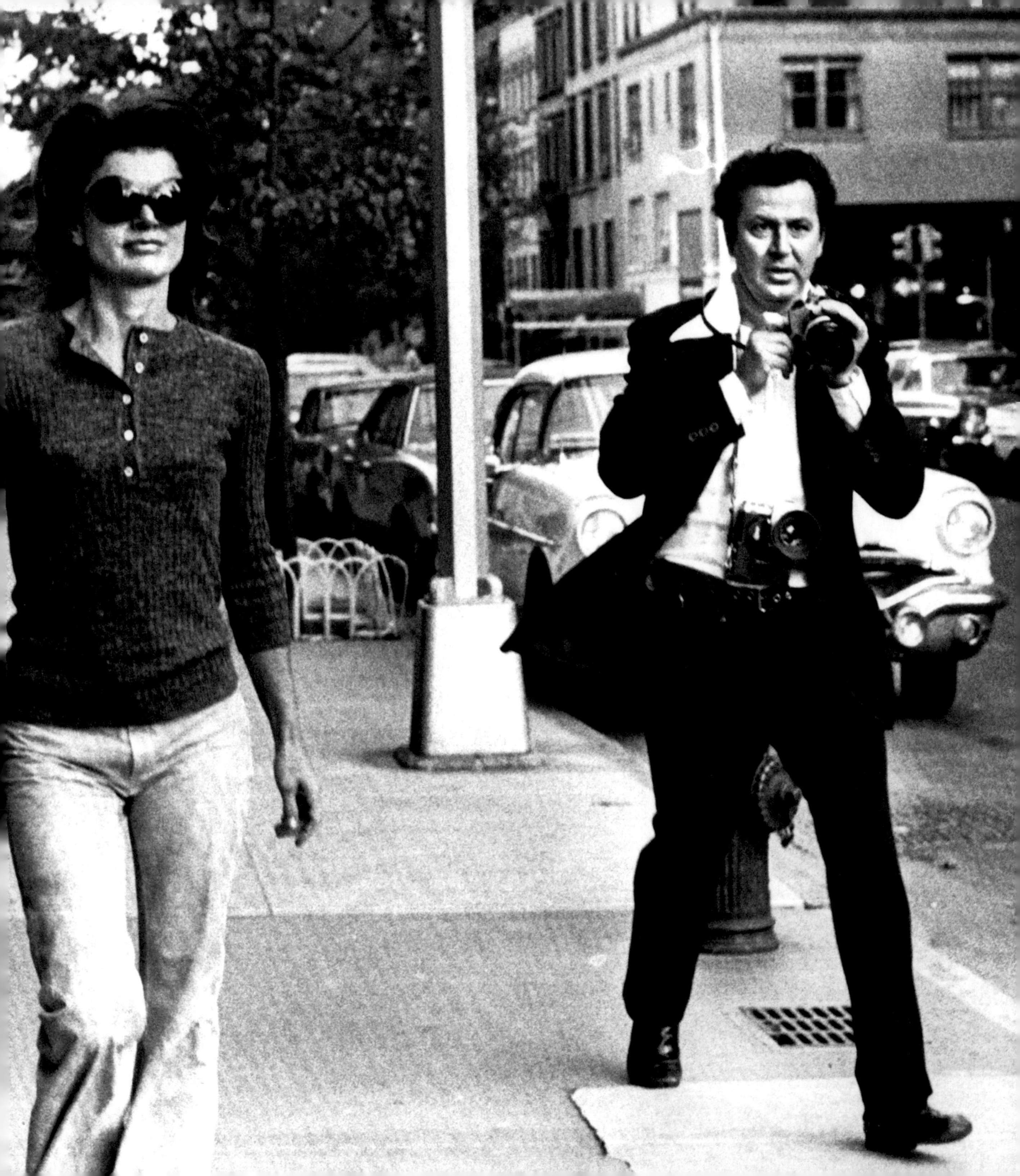

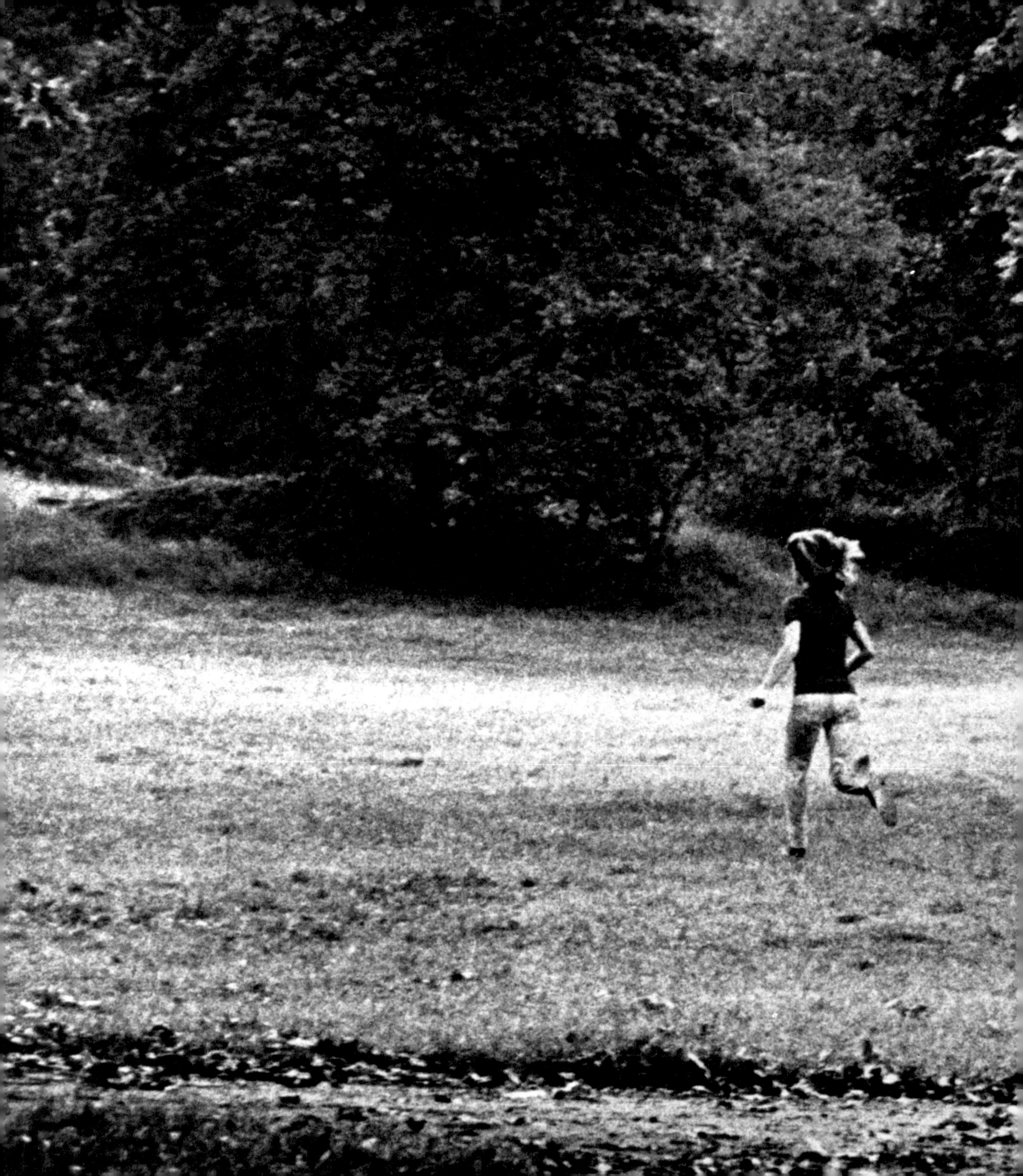

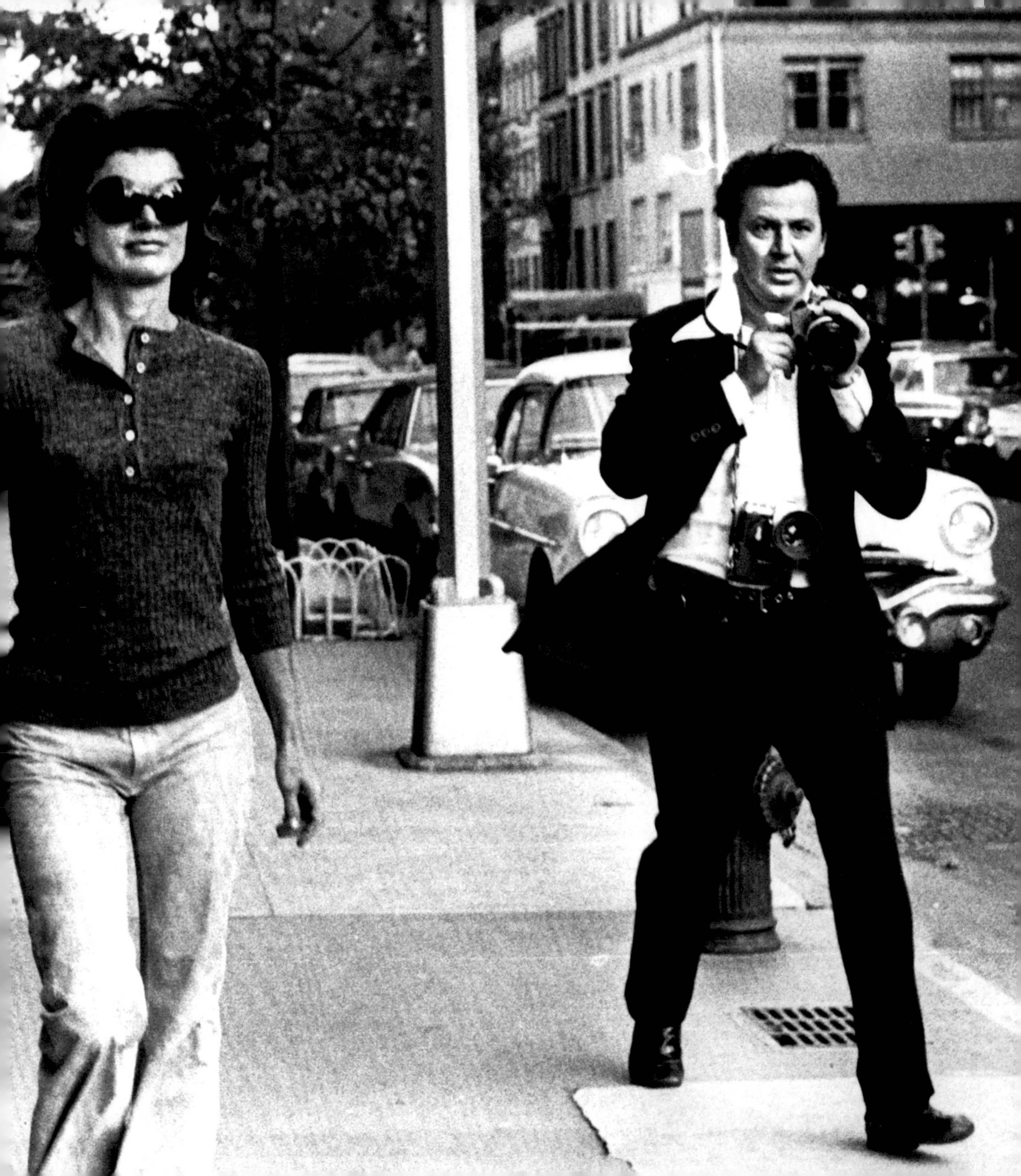

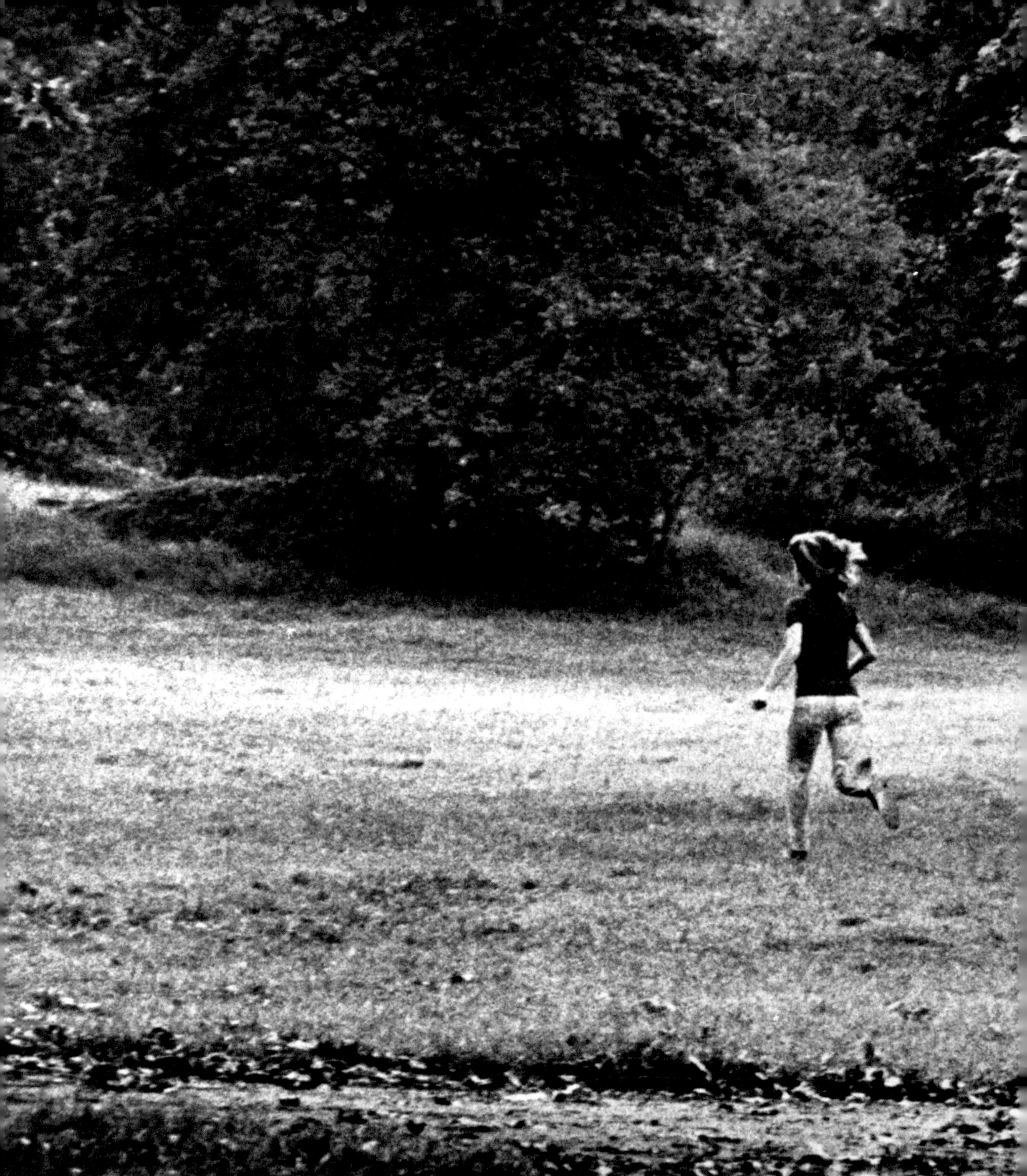

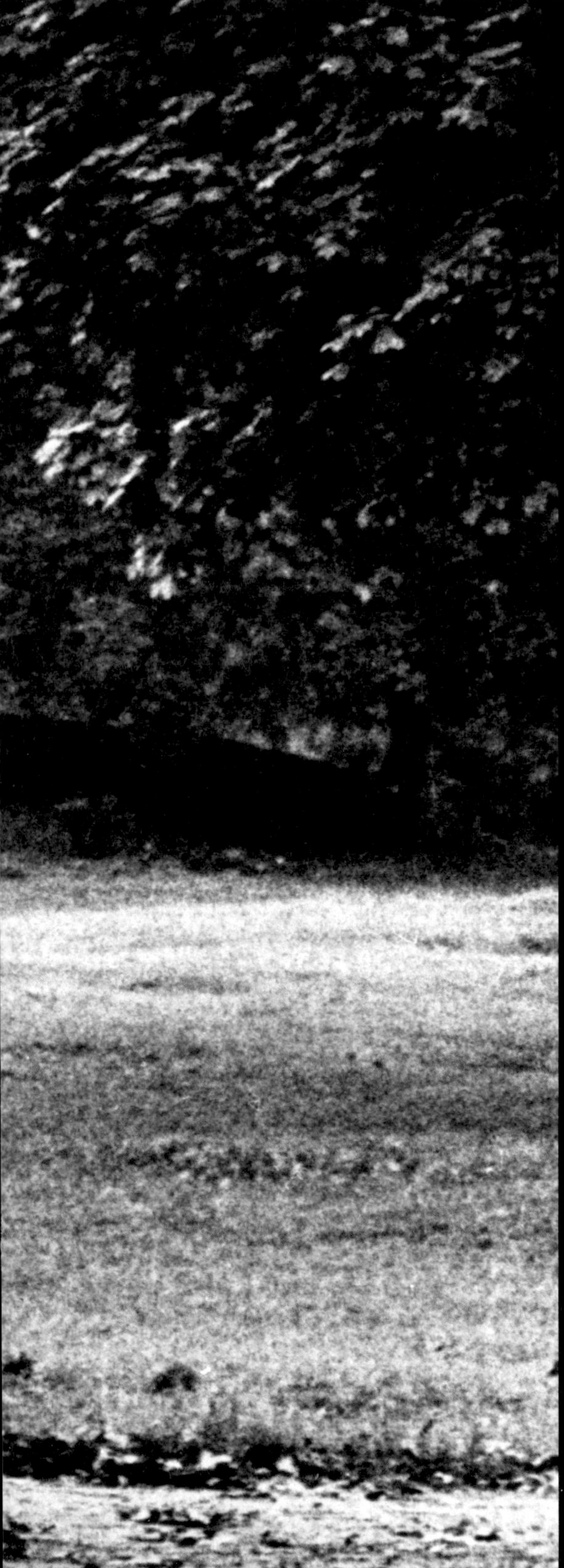

JACKIE

4. Oktober 1971: New York – Jackie Onassis im Central Park.
Der Joggingstrecken-Fall – Letzten Oktober im Central Park, be-
richtete Jackie dem Gericht, wurde die Tennisstunde ihrer Tochter
durch das Erscheinen des Fotografen Galella unterbrochen. »Er rief
zu Caroline herüber,« sagte Jackie aus, »›Schätzchen, ich mache
dich doch nicht nervös, oder?‹ und sie antwortete, ›Doch.‹ Sie
drehte sich mit Tränen in den Augen zu mir herum.« Einen Moment
lang noch stand Jackie neben einem finster dreinblickenden
Geheimdienstagenten an der Seitenlinie. Dann, als Galella anfing,
Fotos zu machen, flüchtete sie und rannte zur anderen Seite des
Parks. Mit Galella im Nacken lief Jackie einen kleinen Hügel hinauf
und an einer Polizeistreife vorbei, deren Besatzung diese Verfolgungsjagd für den Central Park anscheinend nicht ungewöhnlich
fand. Schließlich endete Jackie auf der Joggingstrecke des Parks.
Galella, jetzt völlig außer Atem, konnte ein letztes Mal abdrücken,
bevor sie um die Kurve sprintete und aus seinem Sichtfeld
verschwand.

October 4, 1971: New York—Jackie Onassis in Central Park.
The jogging track incident—Last October in Central Park, Jackie
told the court her daughter Caroline's tennis lesson was interrupted by the apperance of photographer Galella. "He yelled to
Caroline," Jackie testified, "'I'm not making you nervous, am I
honey?' And she said, 'Yes, you are.' She turned toward me and
there were tears in her eyes." For a moment longer, Jackie stood
at the sidelines beside a glowering Secret Service agent. Then, as
Galella's camera records, she bolted away and ran across the park.
With Galella in pursuit, Jackie dashed up a slight hill and past a
police cruiser, whose occupants apparently did not find the chase
out of the ordinary for Central Park. Finally, Jackie wound up on
the park's jogging track. Galella, winded by now, was able to squeeze
off one last shot before she sprinted around the bend and out
of his sight.

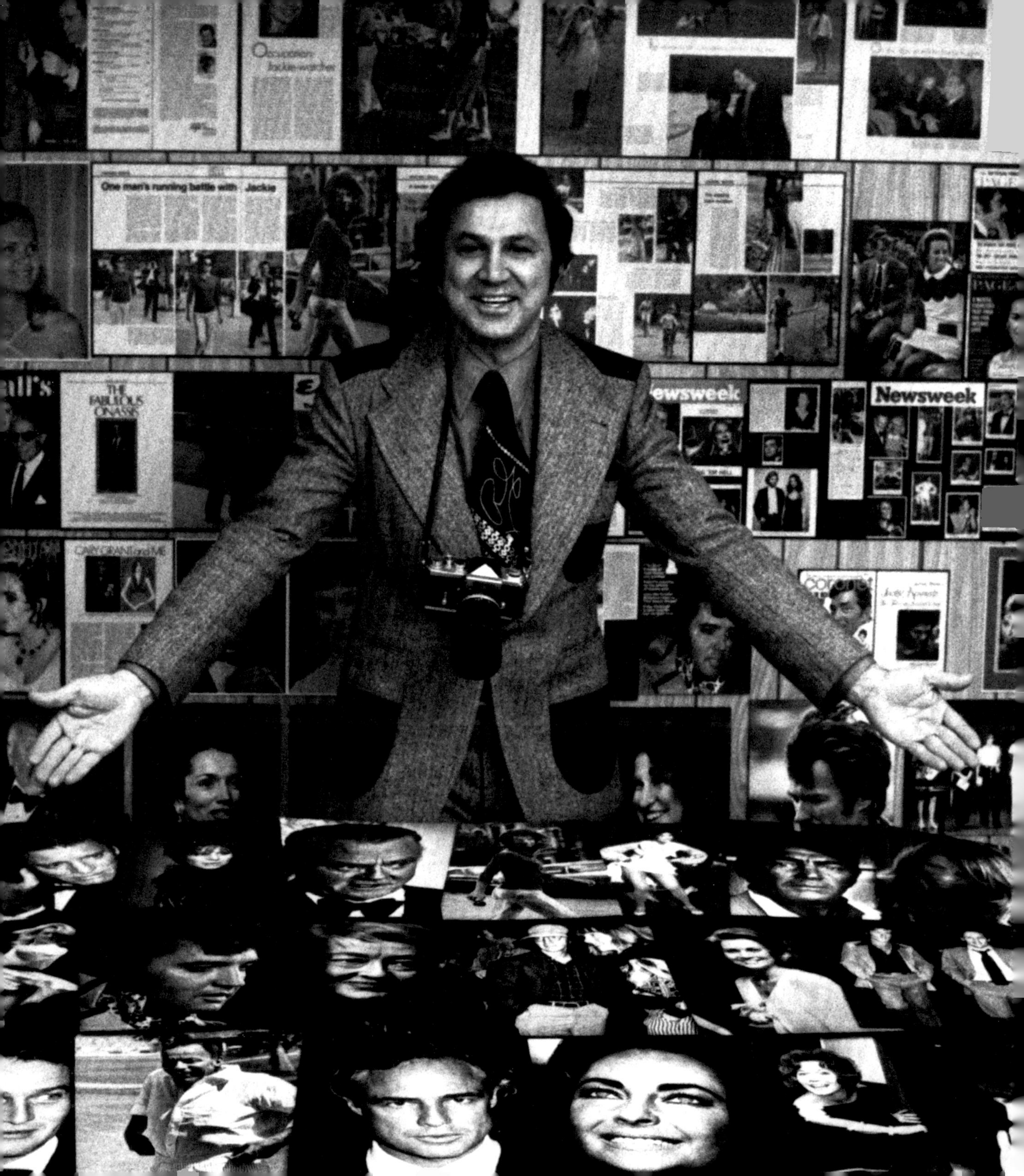

BIOGRAPHY

Ron Galella

1931 in New York geboren, diente Ron Galella während des Korea-Konfliktes als Fotograf bei der US-Luftwaffe bevor er das Art Center College of Design in Los Angeles besuchte, wo er seinen Abschluss in Fotojournalismus machte.

Über Ron Galella ist viel geschrieben worden. Er gilt als der berühmteste und widersprüchlichste Prominentenfotograf weltweit – *Newsweek* titelte »Paparazzo Extraordinaire« und für *Time* und *Vanity Fair* war er der »Pate der amerikanischen Paparazzo-Kultur«. Tatsächlich risikierte Galella viel für das perfekte Bild. So hat er zwei Gerichtsverhandlungen mit Jacqueline Kennedy Onassis, einen von Marlon Brando gebrochenen Unterkiefer und eine heftige Schlägerei mit Richard Burtons Bodyguards überstanden, bevor er im mexikanischen Cuernavaca ins Gefängnis kam. Aber schließlich ist es Galellas Leidenschaft für die Fotografie, verbunden mit einem dezidierten Do-it-yourself-Zugang zu seinem Handwerk – nur wenige Fotografen erreichen sein Niveau bei der Entwicklung der eigenen Abzüge –, der es zu verdanken ist, dass sein Werk weltweit in Museen und Galerien ausgestellt wird, darunter das Museum of Modern Art in New York und San Francisco, die Tate Modern in London sowie die Helmut Newton Stiftung in Berlin. Galellas Passion für den Fotojournalismus führte zu vielen hochgelobten Büchern, darunter *Disco Years*, das 2006 von der *New York Times* als Bestes Fotobuch ausgezeichnet wurde. Außerdem erhielt *Smash His Camera*, ein Dokumentarfilm über Galellas Leben und Werk von Regisseur und Oscar-Gewinner Leon Gast (*When We Were Kings*, 1996), der 2010 auf dem Sundance Film Festival seine Premiere hatte, den Großen Preis der Jury für Regie in der Kategorie US-Dokumentarfilm. Der Film war auch erfolgreich beim 54. BFI London Film Festival, bevor die BBC ihn in Großbritannien und Europa ausstrahlte.

Gleichbedeutend mit seiner Anerkennung in den USA wurde Ron Galella, dessen Vater Vincenzo Galella in Muro Lucano geboren wurde, im Jahr 2009 zum Ehrenbürger der italienischen Region Basilicata ernannt. Dort, in der Carlo-Levi-Halle im Palazzo Lanfranchi in Matera, wurde auch die Wanderausstellung *Ron Galella. Italian Icons* mit über siebzig seiner Arbeiten eröffnet. Im Zusammenhang mit dieser Ausstellung erschien *Viva l'Italia!* – eine Sammlung von mehr als 225 Bildern von italienischen und italo-amerikanischen Prominenten von Frank Sinatra bis Sophia Loren.

Born in New York, in 1931, Ron Galella served as a U.S. Air Force photographer during the Korean conflict before attending the Art Center College of Design in Los Angeles, where he earned a degree in Photojournalism.

Much has been written of Ron Galella. Widely regarded as the most famous and most controversial celebrity photographer in the world—he's been dubbed "Paparazzo Extraordinaire" by *Newsweek* and "the Godfather of U.S. paparazzi culture" by *Time* and *Vanity Fair*—Galella is clearly willing to take great risks to get the perfect shot. As a result, he has endured two highly publicized court battles with Jacqueline Kennedy Onassis, a broken jaw at the hands of Marlon Brando, and a serious beating by Richard Burton's bodyguards before being jailed in Cuernavaca, Mexico. But ultimately, it is his passion for the fine art of photography, coupled with a dedicated do-it-yourself approach to his craft—few artists can claim his level of skill in making their own prints—that sees Ron's body of work exhibited at museums and galleries throughout the world, including the Museum of Modern Art in both New York and San Francisco, the Tate Modern in London, and the Helmut Newton Foundation in Berlin. Ron's passion for photojournalism has also given rise to many highly acclaimed books including *Disco Years,* which was honored as Best Photography Book of 2006 by *The New York Times,* and *Smash His Camera,* a documentary of his life and career by Oscar-winning director, Leon Gast (*When We Were Kings,* 1996), which premiered at the 2010 Sundance Film Festival and received the Grand Jury Award for Directing in the U.S. Documentary category. The film was also well-received at the 54th BFI London Film Festival prior to airing on the BBC throughout the United Kingdom, and Europe.

Tantamount to his recognition here at home, the government of Basilicata graciously honored Ron, whose father, Vincenzo Galella, was born in Muro Lucano, by making him an honorary citizen of the Italian region in 2009. Basilicata also opened *Ron Galella: Italian Icons,* a traveling exhibit of over 70 of Ron's photos, at Palazzo Lanfranchi's Carlo Levi Hall in Matera. In conjunction with the opening, Ron launched *Viva l'Italia!*—a collection of over 225 images of Italian and Italian-American celebrities from Frank Sinatra to Sophia Loren.

Diese Publikation erscheint anlässlich
der Ausstellung / This book is published
in conjunction with the exhibition
Ron Galella. Paparazzo Extraordinaire!

C/O Berlin, Berlin
10. Dezember 2011 – 26. Februar 2012
December 10, 2011 – February 26, 2012

Herausgeber / Editor:
Felix Hoffmann, C/O Berlin

Mitarbeit / Production:
Karin Hänsler, C/O Berlin

Übersetzungen / Translations:
Gillian Morris, Laura Kahle

Konzept, Design / Concept, design:
Naroska, www.naroska.de

Satz / Typesetting:
Laura Köpke, C/O Berlin

Schrift / Typeface:
Vitesse

Verlagsherstellung / Production:
Nadine Schmidt, Hatje Cantz

Reproduktionen / Reproductions:
Repromayer, Reutlingen

Druck / Printing:
Offsetdruckerei Karl Grammlich GmbH,
Pliezhausen

Papier / Paper:
LuxoArt Samt New, 150 g/m²

Buchbinderei / Binding:
Lachenmaier GmbH, Reutlingen

Erschienen im / Published by
Hatje Cantz Verlag
Zeppelinstrasse 32
73760 Ostfildern
Deutschland Germany
Tel. +49 711 4405-200
Fax +49 711 4405-220
www.hatjecantz.com

Informationen zu dieser oder zu anderen
Ausstellungen finden Sie unter www.kq-daily.de. /
You can find information on this exhibition and
many others at www.kq-daily.de.

Hatje Cantz books are available internationally at
selected bookstores. For more information about
our distribution partners, please visit our website
at www.hatjecantz.com.

ISBN 978-3-7757-3324-3

Printed in Germany

Umschlagabbildung / Cover illustration:
29. August 1986: New York – Sean Penn vor
seiner Wohnung in der West 64th Street. /
August 29, 1986: New York—Sean Penn
in front of his West 64th Street apartment.

In Zusammenarbeit mit / In collaboration with:
La Fábrica, Madrid

MICK & JERRY

19. September 1984: New York – Ein Schnappschuss von
Mick Jagger und seiner Freundin, dem Model Jerry Hall, beim
Verlassen des Nachtclubs The Limelight nach einer Party für
den Produzenten der Rolling-Stones-Videos, Reid Rogers.

September 19, 1984: New York—Mick Jagger and his girlfriend,
model Jerry Hall were snapped as they departed The Limelight
where they attended a party for Reid Rogers who produced the
Rolling Stones videos.

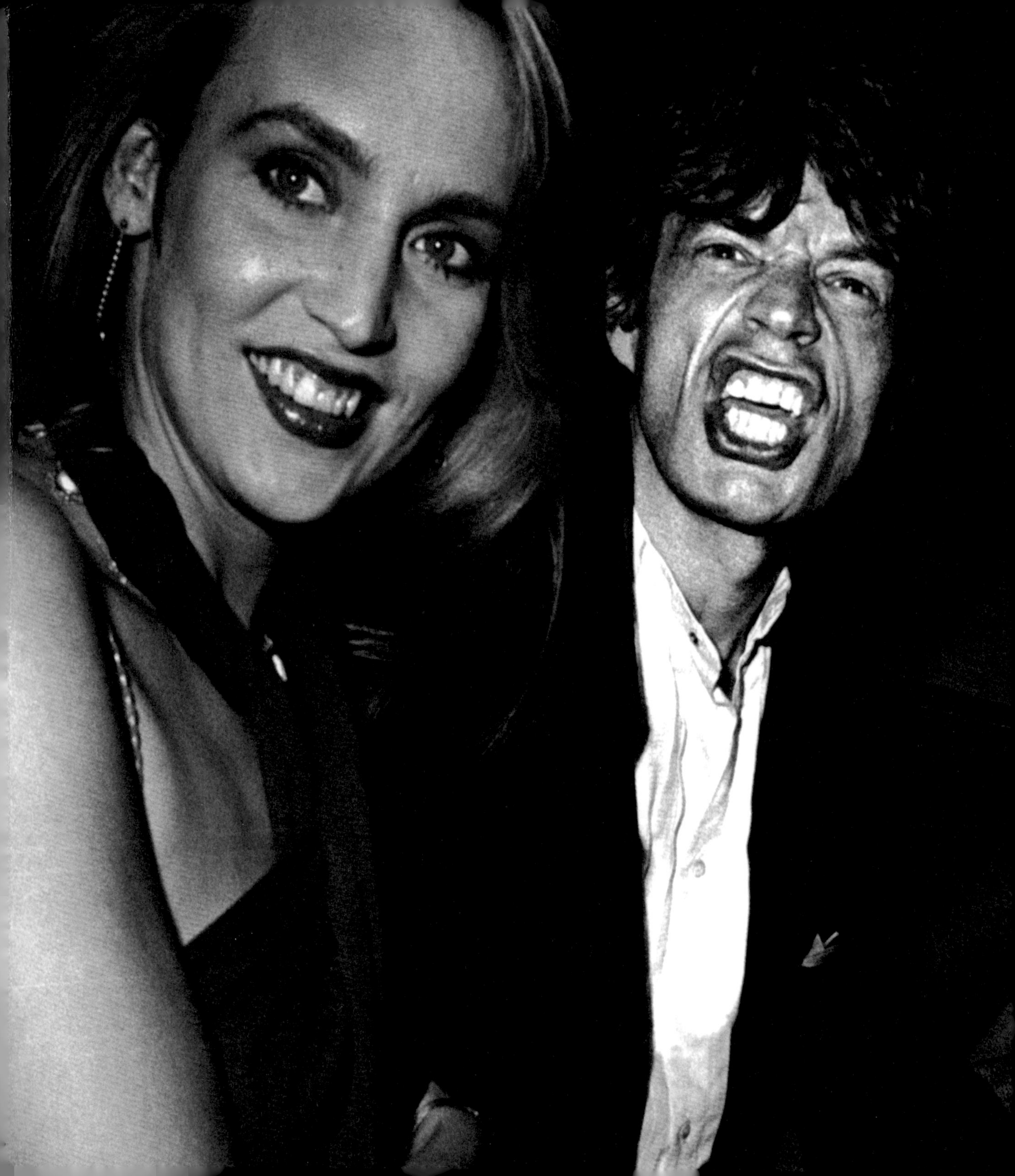

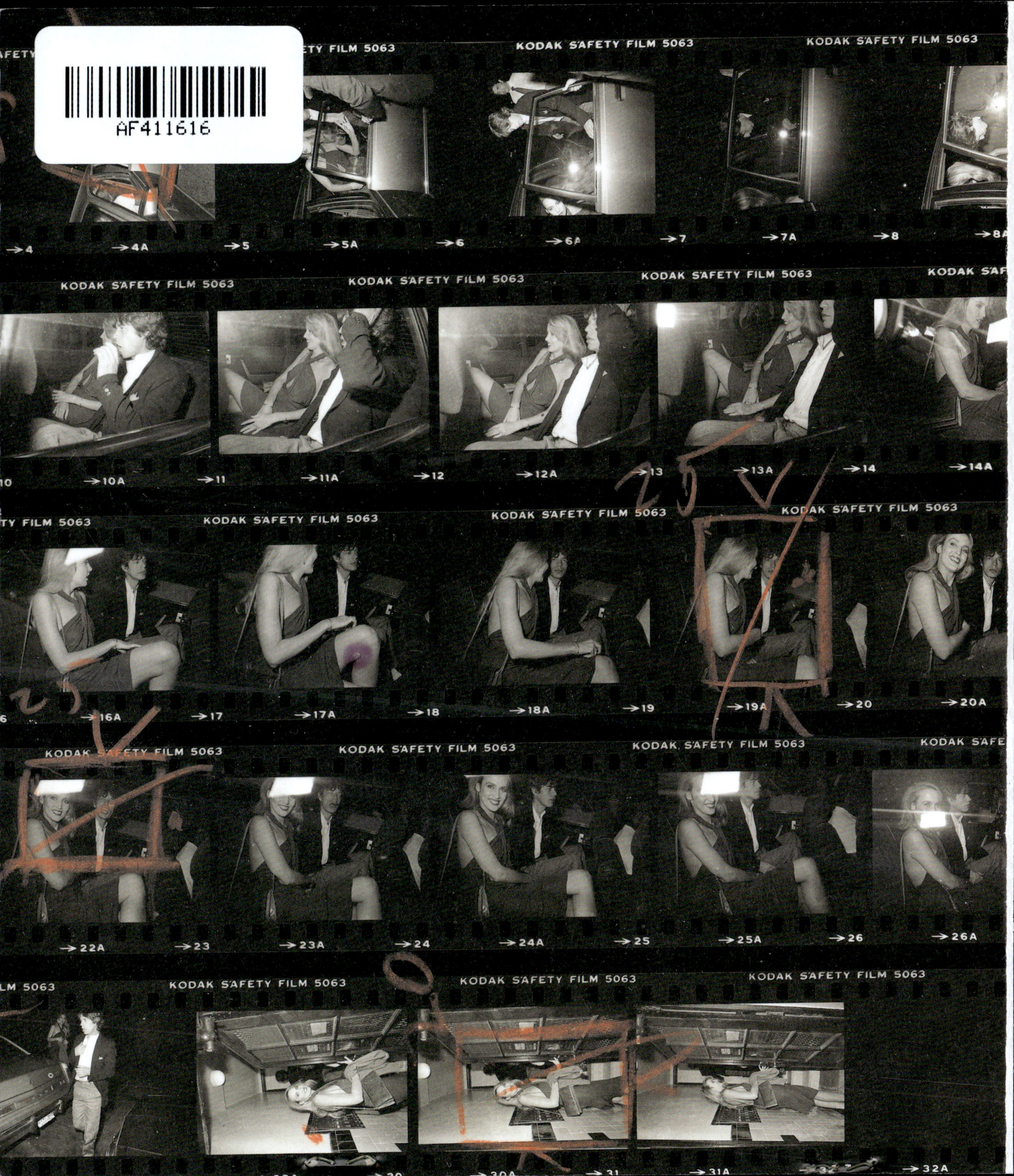